East Asian Social Science Monographs

Ethnicity and the Economy

Ethnicity and the Economy
The State, Chinese Business, and Multinationals in Malaysia

James V. Jesudason

SINGAPORE
OXFORD UNIVERSITY PRESS
OXFORD NEW YORK
1989

Oxford University Press

Oxford New York Toronto
Delhi Bombay Calcutta Madras Karachi
Petaling Jaya Singapore Hong Kong Tokyo
Nairobi Dar es Salaam Cape Town
Melbourne Auckland
and associated companies in
Berlin Ibadan

Oxford is a trade mark of Oxford University Press

© Oxford University Press Pte. Ltd. 1989

Published in the United States by Oxford University Press, Inc., New York

ISBN 0 19 588913 4

British Library Cataloguing in Publication Data

Jesudason, James V. (James Vijayaseelan),
    1954–. Ethnicity and the economy: the
    state, Chinese business, and multinationals in
    Malaysia. – (East Asian social science monographs)
    1. Malaysia. Economic development, 1957–1987
    I. Title   II. Series
    330.9595'04

    ISBN 0–19–588913–4

Library of Congress Cataloging-in-Publication Data

Jesudason, James V., 1954–
    Ethnicity and the economy.

    (East Asian social science monographs)
    Bibliography: p.
    Includes index.
    1. Malaysia—Economic conditions. 2. Malaysia—Economic policy.
    3. Malaysia—Ethnic relations. 4. Chinese—Malaysia.
    5. International business enterprises—Malaysia.
    I. Title.   II. Series.
    HC445.5.J47   1989   338.9595   88–31406
    ISBN 0–19–588913–4 (U.S.)

Printed in Malaysia by Peter Chong Printers Sdn. Bhd.
Published by Oxford University Press Pte. Ltd.,
Unit 221, Ubi Avenue 4, Singapore 1440

To Judy

Preface

ECONOMIC development, especially in the Third World, is not an autonomous process. State élites play a central role in the economy, sometimes to lay the basis for growth, but often to ensure that the course of development takes place along lines that bring support for the regime. In this book I examine how the roles of key economic actors, such as multinationals, state enterprises, and private local capital, emerged from the politics of multi-culturalism in Malaysia. These groups are not faceless units of capital which national leaders can combine in the right mix to maximize growth. They represent different ethnic, national, and cultural segments, whose roles have important consequences for the political and cultural development of society. State élites, thus, have an interest in mediating these roles, and the economic arrangements adopted might entail high national economic costs, although these arrangements might bring significant political pay-offs, at least for a while, to the rulers.

There were two main concerns that led me to explore the role of ethnicity in shaping development processes and outcomes in Malaysia. The first was partly biographical in nature. I remember as a young boy in the 1960s how frequently Malaysia was praised as an economic and political success in Asia. Economically, it was ahead (in per capital GDP terms) of Taiwan and South Korea, the present 'economic miracles', and its political system had many attractive pluralistic features. Yet by the early 1980s, as I embarked on this study, it was apparent that the country was experiencing a relative decline within the East Asian region. Its political system was also becoming less pluralistic, although racial disaffection and political cynicism were not as evident at that time. Neither dependency nor world-system approaches, with their focus on external determinants, had much to offer as an explanation. I wanted to study the relative decline of the Malaysian economy giving due recognition to internal social–structural arrangements, and, in particular, to the role of ethnic structures.

My other concern was that while ethnic studies have become a 'growth industry', their focus has been rather narrow. In the economic area, scholars have been much more interested in examining the characteristics of small, economically successful ethnic groups—such as middlemen minorities—rather than in the macro-economic consequences of ethnic divisions. I feel there is a need to consider ethnicity beyond middlemen minorities and examine its impact on how national economic choices and policies are made.

The other preoccupation among scholars of ethnicity, following the resurgence of interest in collective behaviour, has been the study of the conditions and bases for ethnic mobilization. Like 'ethnicity identity', 'ethnic mobilization' is treated as an abstract concept needing explanation. The effort has led to useful economic and political frameworks for understanding ethnic conflict and mobilization, such as theories of internal colonialism, split and segmented labour market models, state-building processes, and the role of political entrepreneurs. Yet these studies have not moved on to consider what happens, once ethnic mobilization occurs, to the society's development. For example, how do ethnically based polities cope with divergent demands, such as meeting ethnic pressures while trying to provide for economic growth? How do key actors, such as the state, multinationals, and majority and minority business groups, interact in these societies? I feel that these questions can be asked of several multi-ethnic societies, leading to fruitful comparative work. By examining Malaysia, I hope to take the first small step.

Using ethnicity as an analytical entry point to the study requires some justification. In a sense, studies taking ethnicity seriously may be regarded as phenomenological, in contrast to analyses based on class, which appear more structural. Since ethnic phenomena seem immediately observable, resorting to ethnic explanations seems to be practising 'obvious' sociology, while class analyses promise to lay bare the hidden, deeper dimensions of social life. For a variety of historical reasons, ethnicity in Malaysia is a reality *sui generis*, and cannot be reduced to class. My position is that if analysts brush ethnicity aside, they will be making an obvious error, since a critical and felt element in the society will be ignored. However, I have tried not to treat ethnicity and class as competing analytical categories, since I recognize that both can and should be taken into account. I have emphasized ethnicity because it cannot be wished away and, equally important, it also allows me to capture Malaysia's political economy in a more comprehensive manner.

This study was undertaken in partial fulfilment for the Ph.D. degree in Sociology at Harvard University. The interviews for the analysis were conducted in early 1985, and the study completed in October 1987. A few revisions have been made to update the reader on important new events in Malaysia, but a complete analysis will have to wait for a clearer pattern to emerge from the current political turbulence. I have undertaken to publish the dissertation now because I believe the analysis is relatively self-contained in terms of the issues covered and, in addition, it might serve as a useful backdrop for other scholars to interpret future events.

In the course of this study I have relied on the ideas and encouragement of numerous people. I would like to thank my dissertation advisers, Professors Orlando Patterson, Ezra Vogel, and Donald Warwick. Professor Patterson has been a source of inspiration to me throughout my graduate career. Professor Vogel provided the right encouragement during hard times, and crucial feedback at important points in the analysis. Professor

Warwick helped enormously in making the presentation more readable and in forcing me to clarify my ideas. I am also grateful to Professor James Scott at Yale for his comments on the first chapter and to Professor Theda Skocpol for making me interested in political sociology. I thank them for their criticisms and advice, although I have not been able to incorporate all their suggestions because of various constraints. The shortcomings of the book are entirely my own.

My friends and colleagues have also played an important role in this study. I am grateful to Khong Yuen Foong for his support during moments of despair, and to Leong Choon Heng and Subha Segaram for sending me useful material from Kuala Lumpur. I also thank Marta Gil, David Harris, Habib Khondker, Kamaruddin Said, Michael Shifter, Stephen Turner, and Yoon Jeong-Ro for lengthy discussions and their good cheer.

My family has been very kind to me during the long gestation period of the work. I am grateful to my mother for always standing behind me, even when I decided to become a sociologist. I also thank my father, Christopher, Rohini, Nalini, and Peter for their concern and confidence in my ability to finish this study. My in-laws, too, have been most helpful.

My dear wife Judy, to whom this book is dedicated, was untiring in her patience and encouragement, without which this study would not have been completed. She came with me to Singapore so that I could carry out my work and turned down many good offers that would have advanced her mathematical career. I hope I can begin to repay my many debts to her.

I also want to express my gratitude to the Institute of Southeast Asian Studies for making available to me its excellent facilities. Finally, I want to express my indebtedness to those individuals who allowed me to interview them for the study.

Singapore   JAMES V. JESUDASON
June 1988

Contents

Preface		vii
Tables		xiii
Figures		xiv
Abbreviations		xv
Note		xvi

1 The Ethnic Factor in Development — 1
- Introduction — 1
- The Limits of Rational Economic Models — 4
- The Psychology and Politics of Ethnic Claims — 9
- The Ethnic Framework of Development — 14
- Methodology, Propositions, and Data — 20

2 The Colonial Impact — 24
- Introduction — 24
- Historical Background — 24
- Ethnicity and Economic Segmentation — 30
- The Making of Ethnic Political Structures — 39

3 The Restrained Role of the State, 1957–1969 — 47
- Introduction — 47
- Departing from the Colonial Framework — 47
- Constraints to State Expansion — 52
- Preserving the Foreigners' Role — 56
- The Spread of Chinese Business — 60
- Malay Business Developments — 64
- The Breakdown of the *Laissez-faire* Framework — 67
- Conclusion — 73

4 The Enlarged State — 76
- Introduction — 76
- Gearing for State Expansion — 76
- The State as Entrepreneur — 84
  - Pernas and PNB — 86
  - The SEDCs — 98
- The State and Private Malay Capitalists — 100

Group Worth and Support for the State   109
The Over-burdened State   119
Conclusion   123

5 **The State and Chinese Business**   128
   Introduction   128
   The Emerging Economic Environment   128
   The Limits and Possibilities of Economic Protest   134
   The NEP and Chinese Strategies of Accommodation   147
   The Failure of a State–Capitalist Alliance   159
   Conclusion   163

6 **The Role of Multinationals**   166
   Introduction   166
   State Interests and the Business Climate   166
   Capitalizing on International Diversity   172
      Labour-intensive, Export-oriented Production   173
      Casting the Multinational Net Widely   180
   Foreign Investment and Economic Crisis   186

7 **Conclusion**   193

   Bibliography   201
   Index   211

Tables

1.1   Comparative Data on Selected Ethnic Societies   3

1.2   Evans's Model of Dependent Development Compared with the Ethnic Framework of Development in Malaysia   15

1.3   Possible Chinese Business Responses to State Policies   17

2.1   Population by Ethnic Group and Sex, Peninsular Malaysia, 1911–1957   29

2.2   Occupation by Ethnic Group, 1957   37

3.1   Public Development Spending, 1956–1970   51

3.2   Ownership of Pioneer Companies, 1962 and 1969   57

3.3   Foreign Ownership in the Malaysian Economy, 1970   59

3.4   Employment by Occupation and Ethnic Group, 1970   68

3.5   Parliamentary Election Results, Peninsular Malaysia, 1959–1969   69

3.6   State Election Results, Peninsular Malaysia, 1959–1969   70

3.7   Ownership of Shares in Limited Companies, 1970 and 1990 Targets   72

4.1   Public Sector Financing and Expenditure, 1966–1985   81

4.2   Sectoral Breakdown of Development Expenditure, 1966–1985   83

4.3   Public Allocations to Selected State Corporations, 1971–1985   85

4.4   Pernas's Subsidiary Companies in 1984   94

4.5   National Equity Corporation (PNB) Group Shareholdings by Sector, 1985   96

4.6(a)   Results of Parliamentary Elections, Peninsular Malaysia, 1969 and 1974   110

4.6(b)   Results of Parliamentary Elections, Peninsular Malaysia, 1978 and 1982   110

4.6(c)   Results of Parliamentary Elections, Peninsular Malaysia and East Malaysia, 1986   111

4.7   Employment by Occupation and Ethnic Group, Peninsular Malaysia, 1970 and 1980   112

4.8   Malay Occupational Distribution, 1970 and 1980   113

4.9   Enrolment in Tertiary Institutions, 1970 and 1985   113

4.10   Household Income by Ethnic Group, 1970, 1979, and 1984   114

4.11   Incidence of Poverty, 1970–1984   115

4.12   Exports and Prices of Major Primary Commodities,
        1975–1987   121
4.13   Public Sector Revenue and Financing, 1981–1987   122
5.1   Public and Private Investment/Expenditure, Fourth
        Malaysia Plan, 1981–1985   147
5.2   Japanese Investments and Ownership Structure,
        1970–1980   153
5.3   Return on Shareholders' Funds in a Sample of Chinese
        Public Firms, 1974–1982   155
6.1   Number of Strikes and Man-days Lost, 1978–1986   170
6.2   Monthly Wages in Selected Industries, 1974 and 1980   171
6.3   Comparison of Electronics Sector with Selected Countries,
        1982   175
6.4   Main Foreign Investors in Textiles, 1983   179
6.5   Top Ten Foreign Investors (Fixed Assets) in Malaysia as
        of 31 December 1983   180
6.6   Sectoral Distribution of Fixed Assets by Nationality
        (Selected), 1983   181

Figures

5.1   Non-Bumiputra Equity in Manufacturing Projects Granted
        Approval, 1971–1985   143
5.2   Non-Bumiputra and Foreign Equity in Manufacturing
        Projects Granted Approval, 1971–1985   145
5.3   Non-Bumiputra and Bumiputra Equity in Manufacturing
        Projects Granted Approval, 1971–1985   146
6.1   Structure of the Pen-Group   178

Abbreviations

ACCC	Associated Chinese Chambers of Commerce
ACCCIM	Associated Chinese Chambers of Commerce and Industry Malaysia
ASN	Amanah Saham Nasional (National Unit Trust Scheme)
CIC	Capital Issues Committee
CPM	Communist Party of Malaya
DAP	Democratic Action Party
EPU	Economic Planning Unit
Felda	Federal Land Development Authority
FIC	Foreign Investment Committee
FIDA	Federal Industrial Development Authority (See also MIDA)
Fifth MP	*Fifth Malaysia Plan*
First MP	*First Malaysia Plan*
FMM	Federation of Malaysian Manufacturers
FoMP	*Fourth Malaysia Plan*
FTZ	Free Trade Zone
GDP	Gross Domestic Product
HICOM	Heavy Industry Corporation of Malaysia
ICA	Industrial Coordination Act
IMP	Medium and Long Term Industrial Master Plan
KLSE	Kuala Lumpur Stock Exchange
MARA	Majlis Amanah Rakyat (Council of Trust for the Indigenous People)
MCA	Malaysian Chinese Association
MIC	Malaysian Indian Congress
MICCI	Malaysian International Chamber of Commerce and Industry
MIDA	Malaysian Industrial Development Authority
MPAJA	Malayan People's Anti-Japanese Army
MPH	Multi-Purpose Holdings
MTR FoMP	*Mid-Term Review of the Fourth Malaysia Plan*
MTR SMP	*Mid-Term Review of the Second Malaysia Plan*
MTUC	Malaysian Trade Union Congress
MUI	Malayan United Industries
NEP	New Economic Policy

NOC	National Operations Council
OCBC	Overseas Chinese Banking Corporation
PAS (PMIP)	Parti Islam SeMalaysia (Pan-Malayan Islamic Party)
Pernas	Perbadanan Nasional (National Corporation)
Petronas	Petroliam Nasional (National Oil Corporation)
PMFTU	Pan-Malayan Federation of Trade Unions
PNB	Permodalan Nasional Berhad (National Equity Corporation)
SCCC	Selangor Chinese Chamber of Commerce
SEDC	State Economic Development Corporation
SMP	*Second Malaysia Plan*
TMP	*Third Malaysia Plan*
UMNO	United Malays National Organization

Newspapers and Magazines

AB	*Asian Business*
AF	*Asian Finance*
AWSJ	*Asian Wall Street Journal*
BT	*Business Times*, Malaysia
BT (S)	*Business Times*, Singapore
BW	*Business Week*
FEER	*Far Eastern Economic Review*
MB	*Malaysian Business*
NST	*New Straits Times*
SP	*Suara Pernas*
ST	*Straits Times*, Malaysia
ST (S)	*Straits Times*, Singapore

Note

Unless otherwise indicated, all currency values are in Malaysian dollars (*ringgit*). In mid-June 1988, the exchange rates were approximately US$1 = M$2.60; £1 = M$4.70; and Australian $1 = M$2.10.

1 The Ethnic Factor in Development

Introduction

THIS book examines the impact of ethnic divisions on state economic policies and development outcomes in Malaysia.[1] It argues that ethnic considerations decisively influenced the political élite's choices over critical development issues, such as the degree of state intervention in the economy, the choice of entrepreneurial groups to promote, the level of tolerance for economic inefficiency, and the degree of strain to impose on the state's fiscal position. In short, the essential motor of the development process, extending to macro-economic policies, was driven by powerful ethnic sentiments and patterns of ethnic political mobilization.

When Malaysia became independent from Britain in 1957, the ethnic composition of the 6.28 million population was 50 per cent Malay, 37 per cent Chinese, and 11 per cent Indian. The numerically dominant Malays, who considered themselves indigenous, were the paramount group controlling the political sphere and the bureaucracy, while the Chinese were essentially the domestic capitalist class. This traditional ethnic split between political power and economic predominance made the balance between the public and private sectors a politically sensitive one, subject to changing political constellations.

Compromises between the top ethnic leaders resulted in a relatively *laissez-faire* economic framework between 1957 and 1969. There was comparatively little state interference in the operations of the Chinese and foreign business groups. Although the development model was relatively successful in generating national income and diversifying the economy, the Malays—across class lines—did not see sufficient benefits for themselves in the existing economic arrangements. The economic model gradually became discredited, and was discarded after bloody race riots in 1969; the leader, Tunku Abdul Rahman, paid a high price for adopting this model and was made to resign.

After 1970, a younger group of Malay leaders pushed the state toward a highly interventionist role in the economy under the banner of the New Economic Policy or NEP (1970–90). They wanted greater control over the nation's economic resources, both to increase Malay economic power as well as to expand their political base. Targets were set so that by 1990, Malay corporate ownership would be 30 per cent, non-Malay

40 per cent, and foreign 30 per cent in contrast to 1.9 per cent, 37.4 per cent, and 60.7 per cent respectively in 1970 (*Mid-Term Review of the Second Malaysia Plan*, henceforth *MTR SMP*, 1973: 86–7, Table 4.9). To effect this change, the political élites embarked on the rapid expansion of the state enterprise sector and the creation of a Malay bourgeoisie.

In the interventionist phase, the Malay leaders, while hoping that the Chinese and the foreigners would participate in national growth and employment creation, also wanted to regulate them to meet their politico-cultural goals. Conflicts, compromises, and hard bargaining inevitably resulted among the main entrepreneurial groups.

The main units of analysis are the state (including state enterprises), domestic Chinese capital, and multinationals. Our concern is how their respective roles and alliances were shaped and constrained by ethnic contention—in particular, of the type that arises when there is a split between political and economic power. The major tasks are to investigate why the liberal economic policies of the 1960s failed, to examine the capacities of the state to pursue economic and political goals that might go against established economic groups, to determine how the major entrepreneurial groups participated in the economy, and to evaluate the overall economic and political outcomes of the state's policies.

Our study can be situated among those sociological works that have tried to go beyond the simplistic dependency view of economic development by incorporating key internal variables, such as the role of the state and cultural traditions, in determining national economic outcomes. In particular, recent studies on the interplay of the state, local private capital, and multinationals in such places as Brazil, Taiwan, and South Korea provided the major impetus for this analysis (Evans, 1979; Gold, 1981; Lim Hyun-Chin, 1982). These studies have added sophistication to the sociology of development by taking into account the more successful economies in Latin America and East Asia.

Yet, because these studies have focused on relatively homogenous societies, they are not helpful in illuminating economic processes in multi-ethnic societies. The omission of ethnic structures in theoretical models and analyses of development has meant that we have had a less than complete view of the broad drama of contemporary development processes.[2] We know that ethnically homogenous states are the exception rather than the rule, and in as many as 30 per cent of all countries, the largest ethnic group does not even constitute the majority of the population (Stone, 1985: 87).

The impact of ethnic divisions on development choices and processes is not unique to Malaysia. To illustrate the point, let us briefly consider Sri Lanka, Zimbabwe, and Trinidad. They are all multi-ethnic societies where the majority group wields political power but is relatively weak in the economy. In Sri Lanka, the Sinhalese comprise 74 per cent of the 16 million population while the minority Tamils comprise 18 per cent (see Report of the Committee for Rational Development in Tambiah, 1986: Appendix 3). In Trinidad, the Black majority comprise 42.8 per cent of the 1.2 million population while the East Indians comprise 40.1 per cent, Whites 1.2 per cent, Chinese 1.0 per cent, and Mixed 16.3 per cent

(Hintzen, 1985: 110). In Zimbabwe, Blacks comprise 95 per cent of the 8 million population, followed by Whites (4 per cent), and Asians (1 per cent). The Whites and East Indians in Trinidad, and the Whites in Zimbabwe are much more entrenched in the private sector than the majority group. In Sri Lanka, where the private sector is very weak, the Tamils are slightly over-represented in small businesses and the professions.[3]

Table 1.1 provides data on government expenditure, public deficit, and manufacturing output for the above countries. As a yardstick, the average figures for each country's income group, as defined by the World Bank, are also shown. In all of them, central government expenditure in 1983 was significantly higher than the norm in their respective income categories. All the countries, with the exception of Trinidad, also had higher budget deficits than the group average. Trinidad's high oil and natural gas revenues in relation to population size appear to have put its public finances in better shape. The data suggest that there are strong pressures on the state to over-strain national resources, as might occur when the state is made to play a central role in sponsoring the mobility of the majority group. As for manufacturing, which is used as a proxy for national effectiveness in upgrading the economy, there are also some parallels. In 1984, manufacturing's share of GNP was below the group norm in Sri Lanka, Malaysia, and Trinidad. In fact, there was a shrinkage in the manufacturing share in Sri Lanka and Trinidad between 1965 and 1984. Only in Zimbabwe was manufacturing well developed, but this can be explained by the open policy toward foreign investment during the period of White rule. There are constraints, it appears, to forging an effective entrepreneurial alliance for development because of ethnic considerations.

TABLE 1.1

Comparative Data on Selected Ethnic Societies

Country	Government Expenditure/GNP (Per Cent)		Government Surplus/GNP (Per Cent)		Manufacture Share/GNP (Per Cent)	
	1972	*1983*	*1972*	*1983*	*1965*	*1984*
Low Income						
Sri Lanka	25.4	33.6	−5.3	−11.0	17	14
Group Average	18.2	16.3	−4.3	−6.6	14	15
Lower Middle Income						
Zimbabwe	—	36.3	—	−6.9	20	27
Group Average	16.8	24.4	−2.4	−4.7	15	17
Upper Middle Income						
Malaysia	32.7	41.0[1]	−9.8	−15.9[1]	10	19
Trinidad	—	31.0[1]	—	3.3[1]	19	13[2]
Group Average	21.3	26.9	−3.3	−6.2	22	25

Source: *World Bank*, 1986: 184–5, 222.
Notes: [1]1982 figure.
       [2]1981 figure.

This single-case study on Malaysia aims to bring out the relationship between ethnicity and development more fully. Although the analysis dwells on state bargaining capacities, private sector power, and the role of multinationals, these cannot be abstracted from the society's ethnic social structure and the nature of group mobilization. No claim is made that the Malaysian case is directly applicable to other ethnically divided societies. It would be sufficient if the analysis points to the need for sharper analytical distinctions in the sociology of development, and serves as a useful bench-mark for studying other ethnic societies, especially those where economic and political power are controlled by different ethnic groups. These countries include Guyana, Sri Lanka, Trinidad, Fiji, Zimbabwe, and perhaps Lebanon.

The Limits of Rational Economic Models

Two contrasting rational models of economic development can be identified: the market model of the neo-classical economists and the 'broker state' model of the dependency theorists. Both approaches contain implicit pre-scriptions regarding what the ideal or most rational set of policies or actions might be for successful development. Although they contain antithetical views on the proper role of the state, they share the common weakness of abstracting away from the complex social and political structures of Third World nations. The fact is, however, that political leaders are usually faced with multiple and contradictory goals and demands, including assuaging powerful groups—class, ethnic, and religious—and anxieties over questions of relative power in society, as well as their foremost concern of securing their own political power and prestige in the polity (Clapham, 1985: 91). Leaders are also not adverse to using the state to build their own economic fortunes. It is not surprising, then, that rational models are seldom realized in practice or, if so, are realized for very brief periods only.[4]

Deepak Lal, a research administrator in the World Bank, strongly re-affirmed the role of the market economy in Third World development in his recent book, *The Poverty of Development Economics* (1985). He attacked the '*dirigiste* dogma', as manifested in the works of Albert Hirschman and Gunnar Myrdal, for advocating the replacement of the market by various forms of government control. Lal faulted the *dirigistes* for seeing state in-tervention as a superior and necessary method to promote development in lieu of the market. Strong criticisms were levelled at state enterprises, import-substitution industrialization, controls on foreign investment, industrial licensing and other state policies with the argument that they had not led to better outcomes than in societies where decisions were market-determined.[5]

The reasons Lal provided for the continued existence of the *dirigiste* state were intellectual confusion and the patronizing attitude of policy-makers, bureaucrats, and scholars toward the people of the Third World. On the intellectual plane, he states (1985: 103):

The empirical assumptions on which this *dirigisme* was based have been belied by the experience of numerous countries in the post-war period. The most serious current distortions in many developing countries are not those flowing from the inevitable imperfections of a market economy but the policy-induced, and thus far from inevitable, distortions created by irrational *dirigisme*.

And because of the patronizing attitude of policy-makers (1985: 104):

It is easy to suppose that these half-starved, wretched and ignorant masses could not possibly conform either as producers or consumers, to the behavioral assumption of orthodox neo-classical economics that 'people would act economically; when the opportunity of an advantage was presented to them they would take it.' This has been termed the 'Economic Principle' by Hicks, and denying it is the hallmark of much development economics—together with the assertion that some ethereal and verbally sanitized entity (such as 'government', 'planner', or 'policy-makers') which is both knowledgeable and compassionate can overcome the defects of these stupid or ignorant producers and consumers and compel them to raise their living standards through various *dirigiste* means.

It is incontrovertible that if the logic of the market is severely undermined by bureaucratic controls and interventions, numerous economic distortions and problems will result. However, the question is why so many Third World governments routinely thwart market mechanisms in spite of knowing the costs involved. The only consistent answer Lal supplies is that leaders and policy-makers are irrational in their beliefs and actions. Such a view is plainly inadequate and stems at bottom from an image of society that is based on atomistic, economically opportunity-seeking individuals. As Hirschman (1986: 142) says: 'Economics as a science of human behaviour has been grounded in a remarkable parsimonious postulate: that of the self-interested, isolated individual who chooses freely and rationally among alternative courses of action after computing their prospective costs and benefits.'

A more complex view of social action that views individuals as having wider affiliations and networks as well as greater inter-connectedness in society is needed. Individual needs, wants, and actions do not stem from individually given preferences, but are powerfully shaped by inter-personal comparisons of status, well-being, and power. On the positive side, it can lead to individuals emulating or being inspired by their more successful peers. But, as is often the case, strong feelings of envy, insecurity, and relative deprivation also result. Individuals are not neutral to the outcomes of the market place. Individuals who feel relatively deprived have a strong incentive to go beyond merely maximizing opportunities as they freely encounter them by actually modifying the whole structure of rewards and opportunities in society, whether based on the market or not.

Deprived individuals and their leaders, especially if they possess strong cultural and affective ties, are particularly prone to using the state to supplant or transform market mechanisms for their own benefit. The question of when such groups attempt to modify the opportunity structure of society, and whether they can be successful, depends on many other political and economic factors, which will not be pursued here. However, the argument for the market appears to be most realizable only when society is composed of highly atomized individuals who have no particular desire to participate in groups or in politics. Otherwise, the market itself is a contested terrain for mobilizing leaders and groups, and one in which routine violations of market mechanisms can bring broad political support.

From the opposite angle, the new dependency theorists have also been concerned to lay out the necessary structures and conditions for backward (peripheral) societies to move to a more advanced position in the international economy.[6] While they do not make explicit policy prescriptions, they are interested in showing the common economic and political prerequisites for 'dependent development'. This term is used to convey the heavy reliance and dependence of Third World nations on foreign capital inflow and investment for their economic growth. While the market economist accounts for economic success or failure in terms of how much the market model has been followed or undermined, the dependency theorists do so in terms of how effectively the state has been able to enlist and yet control foreign multinationals.

A prime example in this genre is the work by Peter Evans in *Dependent Development: The Alliance of Multinational, State and Local Capital in Brazil* (1979). From his study of Brazil, Evans proposed a general model of dependent development as seen to occur in the more advanced Third World countries—in places where development has been 'accompanied by increasing differentiation of the economy, that is to say, by some degree of industrialization' (1979: 51). Evans's model provided the point of departure for this analysis; for this reason it is worth elaborating on its strengths and weaknesses.

Evans argues that because of the relative weakness of the domestic capitalist class in peripheral societies, dependent development needs a particular mix of state, local capital, and multinational participation in the economy. The interests, role, and behaviour of the three actors can be characterized in the following way:

The state: Its central interest is to maximize long-run growth. To achieve this end the state intervenes in the economy by setting up state enterprises. State enterprises perform two critical functions. The first is to solve bottlenecks and undertake high-risk, long-term investments (for example, raw materials refining and petroleum refining) in which local capital is unable to participate and in which multinationals consider the risks too high and the returns too low. The other important role is to buttress the 'nationalist logic' of accumulation (Evans, 1979: 227). Multinationals, albeit necessary for dependent development, gear their activities toward a 'global logic' of accumulation—the results are the removal of profits from the host country, low commitment to local R and D operations, and the displacement of local entrepreneurship. The state, therefore, steps in as a partner in joint ventures with multinationals to protect the national economy and to encourage local diversification. It is able to induce multinationals to form partnerships by offering a large domestic market, natural resources, special incentives, an exploitable labour force, and high growth rates (Evans, 1979: 44).

Local capitalists: Being relatively weak, local entrepreneurs survive predominantly by finding special niches in the economy, particularly in sectors where scale and technology are not vital for growth and where they are tied to a dense network of local distributors (as in textiles and leather goods). Even large entrepreneurs differentiate themselves from multi-nationals by gravitating toward commercial rather than industrial ventures (Evans, 1979: 162). However, a fraction of the local capitalist class—the élite local capitalists—are able to enter the more dynamic industries by collaborating with multinationals; their resource is their integrative role in serving as intermediaries between the firm and the government and as use-ful interlocks for competing multinationals.

Local capitalists also have another important asset—their 'political legitimacy' (Evans, 1979: 240). Evans does not provide a satisfactory defi-nition for it but he means to convey the idea that the state élites try to protect the local capitalist class in the economy whenever possible but not at the expense of high growth. Local capitalists' 'political legitimacy' appears to be a combination of their close ties to the state élite, a buried belief amongst the state élite that local capitalists ought to be the primary economic agents, and the potential ability of local capitalists to mobilize against the state (Evans, 1979: 268). Thus local capitalists are brought in as partners when the state initiates projects with multinationals. The relationship between the state and the local capitalist class is a mutually supportive one: local capitalists need the state to defend against multi-nationals and the state needs the local capitalist class as a political base.

Multinationals: They provide the key technological input for dependent development, making diversification and growth possible. However, multi-nationals also bring some important problems. The first is that they are relatively unconcerned with local development *per se* since their main objective is a global profit maximization strategy. The second problem is that they contribute to worsening economic and political conditions for the general populace. Their origins in rich countries result in highly capital-intensive production, which does little to solve already high unemployment (Evans, 1979: 38). Evans also claims that multinationals 'have both an interest in keeping wages low so that they can make a profit on routine manufacturing operations and an interest in income concentration so that they will have a market for the kinds of products [that is, luxury goods] they are trying to sell' (Evans, 1979: 38). The state, for its part, is interested in reorienting the behaviour of multinationals as far as the first problem is concerned but not the second; here the interests of multinationals in low wages coincides with the interests of the domestic capitalist groups and the state.

In short, the imperatives of capitalist development in the Third World require a particular division of labour amongst the three segments of capital—multinationals provide the technological base; local capitalists, the political base; and the state, the nationalist base. These groups form a class—the 'triple alliance'—united by common interests such as high profits, high growth, and the economic and political repression of the population. An authoritarian structure, although not necessarily a military regime, is necessary for this form of development because of the need to insulate the dominant class factions from the economic and political demands of those groups that are not benefiting economically.

Evans's contribution is to make the case for the systematic analysis of the interplay of the main entrepreneurial actors in development and to show the economic and political implications of their interactions for the society. Studies which focused on just one actor often failed to convey how their activities and roles were contingent on the behaviour and interests of the other entrepreneurial groups.

This said, however, there are many questionable propositions in Evans's analysis, especially regarding the behaviour of multinationals. The most serious is treating dependent development as an independent variable shaping the nature of the regime, the class structure, and the fate of the general population. It neglects to show how differing internal political arrangements and social structures affect development choices and out-comes. Evans (1979: 13) says:

> . . . the argument has been developed in terms that suggest that the characteristics of Brazil's dependent development are not peculiar to Brazil or even to military regimes. Many countries of the periphery may not have sufficient resources or markets to attract the cooperation of multinationals and undertake dependent development, but those which do are likely to experience a form of industrialization that follows the pattern described here.

The primary prism through which development is viewed is whether the state has the capability to attract and bargain with multinationals. If it is successful in doing both, then dependent development will occur and, if not, the country remains in the periphery. Since Evans chose to base his model of dependent development on an authoritarian polity, key inter-vening variables, such as the nature of group cleavages in society and patterns of political mobilization, are ignored in the fashioning of development.

Evans's model might be useful for class-based societies composed of horizontal cleavages,[7] but it is inadequate for studying societies with strong vertical cleavages (whether ethnic, religious, language, or regional). In societies with strong class cleavages, the main source of potential contention is the distribution of development gains between the classes (and if highly radicalized, the nature of the whole production system itself). Those who are not entrepreneurs rarely struggle to replace existing entrepreneurs. In vertically divided societies, on the other hand, there is often a serious con-flict over which groups ought to be the entrepreneurs in the *existing* system of production; the question who is most skilful and able is often not rel-evant, and has important implications for the interrelationships among the state, local capitalists, and multinationals. One can expect significant departures from Evans's model in such issues as the 'political legitimacy of local capital', the nationalist role of the state, and the way multinationals are used by the state to solve economic and political problems.

In a later section, we will delineate how an ethnic framework of develop-ment, as illustrated in Malaysia, differs from the Evans model. But before that, we need to probe further into the character of group interests and

demands in a society with salient ethnic cleavages. It will help us understand why political leaders in these societies might be willing to pay a high
economic cost in dealing with strong passions generated in society.

The Psychology and Politics of Ethnic Claims

Since there are many perspectives on ethnicity, it is important to make a
number of qualifications regarding our treatment. First, we are primarily
concerned with ethnic groups that are large and constitute a significant
segment in a society and whose struggles permeate the centre of national
politics. The relations, behaviour, choices, and interests of ethnic groups
in a society comprising a tiny ethnic group in the midst of an overwhelming
ethnic majority are certainly very different from ethnic groups which are
closely matched in size.

Secondly, we are essentially looking at unranked ethnic groups
(Horowitz, 1985: 22). Unranked groups are divided into vertical cleavages,
with each group having its own set of élites and followers. One group may
have greater power in a particular social sphere, but there is no hierarchical
ordering between them, as in the quintessential case of plantation slavery.
In unranked groups there is less generalized domination, and more uncertainty in the power relations between the ethnic groups (Horowitz,
1985: 28–9).

Thirdly, we are concerned with ethnic relations at the macro level rather
than the micro level. At the micro level—in settings such as the school,
company, or office—individuals often have the choice as to whether they
want to accentuate or play down their ethnic differences. However, at the
macro level—the level where national political decisions are made and
where there are strong pre-existing ethnic organizations and political
parties—organized ethnic groups tend to act in ways that maximize the
advantages that flow to the group. For example, a Malay and a Chinese in
Malaysia or a Tamil and Sinhalese in Sri Lanka might co-own a business
and belong to the same social clubs. They are socially integrated and
co-operative at the micro level. But this does not mean that at the macro
level of group contention they will not press for beneficial policies (in terms
of resource allocation, employment, educational, and ownership quotas, and
language policies) for their group. Getting greater system-wide power for
the group can be advantageous for the individual in increasing his or her
leverage and power in micro-level interactions with ethnic outsiders.

It is important to approach ethnicity in a way that takes into account both
the specific interests of particular ethnic members and the general interests
of the ethnic group. Most studies have tended to do one or the other.
Marxist approaches often view ethnicity as a mask or instrument for advancing underlying material interests. The common argument made is that
a specific class faction, most often the élite, makes general appeals along
ethnic lines to gain advantages for itself. The cultural pluralists, on the
other hand, view ethnicity as constituted by groups having diverging values
and institutions (for example, Smith, M. G., 1965). Groups have a general
interest in dominating one another because of their fundamental and in-

compatible moral and cultural differences.

Close observations of the dynamics of ethnic mobilization, however, usually reveal a complex mix of specific interests and general interests at work. Both have to be included to understand ethnicity as a macro-level unit of action. An important work that takes both of these interests into account is Donald Horowitz's *Ethnic Groups in Conflict* (1985). Horowitz wants to find out what is common to all members of an ethnic group—in societies with large, unranked ethnic groups such as Sri Lanka, Malaysia, and Nigeria—in spite of class differences amongst them. His thesis is that the primary struggle in ethnically divided societies is the struggle over relative group capacity and worth. The main axis of conflict is usually between a 'backward' group, often comprising the indigenous group, and a more 'advanced' group, often comprising immigrants who came to work under the colonial economic system.[8] This evaluation of groups into backward and advanced categories began with the colonial authorities, who introduced a different evaluative framework that diverged from antecedent standards but was apt for measuring success in the new system of competitive economic values. The 'advanced' immigrant groups, who became economically more successful,[9] were labelled as industrious, competitive, and resilient, while powerful negative stereotypes were attached to the indigenous group. For the indigenous groups—such as the Hausa, Malays, Assamese, Sinhalese, and Lulua—the sense of backwardness was profoundly unsettling, giving rise to fears of weakness, unworthiness, and inefficacy.

The common psychological manifestations of this unease were fears of group extinction and a feeling of weakness and helplessness (Horowitz, 1985: 178):

These apprehensions about survival, swamping, and subordination reflect the enormous importance accorded to competitive values: a group that cannot compete will be overcome or will die out. Such sentiments have tended to be uttered at times when the groups entertaining them have been politically in a strong position.

The élites of 'backward' groups, even though they might enjoy powerful political and bureaucratic positions, also feel a sense of diminished worth. As Horowitz (1985: 185) puts it:

If the need to feel worthy is a fundamental human requirement, it is satisfied in considerable measure by belonging to groups that are in turn regarded as worthy. Like individual self-esteem, collective self-esteem is achieved largely by social recognition. Everywhere, but especially in developing countries, where the sphere of politics is unusually broad and its impact powerful, collective social recognition is conferred by political affirmation. For this reason struggles over relative group worth are readily transferred to the political system.

These powerful passions motivate the threatened group to use the political system for the assertion of group worth. The threatened group often attempts, if it has the political capacity, to tighten its political control even more and to impose its ethnic symbols on the rest of society. In order to play a desperate catching up game with the 'advanced' group, the leaders of the 'backward' group also commonly use the state to advance the group in the educational and economic fields.

Horowitz concedes that many of the measures taken by the leaders to benefit the 'backward' group often bring disproportional benefits to the élite members of the ethnic group. However, in nearly all circumstances, the non-élite members support the goals of the élite. This critical observation is often left out in class and Marxist approaches to ethnicity. There is a wider psychological dimension that transcends material interests in ethnic conflict.

Horowitz's argument that ethnic conflict is primarily a struggle over relative group worth and capacity is a powerful one. It gets to the heart of the emotional and sometimes bloody side of ethnic contention. However, Horowitz's analysis needs to be extended to help us understand how the leaders of a 'backward' group might act with regard to the economy. Since Horowitz's basic argument is rooted in group psychology, he uses the terms 'group worth' and 'group capacity' interchangeably. However, group worth is a psychological construct while group capacity is a system-wide capacity. When leaders try to gain greater system-wide capacity, and specifically greater economic capacity, many objectives are served. Besides increasing group worth, greater economic power allows political élites to channel greater material benefits to their supporters. Since these élites also face political competition from other co-ethnics, who often mobilize for even more extensive group rights and entitlements, dispensing patronage becomes central for maintaining power.

There are three ways in which increasing economic group capacity helps the ethnic leaders of the 'backward' group realize the goals of maintaining political power and bolstering group worth. Two of them can be regarded as bestowing material benefits to the ethnic group while the third is psychological and in line with Horowitz's notion of increasing group worth.

The first is the provision of tangible material benefits to the group. Through regulating the enterprises of ethnic outsiders and expanding the state enterprise sector, new opportunities for wealth, income, and employment can be provided to the ethnic group. There is plenty of room for the élite segments of the group to benefit disproportionately. But if the leaders depend on a wide segment of the population for support, there will be pressures to distribute material benefits in a positive sum manner for the ethnic group.[10] Vastly increasing group economic control facilitates such a distribution.

Secondly, increasing group economic capacity can bring support for the leaders even from ethnic members who are not benefiting presently from existing policies. This is because the group's increased control of resources is preferable to non-control, since the chances for benefit later are greater. From visible evidence that some members of the community have become better off, the individual can hope that his time or his children's will come. Albert Hirschman has termed this phenomenon the 'tunnel effect' (Hirschman, 1973). During rapid growth, those left behind might be willing to tolerate some degree of inequality because they take the increase of living standards of their peers as a predictor of their future situation. The present Prime Minister of Malaysia, Datuk Seri[11] Dr Mahathir Mohamad, expressed a view approximating Hirschman's 'tunnel effect' in his book, *The Malay Dilemma* (Mahathir bin Mohamad, 1970: 44), when he defended the small group of Malay company board directors that emerged in the 1960s:

These few Malays, for they are still only very few, have waxed rich not because of themselves but because of the policy of government supported by a huge majority of poor Malays. It would seem that the efforts of the poor Malays have gone to enrich a select few of their own people. The poor Malays themselves have not gained one iota. But if these few Malays are not enriched, the poor Malays will not gain either. It is the Chinese who will continue to live in huge houses and regard the Malays as only fit to drive their cars. . . .

Finally, going beyond the utilitarian logic of tangible and expected benefits, increased group economic capacity also enhances group worth, in the sense Horowitz uses the term. When a few members of the 'backward' ethnic group achieve success in areas where the group was widely regarded as not capable, the rest can now view themselves in a more positive light. Feelings of envy and jealousy might well occur within the group, but within the broader system of inter-ethnic contention for recognition and worth, the less successful might have a stake in defending the *nouveau riche*. It is difficult to know how long individuals who are not benefiting from policies that increase group worth and capacity will continue to support a regime. Just as the hope for future benefits must at some point square with the receipt of actual benefits, once group members take for granted their efficacy and competence, their demands will probably shift to the material sphere.

The goal of increasing group economic control places constraints on the maximization of economic growth and the pursuit of rational economic policies. It is difficult to have a stable division of power between one ethnic group predominating in the economic sphere, even if more capable, and another in the political sphere, especially if political mobilization is permitted and does exist.[12] A political bottleneck exists because of the problem of translating the economic progress of minority businessmen into support and electoral votes for the regime. For not only are questions of ethnic worth at stake for the 'backward' group, but also minority businesses tend to be family oriented and exclusive, offering few benefits to outsiders. Even if state finances were to be bolstered by good economic performance of the advanced group, which presumably might allow for greater state spending on the 'backward' group, the link between the capabilities of the former group contributing to the latter is too indirect and difficult to see.

A point of contrast can be made to Olson's argument in his book, *The Rise and Decline of Nations* (1982). Olson argued that the efficiency and rate of economic growth are directly associated with the type of interest groups in society. Interest organizations which encompass a substantial portion of societal members, such as a large trade union or political party, have an incentive to promote efficiency and growth (Olson, 1982: 47). Examples of such organizations are the trade union organizations of Sweden and

Norway, and political parties whose clients comprise half or more of the population. These encompassing organizations can take a long-term view of economic rationality because if they violate market rules of efficiency for temporary gain, their own members will have to bear a large part of the social costs (Olson, 1982: 53):

Encompassing organizations have some incentive to make the society in which they operate more prosperous, and an incentive to redistribute income to their members with as little excess burden as possible, and to cease such redistribution unless the amount redistributed is substantial in relation to the social cost of the redistribution.

Small interest groups, however, have little incentive to make any sacrifices in the interest of society. The members' interests are best served by implementing regulatory rules to gain as much of society's production as possible because the long-term social costs can be passed on to others.[13] 'This will be expedient, moreover, even if the social costs of the change exceed the amount redistributed by a huge multiple' (Olson, 1982: 44).

However, an encompassing organization such as the party of a 'backward' ethnic group, has little incentive to take a long-term economic view. When ethnic passions are high, feelings of group unworthiness rampant, and the economic power of rival ethnic groups threatening, such an ethnic organization is likely to act more in line with Olson's narrow interest group. Short-term interests predominate across the organization. These include leaders who want to consolidate political power quickly, influential groups who see the chance for quick wealth, and even the larger membership, who see more benefits under the new redistributive arrangement than in the previous system.

The additional problem is that politicians and bureaucrats may fail, from lack of adequate knowledge and historical experience, to comprehend the ill-consequences of violating market norms markedly. Problems tend to creep up slowly and it is usually only with hindsight that a particular policy is deemed defective. There are many factors that can camouflage the structural problems and inefficiencies of an economy—such as good prices for the country's exports, access to foreign loans, and inflows of foreign capital investment. As Olson (1982: 52) also points out, an encompassing organization, especially if it is popular with its members, may not enjoy the necessary feedback to correct its poor economic policies:

If a society is composed only of highly encompassing organizations and institutions, there also may be less diversity of advocacy, opinion, and policy, and fewer checks to erroneous ideas and policies. Encompassing organizations and institutions may therefore perform unusually badly in some cases or periods and unusually effectively in others.

We thus conclude this section on the nature of ethnic claims and their impact on economic development with the following points: (1) in situations of strong ethnic passions and contention, encompassing organizations of the 'backward' group are willing to forgo national economic efficiency for political support building, group empowerment, and building up the economic capacity of the group, and (2) the high costs of economic policies do not reveal themselves immediately but over time. Temporary props to the economic system, such as favourable external economic conditions and strong political support for the regime, deflect attention from present, underlying economic inefficiencies.

The Ethnic Framework of Development

We now turn to how a state, relying on an indigenous ethnic political base, might shape the role of state enterprises, local capital (primarily from the advanced group), and multinationals. Our argument has thus far been that such a regime is constrained from aiming for full-scale economic rationality and efficiency. As a way of framing the rest of our analysis, it will be useful to compare the ethnic framework of development in Malaysia and Evans's model of dependent development, with its claim about the 'triple alliance'. Our concern will be how the roles and leverage of the entrepreneurial groups vary in each case, and how their respective economic and political trajectories might differ (see Table 1.2 for a summary).

In Evans's model, state enterprises were portrayed as the essential guarantors of national capitalist development. Their objective was to solve bottlenecks in the economy and to counteract the negative effects of multinational participation (see Petras, 1976; Freeman, 1982; Duvall and Freeman, 1981, for similar views). Evans, however, blocked out the impact of wider political issues on the role of state enterprises since he started with the premise of authoritarianism; hence he failed to consider how state enterprises could act as agents of internal political management. Edwin Jones (1981: 40), in looking at the Caribbean, gives an alternative view:

. . . in all competitive milieux . . . there is the contradictory need for the political elites to build personal reward systems and public purpose organizations. The public enterprise system conveniently satisfies both imperatives. It facilitates the use of public resources to strengthen the political base of representatives of the state. Simultaneously, it allows for the creation of counterpart bureaucracies which are not constrained by the traditional ethos of the general bureaucracy and which, therefore, allow state representatives to distribute political rewards with greater flexibility.

If we consider further that in an ethnic society, state élites have an incentive to counteract the economic power of rival ethnic groups, then one can readily see how political and economic objectives can be combined by the promotion of state enterprises.

Thus, the behaviour of state enterprises and their relation to the state in Malaysia may vary considerably from Evans's model. First of all, their desire is to enter into all sectors of the economy and accumulate assets as quickly as possible for the 'backward' ethnic group. Their ethnic agenda does not grant them the role of the third partner in an elaborate division of labour to maximize national accumulation. Secondly, central authorities as a rule do not try to restrain them from offering too much competition to multinationals and local capital. Rather they do the opposite, coming up with elaborate rules and regulations, and the finances for large-scale state

TABLE 1.2

Evans's Model of Dependent Development Compared with the Ethnic Framework of Development in Malaysia

Actors	Evans's Model of Dependent Development	Ethnic Framework of Development
Leaders' goals	Maximize growth in a dependent, internationally constrained context.	Shape development to enhance dominant ethnic party's political base; meet cultural aspirations of 'backward' group.
Bureaucratic behaviour	Harmonize interests between entrepreneurial groups to maximize growth.	Control private sector groups to facilitate expansion of state enterprises and entrepreneurs from 'backward' group; strain national resources for state expansion.
State enterprises	Participate in selected sectors to solve bottlenecks and act as counterweight to MNCs; impose 'national logic of accumulation'.	Pursue an ethnic economic role rather than buttress 'national logic of accumulation'. Counterweight to 'advanced' ethnic group and MNCs. Involved in all sectors; surpluses used for ethnic redistribution.
Local capital	Capable entrepreneurs promoted by the state whenever possible. Its leverage is its 'political legitimacy' and ability to mobilize against the state.	Businessmen from 'advanced' group face constraints imposed by the state. Weak in mobilizing against the state. However, entrepreneurs from 'backward' group strongly promoted by the state.
Multi-national corporations	Provide the vital technological basis for dependent development. Deepen industrialization. Highly capital intensive and exacerbates unemployment. Induced by large market and high income inequality.	Provide the state with an alternative to entrepreneurs from 'advanced' ethnic group. Helps state with employment creation (in labour-intensive, export industries); industrial deepening not a state priority.
Class alliance	State, local capital, and multinationals share common interests in high profits. Agree to a division of labour in the economy to maximize growth.	No national policy of collaboration. No division of labour and much duplication of investments, especially between the state and ethnic capital.
Economic outcomes	Industrial deepening and diversification. High growth rates but high unemployment and falling real wages for the masses.	*Ad hoc* industrial development. Many structural inefficiencies in economy. Growth rates highly dependent on commodity prices. More emphasis on employment

(continued)

TABLE 1.2 (*continued*)

Actors	Evan's Model of Dependent Development	Ethnic Framework of Development
		and on stable real wages for purposes of political incorporation.
Political outcomes	Highly authoritarian state. Need to repress the general populace because of their economic exclusion.	Some degree of pluralism because of ethnic divisions and ethnic political mobilization. Dominant ethnic party able to enjoy political support because of key role in providing material and psychological benefits to 'backward' group.

enterprise expansion. If and when central authorities exert control, their main concern will be only to prevent state enterprises from wasting too many resources—a result not wholly unanticipated since the ethnic agenda of state enterprises can lead to confusion about whether to base performance on commercial or social criteria.

However, given the lack of congruity between the interests of state and the dominant economic groups, it is important that state élites have sufficient leverage over the private sector actors to pursue their objectives. The new dependency theorists provide useful suggestions about how the state might exercise control over private economic actors. For instance, Moran (1978: 82) has hypothesized that the state is better able to control foreign firms when they have high fixed investments, high fixed costs, unchanging technology, and simple marketing procedures. At the political level, Stepan (1978: 238) has argued for the necessity of the political élites to have sufficient internal cohesion and unity to prevent external groups from weakening their commitment to the formulation and implementation of policies. And state élites, according to Hamilton (1982), must also have sufficient political support from subordinate groups to forestall attempts by dominant economic groups to counter-mobilize against unfavourable state policies.

The *sine qua non* for state expansion is undoubtedly the fiscal capacity of the state. Whether it means taking over companies, starting new ones, or forming partnerships with private companies, the state must enjoy a large capacity to mobilize resources. The financial leverage becomes even more critical if the state lacks critical technological and organizational capabilities. Thus, state finances constitute the ultimate restraint to state expansion—it is a vital issue how the state gets its resources, how prudently it manages them, and how long they last.

Turning to the relationship between the state and local private capital, Evans argued that the state, acting within constraints imposed by the pursuit of high growth, accords local capital (particularly 'élite' local capital) a privileged position in the economy. This was due to their 'political legitimacy' and ability to mobilize against the rulers.

In Malaysia, the difficulty of translating Chinese economic progress into Malay political support for the political élites precludes Chinese local capital from having any privileged position *vis-à-vis* the state. Any influence Chinese businessmen might have with the government rests on two fragile stilts: (1) the ability to mobilize and deliver the support of a large segment of the Chinese population for the government, and (2) the willingness on the part of Malay leaders to compromise with the Chinese. Cracks in *either* can quickly make the position of Chinese businesses vulnerable to state controls and restrictions.

Table 1.3 shows the range of possible responses by Chinese businessmen and companies to unfavourable or restrictive state policies, such as requirements to bring in more Malay partners and workers. They can act individually or collectively and they can decide whether to comply or not with state policies. Individual persons and companies that comply with state policies are likely to act on the premise that the benefits, such as expansion possibilities and making good profits, exceed the costs of complying. We can expect the owners of large firms and public companies, because they have the interest and ability to modify their family business structures, to exercise this option. Individuals or companies who do not wish to comply—because of poor remuneration for giving up part of their ownership, the constraints of family business structures, or just plain resentment—might simply not invest further or look for opportunities abroad.

One other way of complying is for existing Chinese organizations, such as political parties and chambers of commerce, to pool their members' funds for productive investment. Since they are already organized for political purposes, they have the ability to mobilize capital from their members.

TABLE 1.3
Possible Chinese Business Responses to State Policies

| | Actor | |
Behaviour	Individual	Group
Compliance	Benefits (e.g., profits, possibilities for expansion) exceed costs of complying. Usually worthwhile for large firms.	Complying, while trying to increase bargaining power *vis-à-vis* leaders and bureaucrats. Pooling of resources by individual units as a strategy to gain strength and leverage.
Non-compliance	Costs of compliance high (economically and culturally). Cease to invest and demoralized. Behaviour usually exhibited by small firms. Large firms look for opportunities abroad.	Organizations try to counter-mobilize against policies. Investment strike used as a weapon. Success depends on (1) state's financial resources and willingness to forgo investments; (2) other alternatives to Chinese investments (e.g., MNCs).

These organizations, on the surface, appear to have greater leverage with state officials than individual businesses because they are larger and have greater access to influential persons. The last option, group non-compliance, refers to Chinese companies failing to invest on a large scale. Whether they do so consciously or not, their leverage lies in demonstrating to the officials that Chinese failure to invest will have serious consequences for the national economy, and ultimately the welfare of the Malays. Their ability to modify unfavourable policies, however, depends on whether the state can find alternatives to the investment shortfalls.

Multinationals, in Evans's model, were depicted as highly capital intensive and oligopolistic. They are attracted only to large markets and are generally reluctant to part with equity ownership. Although they are critical for industrial deepening, they contribute toward economic and political exclusion of the general populace.

The ethnic basis of Malaysia's development policies, however, suggests a different role for multinationals. The ethnic agenda of state enterprises and the restrictions on local capital hinder a strong developmentalist role by both. Multinationals can help compensate for these weaknesses. We can expect many multinationals in Malaysia to be engaged in relatively simple production, which would be carried out by locals in other countries of comparable per capita GNP.

In a situation of ethnic conflict, multinationals can also help neutralize Chinese business protests against government policies by offsetting their investment shortfalls. This is not to say that multinationals are not regulated, but controls can be so adjusted as to achieve a desired level of foreign investment.

The other difference with Evans's model is that unemployment cannot be so easily dismissed politically. Because there is some degree of pluralism built into the system by ethnic divisions and mobilizing ethnic parties, it is difficult to install authoritarian rule. There is hence greater pressure to meet mass demands. The state élites, therefore, have a stake in multi-nationals absorbing labour.

There is a greater variety of technologies and firm types available in the international economy than large, oligopolistic firms acting on the basis of global rationality. Helleiner noted in the early 1970s that there was a new form of manufacturing investment in labour-intensive industries (1973). Multinationals, experiencing strong price competition, were locating the labour-intensive aspect of their operations in low-wage countries. Fabricated products were then exported back to the home country for further processing. These firms generated few linkages in the economy and made modest contributions to state revenue since governments had to offer generous tax incentives to enlist their participation. However, they were not constrained by the domestic market and absorbed a lot of labour.

Kumar and McLeod (1981) have also noted the rise of multinationals from developing countries setting up companies in other less industrialized countries. Their operations tend to be labour intensive and well adapted to producing low volume products (typically low-priced brand products) quite efficiently. They are therefore suited for the small markets of many

Third World countries, and they are often willing to take minority positions, which dovetail favourably with host governments' requirements for giving sizeable equity participation to locals (see Wells, 1981, Chap. 2; Lecraw, 1981, Chap. 3).

In short, the international economy is not monolithic in structure and governments can draw on a variety of technologies and firm types for their purposes. There might not be a deep contradiction between getting foreign participation in manufacturing and expecting them to enter joint ventures easily and provide high levels of employment. Many of these multinationals cannot be said to play a vital role in deepening the technological capabilities of the nation. But in a country like Malaysia, they can offer a short-to-moderate term solution to underlying economic problems arising from the political dynamics of cultural pluralism.

Clearly, an elaborate, rational division of labour amongst the main entrepreneurial groups does not appear possible in Malaysia. The state élite's desire to increase group economic capacity leads state enterprises to compete against and sometimes supplant the existing entrepreneurs rather than to co-operate with them to create a dynamic economy. Large state resources, for example, are used to buy up established private sector companies in low-growth and declining sectors. This strategy allows for rapid control of the economy and for redistributing existing surpluses to the leaders' supporters. The corollary, however, is the weak effort to modernize and strengthen the physical and educational infrastructure of the nation, so vital for building up new competitive industries.

Despite many structural inefficiencies, it does not mean that high growth rates cannot be obtained. A buoyant external sector and foreign capital inflows can help mask the underlying problems of the economy. However, the weakening of the international props (that is, good commodity prices and adequate foreign capital inflow) can easily lead to serious problems for the economy. Taking corrective action, however, is not easy. The popularity and zeal behind the state's ethnic mission enfeeble vigorous and effective criticisms of development policies.

Politically, however, the economic policies can have high pay-off. The leaders are able to enjoy strong support from the provision of new material and psychological benefits to their ethnic base. This is the fundamental propellant of the politico-economic system. But finding the right balance between economic dynamism and political legitimacy is problematic. When effective growth-promoting policies are pursued, political problems arise because the 'backward' group feels left behind. However, when the system swings to meet political goals, economic rationality is undermined; this results from the increasing expectations of the beneficiaries of the state's largesse, who want to preserve existing policies, as well as the breakdown of effective feedback mechanisms because of highly centralized economic decision-making structures. The ever-present danger is that if the economy fails to perform for extended periods of time, the legitimacy of the leaders will disappear and this may lead to political instability. Such a situation would be the worst of two worlds, a non-performing economy and an unpopular political regime.

Methodology, Propositions, and Data

The study is based on the single-case study approach. The single case has both limitations and virtues. It is not designed, like the comparative method, to generate explicit causal inferences because it suffers from a 'lack of variation in possible causes and effects' (Smelser, 1976: 199). The single case, however, provides plenty of scope for testing existing notions and theories, pointing out inadequacies of existing approaches, refining new relations among variables, and, not least, telling a good, theoretically informed story.

Eckstein (1975) advances the 'crucial-case study' as one type of case-study.[14] Its basic aim is to test existing theories—for example, invalidating a theory by taking a case that ought to fit a theory, but which does not, then proceeding (if possible) to suggest a counter theory.[15]

The starting point in this book is Evans's model of development. In many ways, Malaysia belongs to the set of countries which fit Evans's definition of 'dependent development' (see Evans, 1979: 290–7). The *World Development Report* (1987) by the World Bank ranks Malaysia as a middle-income economy. In 1985, its gross domestic product was US$31.2 billion with a population of 15.6 million; in per capita terms, it ranked above Portugal and Brazil and not much below Mexico and South Korea (World Bank, 1987: 203, Table 1). Its manufacturing base was around 18 per cent of GDP, and it had strong multinational participation. Malaysia is therefore a pertinent case to evaluate and add the necessary distinctions to Evans's model.

We have already noted Evans's failure to take into account variations in internal socio-political arrangements in his model of dependent development. Important divergences in economic arrangements and outcomes can result when ethnicity is introduced as a variable. Thus, the central propositions of the book are as follows: (1) When there is a schism between the interests of the state élites and the local capitalist class, there is a limit to the pursuit of a rational economic course. Local capital is relatively weak against a state with a strong political base. This fact can allow the state to pursue its politico-cultural goals even at the expense of national economic rationality.

The common assumption in most rationalist approaches is the imputed identity of interest between the state and domestic capital (for example, Bennett and Sharpe, 1985: 45). This relationship needs to be examined in each particular case rather than simply asserted because it has important implications for the goals of the regime, including how the state, local capital, and multinationals are promoted.

The temporal variation in our case-study—from a moderately successful *laissez-faire* system to a highly state interventionist economy with deep economic problems—highlights the role of internal domestic arrangements and choices in producing economic problems. Our second proposition is thus: (2) Socio-political structures are as critical in accounting for economic problems such as slow growth, mounting foreign debt, and state fiscal crisis as are adverse global economic conditions. Multinationals play a minimal role in accounting for economic and political problems.

While the international environment, including multinationals and global financial and commodity markets, does have important implications for development, the distinguishing feature of a society is how it adapts to the global economy and builds resiliency in its economy. The 'world-system' approach of Wallerstein (1974: 1976) has, with unfortunate consequences, provided the methodological justification for reducing many local processes to international determinants. This book tries to suggest, from the investigation of a concrete situation, the need to move away from a constrained and determinative view of the international economy to one that emphasizes an internal dynamic in the development process.

The primary sources of empirical data for the study are interviews with government officials and business executives and representatives, and local and regional newspapers. About twenty-five interviews were conducted in all, in early 1985. On the business side, about fifteen interviews were carried out with officials from the Malaysian International Chamber of Commerce and Industry, Associated Chinese Chambers of Commerce and Industry, Malay Chamber of Commerce, Federation of Malaysian Manufacturers, trade representatives (in embassies and business organizations) from the US, Britain, Japan, Germany, and Singapore, and a few local and foreign company executives. The interviews provided important information on the policy positions of business groups and the main patterns of foreign investment in Malaysia. Interviews with owners and executives of companies, however, were difficult to get and the information provided was not much more revealing than that found in business journals and magazines. There was little to offer companies while they had a lot to lose by revealing any information that might displease government officials. It was necessary, therefore, to turn to publicly available company reports, business journals, and magazines—in particular *Malaysian Business (MB)*, *Insight*, and *Asian Finance (AF)*—to get information on company strategies and business personalities. Interviews with government officials provided useful information on the key changes in the priorities of important technocratic and bureaucratic agencies responsible for national economic management.

Extensive use was made of newspapers—especially the *Straits Times (ST)*, *New Straits Times (NST)*, *Straits Times*, *Singapore (ST(S))*, and the *Asian Wall Street Journal (AWSJ)*—for current and historical information on government policies, leaders' policy positions, as well as general statistics. Cabinet ministers sometimes reveal important data on the economy (especially concerning state enterprises and Malay businesses) in newspapers that cannot be found in government documents and publications. Government plan documents and statistics were also used extensively. Unfortunately, information useful to this study, like the Department of Statistics' *Principle Statistics on Ownership and Participation in Commerce and Industry* (1970/1 and1981/2), are top secret and only snippets of this information appear in government documents. Such is the sensitivity of ethnic ownership patterns in Malaysia. Although the author cannot claim to have taken a random sample of firms and government officials, every effort has been made to select important companies (state, Malay, Chinese, and foreign), key policies, and the main patterns of foreign investment to make this study and claims of Malaysia's development process as convincing as possible.

1. This analysis is confined to Peninsular Malaysia where 82.1 per cent of the 15.8 million population (in 1985) reside. The East Malaysian states of Sabah and Sarawak (in North Borneo) have a different history and ethnic structure from that of West (or Peninsular) Malaysia, and there is not much data on them.

2. The book by Snodgrass, *Inequality and Economic Development in Malaysia* (1980), is one of the few that explicitly treats the role of ethnicity in economic development. His broad analysis is mainly concerned with the links between ethnicity, inequality, and state redistributive policies. Our analysis focuses more directly on the role and bargaining capacities of the key entrepreneurial groups as they relate to the Malay leaders' politico-cultural goals.

3. Because of the weak private sector, the main avenue to mobility has been the professions and government jobs. Ethnic contention has been bitter over tertiary educational recruitment, the critical ladder to professional status.

4. While the maximization of economic growth can help solve these conflicting goals in the long run, the fact that individuals and groups primarily conduct their affairs over a much shorter term places the issue of rational economic policies and arrangements in a secondary place among national priorities.

5. In typical fashion, the successes of Hong Kong, Taiwan, and South Korea are cited as examples of the market mechanism being superior in generating growth and alleviating poverty (Lal, 1985: 87, 102). The high degrees of state co-ordination and control in the latter two cases are usually not addressed in the analyses.

6. The new dependency theorists differ from the orthodox dependency theorists (as represented by theorists such as Frank (1967) and Dos Santos (1970)) in rejecting economic development as a zero sum game between the core (or advanced countries) and the periphery (poorly developed countries). They have been inspired by the work of Cardoso and his collaborator, Faletto, who in their book, *Dependency and Development in Latin America* (1979), brought a greater internal focus to development processes (as opposed to sheer external determination) and gave a greater degree of freedom to domestic actors to shape their societies. The new theorists, while still seeing the international economy as benefiting primarily the core countries and producing various circumscribed social arrangements in the periphery, nonetheless do allow for development to occur in dependent situations. They are concerned with the bargaining capacities of the domestic actors to allow for this form of development. The scholars in this group include Tugwell (1975), Moran (1974, 1978), Evans (1979), Hamilton (1982), Gereffi (1983), and Bennett and Sharpe (1985).

7. Even here, studies done on East Asian countries, such as South Korea and Taiwan, have shown that while these countries can be described as undergoing dependent development, the mix of entrepreneurial participation is very different (that is, comparatively low multinational involvement) and patterns of income distribution, employment, and wages are far more favourable than suggested by Evans (see Gold, 1981 and Lim Hyun-Chin, 1982).

8. These terms are used for analytical purposes only and are by no means meant to be pejorative or judgmental. In any case, the leaders themselves of economically disadvantaged groups often refer to their own groups as 'backward'.

9. Some of the reasons provided by Horowitz (1985: 151–60) are the immigrants' greater mobility to pursue economic opportunities in contrast to indigenous groups who belonged in traditional communities, more favourable facilities for education, and sometimes cultural attributes which favoured the pooling of resources.

10. The terms positive sum and zero sum are analytical terms in game theory. In a zero sum situation, one person or group loses what the other gains and vice versa. In a positive sum situation, both parties can gain from a particular distribution of resources because the total pie increases. It should be emphasized that our emphasis of ethnicity as a critical macro

unit of social action does not deny the presence of significant income or wealth inequality within ethnic groups. We only want to caution against the rigid argument that ethnicity is merely a mask or instrument for class interests. In positive sum situations (not only in the economic sphere but also, as we shall see, in the psychological sphere), élite enrichment and popular support can coexist at the same time.

11. This is an honorific title given by the rulers (sultans) and governors of the states of Malaysia. Roughly equivalent in rank is 'Datuk' or 'Dato'. The other titles that might appear before Malaysian names are 'Tengku' (or 'Tunku'), 'Tun', and 'Tan Sri'. 'Tengku' (or 'Tunku') is a Malay hereditary title denoting royalty. 'Tun' is the highest federal honorific title conferred by the Agong (King). It is roughly equivalent to a British knighthood. 'Tan Sri', which is more liberally given, is next in rank and quite common among prominent Malaysians, particularly those friendly to the government (Mauzy, 1983: 170–4).

12. The model of consociational democracy, advanced principally by Lijphart (1969, 1977), argued that democratic functioning was possible in divided societies if the élites of the various segments, in rational recognition of centrifugal forces, came together to form co-operative political arrangements. The scheme, as it was supposed to work in Malaysia, was based on ethnic leaders agreeing to tolerate Malay political predominance in return for preserving Chinese economic power.

13. Olson accounts for the economic decline of Great Britain by the agglomeration of special interests groups (of workers, businesses, and professionals) in the society, which have gnawed away at the economy.

14. The others are the configurative-idiographic (or rich, interpretative studies); disciplined-configurative study (systematic application of an existing theory to a case); heuristic case-studies (the sequential study of individual cases to improve on a theoretical construct); and plausibility probes (looking for an empirical instance to establish whether a theoretical construct is worth considering).

15. The converse is also valid: confirming a theory by taking a case that ought not to fit the theory, but which actually does (see Eckstein, 1975: 118).

2   The Colonial Impact

Introduction

GROUPS do not confront one another merely because they differ in their norms, cultural practices, and symbols. While individuals sharing common attributes have strong affective ties which serve as initial bases of group differentiation, salient group cleavages and conflict require another important ingredient, a sense of group weakness and threatened status growing out of a common competitive environment. This chapter, on the colonial era, investigates the new economic framework and accompanying set of values the British colonialists brought to the Malay world. The resulting social structure was marked by ethnic pluralism while the emerging export economy was distinguished by segmentation along ethnic lines. The indigenous Malays became marginal in an economy dominated by Europeans (foremost, British) and, to a lesser extent, the large Chinese immigrant group, producing fears of Malay weakness and peril not just about the economy, but in politics as well. These economic and ethnic structures were to shape Malaysia's post-colonial development.

Historical Background

The Malay archipelago was an active trading area for centuries before European intervention. Located between the two great markets of early Asia—India and China—numerous trading ports developed along the archipelago's long coastline to service regional and Asian trade (Courtenay, 1972: 42). Chinese traders were known to have supplied, even prior to the fourteenth century, pottery, silk, and lacquerware in exchange for the region's natural products such as ivory, tortoiseshell, resins, rattan, and tin (Andaya and Andaya, 1982: 29).

A coastal port, through conquest and alliance building, would occasionally establish itself as the regional centre and become the main port of call for foreign and regional traders. These centres, acting as important channels for the permeation of cultural forms and ideas brought by foreign traders, shaped the Malay world fundamentally. Indian influence was very strong before the tenth century. Indian traders introduced Hinduism and Buddhism to the region while Indian concepts of kingship and political power strongly influenced the courtly culture of the Malay rulers. Islam came later but spread quickly throughout the Malay archipelago after the founder of the Melaka sultanate, the hegemonic centre of the fourteenth century, embraced the religion. Islam was to constitute a vital component of Malay identity, differentiating the Malays, in addition to language and custom, from the Chinese and Indian immigrants streaming into Malaya[1] in the nineteenth and twentieth centuries.

For many Malays, especially among the second generation leaders of the post-colonial era, the Melaka sultanate symbolized Malay sophistication in trade and the use of money. In voicing the sentiments of the current generation of the Malay middle class, Dr Mahathir Mohamad, the present Prime Minister, had this view of early Malay commerce (1970: 34):

We do not know when money in the form of coins was first used in Malaya. What we do know is that it antedated the coming of the Chinese. Ancient Malay coins show strong evidence of Indian and Arab influence and very little, if any at all, Chinese influence. It follows that sophisticated commerce involving money instead of barter was already in progress when the Chinese came.

This view echoes a common feeling that it was the coming of the aggressive Europeans and the Chinese which stifled the full flowering of Malay commerce.

The Europeans began to show interest in the region around the fifteenth century with the expansion of their maritime powers and desire to dominate important world trade routes. Successive European nations, as each gained dominance in the European state system, conquered the strategic trading centres of the Malay archipelago. In 1511, the Portuguese, with minimal effort, conquered Melaka to take over the valuable spice trade. In 1641, the Dutch, under the auspices of the Dutch East India Company, seized Melaka. Neither the Portuguese nor the Dutch could so completely dominate trade as to put an end to native trading but their presence inhibited the development of any future regional hegemonic centres in the Malay archipelago.

The indigenous society before British intervention was the product of the decomposition of the Melaka sultanate. Some states in the Malay hinterland were established by princes of the Melaka sultanate, while others were formed by members of regional dynasties setting up their own territories and states in the peninsula (see Gullick, 1958: 9–11; Andaya and Andaya, 1982: 55–62).[2] Each state had a ruler bearing the honorific title of sultan or 'yang di-pertuan besar' (he who is made lord). Below the sultan was the stratum of aristocratic chiefs, who descended from the lesser royal and ministerial lineages of the Melaka sultanate. As members of the ruling class, the sultan and the chiefs enjoyed much prestige and power. They had the right to tax goods traded in their territories and to command the services of the subject classes for household and military purposes. There was little wealth accumulation among the ruling class because available funds (primarily coming from tin taxes) were used for personal and political ends rather than for further economic investment (Gullick, 1958: 131). The principle concern of the ruling class was power aggrandizement. Available resources were used for enlarging the sultan's or chief's retinue, which denoted status and was useful for military purposes, and for indulging in luxurious consumption, again symbolizing status and power.

The lesser authorities were the village headman and the ritual and religious functionaries. The duties of the village headman were manifold, from collecting taxes and organizing corvée labour, to keeping law and order. At the base of the social system was the peasant cultivator. Peasant cultivation, mainly of rice and fruits, was conducted on a household basis, although mutual help was common. Peasant wealth accumulation was minimal since any obvious sign of wealth or surplus quickly invited expropriation by the upper classes. One factor which restrained the rapacity of the ruling class was the great geographical mobility the peasants enjoyed by virtue of the abundant land available. Rulers and chiefs who acted harshly risked losing their manpower and revenue base if their harshness provoked peasants to migrate.

The political system tended toward a high degree of decentralization. There was no evidence of centralization within or between the Malay states before British colonialism. The sultan, lacking an adequate communication and transport network, and a centralized bureaucracy, was limited in his ability to control the chiefs. Conflicts amongst the chiefs and between chiefs and sultans were common. The fissiparous tendencies of the state were made worse by the absence of fixed rules for royal succession, producing numerous skirmishes among rival claimants to the throne.

Malay society was thus far removed from abstract notions of nationalism and economic development. The Malay peasant only dimly perceived that he belonged to a wider world than the village community. Members of the ruling class, while sharing a sense of belonging to a state, were more inclined toward enhancing their personal political positions than preserving the integrity of the abstract state. Chiefs and rulers from different states would constantly form alliances with one another or with foreigners to maintain their power. This system made the Malay states porous to external influences, and explains why the British were able to secure control of Malaya without much resistance.

The British East India Company came to the region in the late eighteenth century in search of trading and military bases to conduct their valuable China trade (Turnbull, 1964: 130). Finding the Malay rulers quite willing to cede territory in exchange for 'protection' and 'recognition' against internal and external threats, the British managed to acquire two strategic islands, Penang and Singapore, off the shores of the Malay peninsula in 1816 and 1819 respectively. In 1826 the two ports, together with Melaka—which had come into British hands earlier in 1795 after Napoleon conquered the Netherlands—were combined under a single administrative unit, the Straits Settlements. British officials initially did not show any desire to intervene further in the Malay states. Britain's main diplomatic interest, mirroring its global commercial hegemony, had become free trade rather than territorial expansion. 'Only the inability of native regimes to maintain themselves in the face of mounting domestic and foreign pressures prompted Britain's direct (and generally begrudging) intervention' (Smith, T., 1981: 100). The officials adhered to this policy of non-interference until pressures to intervene proved too great.

The stable trade conditions in the Straits Settlements attracted many Chinese traders, many of whom ventured into tin-mining in the Malay states. Although Malay chiefs had been involved in tin-mining in the past, particularly when surface mining sufficed, the Chinese now proved useful to the Malay rulers and chiefs because they were able to mine deeper using adapted rice-farming techniques like the wooden chain pump (Lim Chong-Yah, 1967: 47). The Chinese financiers and miners also had liquid capital and, through the use of secret societies, could exert tight control over Chinese labour. Before the 1850s, the Chinese mining communities were relatively small and could be closely monitored and controlled by the Malay chiefs.

However, with the spurt of demand for tin in the 1850s, there was an onrush of Chinese labour and capital into the tin-rich states of Perak and Selangor. Mining settlements increased in size and Malay political control weakened substantially (Gullick, 1958: 126). Chinese secret societies fought each other for tin-mining land, and often took sides with rival Malay chiefs, who also engaged in territorial struggles over tin areas. At stake was their critical revenue base. The civil strife in the Malay states redounded on the Straits Settlements in secret society warfare, threatening trade and investment.

British officialdom, coming under strong pressure from the European and Chinese commercial communities in the Settlements, decided that intervention was necessary to introduce 'good government' in the Malay states. Preferring indirect rule to annexation, the British officials' typical strategy was to support or recognize a particular ruler or claimant to the throne, who then had to accept a British Resident to run the government. The Pangkor Treaty, signed in 1874 when the first state of Perak came under direct British influence, stipulated that the Resident's 'advice must be asked and acted upon on all questions other than those touching Malay Religion and Custom' (Parkinson, 1960: 324).

The British officials did not come with a master plan for colonial rule in Malaya. Important debates took place between the Colonial Office and local British officials regarding the most appropriate land tenure arrangements (see Lim Teck Ghee, 1976: Chap. 1) and the degree of central control in the states (Emerson, 1937). Lacking an explicit strategy, British residents adjusted to the conditions they found themselves in and generally proceeded cautiously in implementing their ideas. Nonetheless, they held in common two central, and sometimes conflicting, objectives. One was to preserve the basic structures of Malay society as far as possible, if only because it best ensured political order and stability. The other was to lay the conditions for a thriving export economy to provide the finances for running the colony. Nothing seemed to fulfil their modernization mission more than the conversion of jungles to plantation agriculture.

British officials carried out major changes in the previous style of administration and revenue use. The powers of taxation and spending were removed from the indigenous power-holders and placed in the hands of new state treasuries. Revenues obtained were now devoted to greater spending on railways, roads, bridges, and telegraphic services, particularly to service

the growing tin-mining industry (Li Dun Jen, 1982: 27).[3] However, the
British Residents were careful to maintain the influence and prestige of the
rulers by giving them a symbolic role in newly created State Councils, and
were mindful of acting as if they were under the sultan's authority. By and
large, the sultans and leading chiefs (the lesser chiefs lost out in the process
of centralization) went along with the British because they were compensated in other ways (Jagjit Singh Sidhu, 1980: 188):

> The Sultans were provided with generous monetary allowances, allowed to enjoy
> the superficial trappings of pomp and ceremony, and freed from the uncertainties
> that could be created by rebellious subjects and court intrigues. In return for this
> security of tenure the Rulers were required to surrender most of their real powers
> and authority.

To promote administrative uniformity and economic co-ordination, the
British undertook the unprecedented step of creating a new federation and
centralized bureaucracy—the Malayan Civil Service—in 1895 to oversee
the states of Perak, Selangor, Pahang, and Negeri Sembilan (which became
known as the Federated Malay States or FMS). Centralized departments
were created in finance, public works, lands and mines, agriculture, and
police. 'The executive ranks of this bureaucracy were wholly European,
and in effect all departments of public life passed under European administrative control' (Roff, 1967: 13). The uniform rules and procedures,
now extended over a much wider territory, were decisive in providing the
necessary security and predictability for entrepreneurs to engage in large-
scale economic activities.

Changes were also made in the indigenous system of land tenure arrangements. In the traditional system, the cultivator had free access to land.
Although in theory, the sultan had the right to dispose of waste or un-
cultivated land according to his wishes, customary law recognized the right
of the cultivator to land as long as he paid a certain rent to the ruler (Lim
Teik Ghee, 1976: 6). The British officials regarded this system as lacking a
well-defined system of proprietorship and security of tenure for the user.
In its place, they introduced a system of individualized land-holdings and
the idea of land as a commercial asset. Peasants were given proprietorship
of the land they were cultivating on condition they paid quit rent but all
unused land passed to the state, thereby freeing vast tracts for modern
agriculture.

In finance, the colonial government set up the Board of Commissioners
of Currency with sole powers to issue standard coins and notes. Transactions in the past were carried out using foreign silver coins, but since there
was a perennial shortage, trade was frequently disrupted (Bank Negara,
1979: 27). Instead, a new Malayan currency was issued fully backed by the
sterling, permitting free exchange between the two currencies. The
Currency Board, by ensuring monetary and exchange stability, was critical
for the export economy's ability to attract foreign capital and to carry out
smooth international transactions (Lim Chong-Yah, 1967: 230).

Finally, the colonial government played an integral role in the export
economy by operating the 'immigration gate'. Malays showed a reluctance

to work outside their village communities in harsh, lowly paid conditions. They had adequate land for cultivation and the colonial government had no desire to forcibly recruit or even persuade Malays to work in the plantations and mines. Instead, the colonial officials turned to the surplus population areas of the world, permitting free immigration, first from China and later from India. The persistent problem of European planters, as they moved to Malaya from Ceylon and elsewhere, was securing labour supplies. Chinese labourers, mainly absorbed in tin-mining, preferred to work in culturally familiar settings, and were in any case tightly controlled by Chinese employers. The shift was therefore made to recruit Indian migrants. The planters themselves showed a marked preference for the more familiar and submissive Tamil labourer. The colonial government actively bargained with the Government of India to permit a greater flow of migrants, even subsidizing steamship fares between the Indian port of Nagapatnam and Penang (see Arasaratnam, 1970). Both Chinese and Indian migration was unregulated until the Depression, when the colonial government implemented a restricted immigration policy which applied until 1947. However, already by the 1930s, the demography of the society had undergone an unalterable change (see Table 2.1). By 1921, there was a rough balance between the indigenous Malay and the migrant populations. Of the 2.9 million population, Malays constituted 48 per cent, Chinese, 29.4 per cent, and Indians, 15.1 per cent (Snodgrass, 1980: 24, Table 2.1). Although the migrant population was predominantly male until the late 1930s, there was little miscegenation and intermarriage with the indigenous women. Religion, language, and tight community surveillance acted as powerful barriers.[4]

For the Malays, the changes wrought by colonialism had a major imprint on their psyche. The experience of external domination weakened their collective self-confidence and drove them, particularly the second generation post-independence Malay élite and intelligentsia, to recover this loss in the symbolic, political, and economic spheres. The first generation leaders were part of the colonial past, and did not reflect abstractly on its meaning for group identity and destiny. The following (and current) generation of the Malay élite, however, began to view with dismay the

TABLE 2.1

Population by Ethnic Group and Sex, Peninsular Malaysia, 1911–1957
(in millions)

Date	Malays		Chinese		Indian		Total
	Male	Female	Male	Female	Male	Female	
1911	0.61	0.61	0.57	0.12	0.18	0.06	2.34
1921	0.69	0.69	0.63	0.22	0.31	0.13	2.91
1931	0.78	0.79	0.87	0.42	0.38	0.20	3.79
1947	1.06	1.10	1.04	0.85	0.32	0.22	4.92
1957	1.38	1.42	1.21	1.12	0.40	0.28	6.28

Source: Snodgrass, 1980: 24.

ease with which foreigners conquered and dominated Malay society. In the 1970s, the symbolic rejection of colonialism expressed itself most visibly in the renaming of street signs; colonial names were erased and replaced by the names of local heroes and personages. But what was probably more unsettling to the Malays was their economic weakness, for it was a daily reminder of their group weakness and loss of place in the society.

Ethnicity and Economic Segmentation

The stable political and economic conditions under the British attracted merchants, financiers, and labour to the Malay peninsula. The most successful groups in the new competitive economic system were the ones which could best mobilize capital, organize and control labour, adapt technology to exploit available resources, and forge close links with the colonial officials. It was the British and, to a lesser extent, Chinese entrepreneurs, who benefited most from the emerging export economy. The Malay role was marginal, handicapped by a weaker commercial impulse, a gravitation to administrative positions, and the community's entrenchment in village structures.

In the nineteenth century, it was actually the Chinese who were more successful economically than the Europeans. Both the wealthy Baba Chinese[5] of the Straits Settlements—who had accumulated capital from land speculation, trading, and as tax collectors for the Straits Government—and newly arrived merchants successfully diversified into tin-mining and plantation agriculture (Andaya and Andaya, 1982: 138). The Chinese made notable achievements in the growing of tapioca, pepper, gambier, and sugar. The Europeans, on the other hand, encountered many problems in mining and plantation ventures because of the difficulty of securing labour.

In long-distance trade, however, the European merchants were firmly established, and later had a decisive edge in exploiting economic opportunities in the twentieth century. As agents for producers and importers in Britain, these merchants sold British manufactured goods to the region and returned with Asian produce. Not independent capitalists as a rule, they often borrowed from the wealthy Straits Chinese or relied on credit from their British principals (Drabble and Drake, 1981: 302). Gradually, their implantation in the import–export nexus brought opportunities for acquiring shipping and insurance agencies. As trade grew, their merchant firms steadily evolved into large-scale agency houses. In the field of commerce, the settled Chinese traders played an interesting middleman role to the British traders. As Drabble and Drake (1981: 303) note:

When the goods arrived at a Straits port, the consignments were broken down and advanced in smaller portions and on credit to Asians (mostly Chinese). In other words, the so-called long credit which the merchant firms received from the English exporters was passed on as shorter credit, often unsecured, to Asian distributors who bought the goods in the Bazaar. To a very considerable extent, barter came into play—Asian traders often discharged their debts by rendering to the merchants local produce (such as spices, sugar, tin), obtained from local cultivators and miners, which the merchants in due course exported to Europe and America.

The subordinate role of the Chinese in trade was to become the general pattern in the twentieth century. Yet the Chinese did have a salient role in the economy. What were the reasons for their success, particularly in comparison to the indigenous Malays? Freedman (1961: 42) captures the pivotal characteristic of the Chinese: they 'knew how to handle money and organize men in relation to money'. Two important notions are buried in this statement—the impulse to accumulate money not for immediate social or political 'consumption', but for an unspecified future use, and the ability to use existing associations and organizations of people for capital accumulation. A critical advantage the Chinese had over the Malays was the concept of business organization. Andaya and Andaya (1982: 139) note:

Their expertise is clearly seen in the *kongsi*, an association of individuals from the same dialect group and the same area of China who held shares in a co-operative venture. . . . In the Yunnan *kongsi* organization, a man with capital brought together a group of men from the same clan or dialect group who, whether managers or wage labourers, were willing to share in the gain or loss of a common endeavour. It was this experience and this tradition, characterized by a sense of group cohesiveness and brotherhood, which the Chinese introduced to the Malay world.

This early commercial orientation encouraged savings and ensured a pool of liquid capital within the Chinese community. The wealthy Chinese, as outsiders in the social and political system of Malay society, had a different route to gaining community status. By giving out loans to fellow clan members and sponsoring their mobility, wealthy Chinese businessmen could become prominent leaders of Chinese society. In contrast, the élite of Malay society sought status through luxurious consumption and maintaining a large retinue of followers, ends which precluded the commercial deployment of resources.

Finally, the Chinese entrepreneurs had a large supply of labour available in the region. Most Chinese left China because of the poverty there and in general were welcomed by British officials.[6] Chinese businessmen, in addition, had various methods of tightly controlling their labour supply, such as using secret society organizations, clan groups, and the credit ticket system (which bound an employee to the employer for a specified period of time without wages as payment for his trip to Malaya). The availability and control of labour was a critical asset of Chinese employers, explaining their early successes over the British and European capitalists.

Despite the early achievements of the Chinese, the British officials never really regarded their activities in plantation agriculture as sufficiently large scale and permanent, believing that the Chinese were in Malaya only transitorily. Only the Europeans, they thought, could fully transform the society economically. As Frank Swettenham (1920: 296), one of the first British Residents, put it:

. . . roads and railways will open up the agricultural capabilities of the country and give us the best thing we can hope for: a settled agricultural population and a body of Europeans who will bring their brains, their energy, and money to convert our jungles into extensive estates of permanent cultivation, a form of enterprise such as no Asiatic has hitherto the ability, experience, or determination to attempt.

Manufacturing was never considered a serious option for the country. The colonial officials subscribed to an international division of labour in which the colonies would produce commodities and the metropole, the manufactured goods. The free trade policy—although conveniently jettisoned from time to time to protect British imports and interests—in general acted against local manufacturing.[7]

After many failures, the decisive change in European involvement occurred after 1905 when demand for natural rubber began to soar in the US and Europe as tyres began to be produced in large volumes. Coffee planters in the region, experiencing a deep coffee slump, diversified into rubber. These early planters soon faced difficulties getting capital since they ran proprietary estates. The merchant firms or agency houses in the Straits Settlements were in a more favourable position. Possessing international marketing and financial expertise, shipping and insurance agencies, and a good reputation in London, they could raise large capital sums for the rubber companies they were floating or helping to float. They got subscriptions from British institutions and the public, and invested their own funds as well. Soon the larger agency houses had numerous rubber companies under their wings; sometimes they were full owners but often their role was managerial and secretarial only. Big names such as Harrisons and Crosfield, Boustead–Buttery, Guthrie, and Sime Darby managed 226,074, 169,555, 156,306, and 109,901 acres respectively (Puthucheary, J., 1960: 46).[8] By 1920, British Malaya had become the dominant producer of rubber in the world. Over 3.5 million acres out of a total of 5.5 million acres under cultivation in 1953 was under rubber (Puthucheary, J., 1960: 26). Half the rubber trees were planted in estates of more than 500 acres. The ethnic distribution of the estate sector, comprising 1.9 million acres, in 1953 was 83 per cent European, 14 per cent Chinese, and 3 per cent Indian—Malay estate ownership was essentially non-existent.

From their foothold in the plantation sector, the agency houses captured a high portion of Malaya's international tradetransactions.[9] Control over shipping and insurance gave them the leverage to market a significant percentage of the society's agricultural produce, including the smallholder's output. In rubber marketing, a similar division of labour operated between Europeans and Chinese as in the Straits Settlements. The Europeans were the main importers and exporters while the Chinese played various intermediary roles at the local level—such as purchasing rubber from the smallholders and the smaller Asian estates with credit supplied by the European exporters, and marketing the produce through the agency houses. It was probably the ubiquitous presence of Chinese traders and shopkeepers in nearly every village that was to make the Chinese economic role seem more threatening and exploitative to the Malays than the European role, although the Europeans were far more dominant economically. Puthucheary estimates that Europeans, including agency houses, mining agencies, and sales branches of foreign manufacturers, controlled as much as 65–75 per cent of the export trade and 60–70 per cent of the import trade (Puthucheary, J., 1960: xiv).[10]

In tin-mining, the Europeans began to out-produce the Chinese. The suppression of secret societies in the 1890s and the abolishment of the ticket credit system freed the flow of labour to the European sector (Yip Yat Hoong, 1969: 150). By 1910, Western mining was producing 22 per cent of the output of the Federated Malay States (Lim Chong-Yah, 1967: 50). However, the real spurt in European tin output came with the introduction of new mining technology. In 1912, Malayan Tin introduced bucket dredging—hitherto used for gold-mining in Australia and New Zealand. It was highly capital intensive and costly but was extremely efficient for deep mining. This technology—affordable only to the Europeans because of their larger organizations and international fund-raising ability—gave them a major advantage over the partnership and sole proprietor business organizations of the Chinese miners. They were additionally favoured by the colonial government's policy of allotting the best mining lands according to the amount of capital invested (Yip Yat Hoong, 1969: 152). In 1929, when Malaya was producing one-third of the world's tin supply, the European sector had out-produced the Chinese.

The dredging companies were controlled and managed by specialist tin-mining agencies; the three largest groups were Anglo-Oriental, Osborne and Chappel, and Neil and Bell. Plantation agencies such as Guthrie, Sime Darby, and Harrisons and Crosfield also held a few tin-mining agencies but, by and large, the mining and plantation companies were under separate control (Allen and Donnithorne, 1954: 157). Anglo-Oriental controlled about twenty companies (forty dredges), producing about one-fifth of Malaya's tin in 1954 (Puthucheary, J., 1960: 85). Neil and Bell controlled nine companies while Osborne and Chappel controlled twenty, producing 15 per cent and 8 per cent of total tin production respectively. The owners of Anglo-Oriental were the London Tin Group, while Neil and Bell had close links with Charter Consolidated, an Anglo-American mining group based in South Africa and controlled by the De Beers and Oppenheimer families. Osborne and Chappel managed companies for the Straits Trading Company, a Singapore-based company first floated by Europeans but which later had substantial Singaporean Chinese interests.[11]

With the development of the export economy, European banks entered Malaya to capture trade financing activities. Chartered Bank pioneered the setting up of branches in the Malayan hinterland from the Straits Settlements. As the rubber industry expanded, Hong Kong and Shanghai Bank and Mercantile Bank also opened up branches. Later other foreign and Chinese banks followed suit, but these three dominated the banking business in Malaya for decades. The European banks dealt primarily with their own nationals, but the banks instituted a 'comprador' system that used Asian intermediaries to get Asian customers. The Chettiars, a caste of South Indian money-lenders, acted as brokers between the smaller Chinese businesses and the Western banking system. They had intimate knowledge of the credit-worthiness of the smaller businesses, and collected commissions according to the amount of business they generated (Allen and Donnithorne, 1954: 205).

By dominating external trade financing and monopolizing government deposits, European banks controlled the bulk of bank resources in the colonial period. In 1959, two years after independence, the five largest banks were foreign incorporated, and accounted for 71.8 per cent of total bank resources (Bank Negara, 1979: 144).

Colonial rule in the twentieth century witnessed European, principally British, interests dominate nearly every facet of the export economy. Nonetheless, the highly favourable climate colonial officials created for Western commerce also benefited the Chinese business sector. A few Chinese businessmen became quite wealthy, and toward the end of the colonial era managed to make some inroads into the Western sector.

The most striking aspect of Chinese businesses was their presence in the distributive and service trades. The statistical data suggest that large numbers of Chinese entered commerce from the wage-earning occupations in tin-mining and plantation agriculture (see Snodgrass, 1980: 38, Table 2.4). It is easy to understand their keenness to enter commerce when one considers the terrible conditions of wage labour (Andaya and Andaya, 1982: 138):

Though most *singkeh* [new men or migrants] were already accustomed to harsh conditions and backbreaking work, the rigours of existence on the edge of the jungle and the depredations of tropical disease took their toll, the death rate in some areas being estimated at 50 per cent. Those who survived exhibited a competitive spirit and determination to succeed which could not but affect the pace of change in the Malay world.

Reflecting the owners' rather humble origins, most of the businesses were small sole proprietorships and partnerships. Trade specialization tended to be along dialect groups, suggesting the key role of mutual help and family ties in financing and operating businesses. The Hokkiens dominated the rubber dealing business; the Teochews, the rice import business and goldsmiths; the Cantonese and Hainanese, the restaurant business; the Hakkas, textile shops and medical halls; and the Cantonese and Hakkas, tin-mining (Goh Joon Hai, 1962: 93–4).

Through hard work and initiative, a few made it from 'rags to riches'. The head of the Teo family in the early twentieth century, who later earned the sobriquet 'Rice King of Malaysia', began life selling salted eggs. From there, he moved into rice and sugar trading, and by cultivating strong clan ties with the Teochew community of rice dealers, became dominant in rice trading. In the 1950s, the family diversified into plantations, insurance and real estate (*Insight*, April 1982: 249). Lim Goh Tong, currently a major resort and casino developer, sold foodstuffs during the Japanese Occupation. He then set up a scrap iron shop, and from buying and selling used mining machinery developed a profitable business in hardware; this experience allowed him to enter construction in a big way in the 1950s and 1960s (*Insight*, June 1980: 22). Penang's tycoon, Loh Boon Siew, now a property developer and holder of the Honda franchise, started out as a mechanic, and saved enough to establish the Penang Yellow Bus Company in 1941. He later diversified into real estate and property development (*MB*, January 1974: 52).

Chinese businessmen already prominent early in the colonial era were usually in tin-mining and plantation agriculture. Many owners of large plantation companies started as rubber dealers, millers, and exporters of smallholder produce, subsequently diversifying backwards into plantation ownership. The most outstanding Chinese in the rubber industry was Lee Kong Chian, a Singaporean, who owned fifteen rubber milling factories and controlled about 18,500 acres of rubber in 1953 (Puthucheary, J., 1960: 127). The Tan family, who came from the Baba community in Melaka, were also prominent rubber owners. Both Tan Cheng Lock and his son, Tan Siew Sin, were to play prominent roles in Malaysian politics in the mid-twentieth century. The family's early business was in regional shipping in the nineteenth century (*Insight*, December 1982: 24–5). Tan Cheng Lock was also a director of Sime Darby, representing one of the few instances of collaboration between Western and Asian interests.

In tin-mining, the Chinese owned about 600 gravel pump mines, producing about 40 per cent of Malayan tin output. Most of the mines were sole proprietorships and partnerships. The Chinese tycoons in tin-mining were Eu Tong Sen, H. S. Lee (who also became a prominent politician), Lau Pak Kuan, Foong Seong, and the Loke family (Puthucheary, J., 1960: 84).

Large Chinese businessmen also diversified into banking, for it served as a useful platform to get more funds and widen existing businesses. Some of the men mentioned were deeply involved in setting up or running banks in the colonial era (Tan Ee Leong, 1961: 454–79). Tan Cheng Lock was associated with the Ho Hong Bank (founded 1917), Lee Kong Chian with the Chinese Commercial Bank (1912), Eu Tong Sen with the Lee Wah Bank (1920), and Loke Yew with the Kwong Yik (Selangor) Bank (1913). These banks did their business principally with the Chinese community and, more specifically, with particular clan groups since the banks themselves were founded and run by people of distinct clans. Many of these banks lacked expertise and connections to engage in foreign exchange transactions, especially in sterling. Chinese banks therefore had to play intermediary roles to the foreign banks, buying foreign exchange from them and selling it to their Chinese and clan clients.[12]

These Chinese banks played an important role in strengthening the position of Chinese traders. By providing credit and financial guarantees, Chinese importers could get their consignments direct from Europe rather than through the agency houses (Allen and Donnithorne, 1954: 237). The importers enjoyed a large internal Chinese market and distributive network, and were gradually able to capture more and more of the trade in consumer goods. However, the Europeans were firmly entrenched in the import of machinery and capital goods since these activities required greater knowledge, capital, and close connections with the European producers.

For most of the colonial era, there was little joint ownership between Western and Chinese interests. In the 1950s, with independence in the offing, some Western investors who were uncertain of Malaya's political and economic future sold off their Malayan assets. Chinese capital bought into many Western companies, especially those which were listed locally.[13]

Many rubber dealers, flush with funds from the Korean War boom, invested in rubber companies for the first time, departing from their historical preference for property, where prices had become inflated (Mamajiwala, 1968: 351). Chinese invested their capital in tin-mining, and by 1954, 22.3 per cent of the shareholdings of locally incorporated dredging companies were locally owned (Yip Yat Hoong, 1969: 351). Most of the investments made by the Chinese were of the rentier type; agency houses and mining agencies continued to control and manage them.

However, in some instances, Chinese businessmen, like Lee Loy Seng, acted more aggressively toward the Western sector. Lee was forced to learn about rubber when his three-generation family of tin miners made the mistake of buying some rubber land for the possibility of mining tin (MB, May 1973: 27). Lee soon discovered that many locally incorporated rubber companies were terribly undervalued although cash rich. He then engaged in a domino-type strategy, buying up one company and using its reserves to buy into another, and so on. Lee Loy Seng quickly established himself as the local 'rubber baron'. While these ownership changes modified the picture of Western and Chinese exclusivity in business, they did not weaken significantly Western control and ownership of the economy.

Colonial rule undoubtedly brought a great deal of economic dynamism to Malaya. It installed a competitive economy in place of a 'quasi-feudalistic' economy and introduced the abstract notion of economic development as an end for the government to pursue. Yet there were two critical problems. The rudimentary manufacturing base was one. The other was the minuscule development of Malay commerce and industry. In large part, both resulted from the colonial government's practice of subjecting economic development to market forces as much as possible, avoiding any project which would not pay commercially or incur a large government deficit.

Malays in the colonial economy for most part kept to their traditional agricultural activities, such as rice cultivation, fishing, small cottage industries, and coconut growing, although diversifying into the commercial cultivation of rubber in smallholdings became increasingly popular. J. Puthucheary (1960: xvii) observed that there was probably no Malay ownership in tin-mining and manufacturing. Malays also had an insignificant share of exporting and only a bit more in importing—in items like dyes for batik cloth (Allen and Donnithorne, 1954: 245). They certainly did not have any role in banking and, at most, a minute level of ownership in medium-sized plantations. Table 2.1 gives the occupational distribution of each ethnic group in 1957.

The concentration of Malays in agriculture and their poor representation in commerce is plain. The reasons for Malay commercial backwardness have been alluded to. Differences in cultural orientation toward capital accumulation were partly responsible. But organizationally, Malays lacked institutions that could mobilize capital and pool economic resources effectively. The Europeans had their international financial networks

TABLE 2.2
Occupation by Ethnic Group, 1957
(in thousands; figures in parentheses represent occupational distribution of
ethnic group)

Industry	Malays	Chinese	Indians
Agriculture, fishing, forestry	749 (73.2)	310 (40.2)	174 (55.7)
Rice	381 (37.2)	9 (1.2)	0.5 (0.1)
Market gardening	23 (2.2)	54 (7.0)	1 (0.3)
Rubber	260 (25.4)	200 (25.9)	150 (48.0)
Mining, manufacturing	36 (3.5)	136 (17.6)	16 (5.1)
Commerce	32 (3.1)	127 (16.5)	32 (10.3)
Other industries and services	180 (17.6)	174 (22.5)	80 (25.6)
Government service	17 (1.7)	5 (0.6)	8 (2.6)
Police, home guard	43 (4.2)	4 (0.5)	2 (0.6)
Armed forces (Malayan and other governments)	15 (1.5)	2 (0.2)	3 (0.9)
Total Economically Active	1,023	771	312

Source: Means, 1976: 16, Table 2.
Note: For the other ethnic groups, agricultural participation, except for market gardening, was predominantly in the form of wage labour in the plantation sector rather than peasant agriculture.

while the Chinese had clan-based organizations—the latter were so ubiquitous that even when Chinese took up agricultural cultivation in smallholdings, they carried it out in *kongsi* form, in contrast to the more individualistic methods of the Malays, which were more prone to failure (Lim Teck Ghee, 1977: 236). Apparently, Malays were co-operative socially but not economically. Also, taking up new and untried economic roles was not so compelling as their economy was quite adequate for a modest living.

For the élite Malays, there was an alternative source of prestige and income in the bureaucracy, which may have diluted whatever inclination they might have shown toward commerce. The aristocratic Malays were carefully cultivated as a reliable ally of British officialdom. A special administrative unit—the Malay Administrative Service—was created in 1910 as the state councils and other posts of native magistrates, judges, and superintendents could not absorb all the displaced traditional élite (Roff, 1967: 24). The children of aristocratic and upper-class Malay families were sent to an élite college—Malay College, Kuala Kangsar (founded 1905)—and trained for positions in the Malay Administrative Service as junior administrators and civil servants to the British.

A few élite Malays felt keenly their inability to compete with the Chinese. There was one example of a teacher in Malay College, Kuala Kangsar, who tried to start a Pan-Malayan business enterprise called the Malay Trading and Craft Company. Unfortunately, the company never came into being, suffering from problems of organization, expertise, and management (Roff, 1967: 186). This example pointed to the rude fact that even when business inclinations existed, problems of organization and managerial expertise remained.

Colonial policies were also not helpful in increasing the pool of savings within the Malay community. Colonial officers were very concerned that Malays remain in rice cultivation—their traditional pursuit—but they never made sustained efforts to help boost rice production. Except for the Krian Irrigation Scheme (1905), no other irrigation projects were implemented until the Depression.[14] When Malay peasants responded positively to the more profitable cultivation of rubber, the colonial government applied official pressure and enactments to prevent the conversion of rice to rubber land, 'persisting in their view that peasants should be subsistence producers and that cash cropping should be the monopoly of the planters' (Lim Teck Ghee, 1977: 94).[15]

When the colonial government acted favourably toward the Malay peasant, it was only to blunt the worst ravages of the new commercial economy. In 1913, the Malay Reservations Enactment was introduced forbidding the transfer of traditional Malay holdings to the economically more powerful non-Malays. The objective was to discourage Malays from making quick profits by selling land to plantation and commercial interests and to prevent indebted peasants from transferring land to creditors. While laudable, it failed to tackle the new problems which the commercial economy inflicted on peasants: perennial indebtedness to traders and money-lenders, and gradually diminishing plot sizes from Islamic laws of inheritance and decreasing land availability.

Colonialism institutionalized new statuses in society. As a result, a different criterion emerged for evaluating the existing groups. The Malays did not do well. The Malay élites had lost their traditional sphere of power and were now subordinated politically to British officers. They also could not enjoy the new status conferred by achievement in the market economy. The frequent assurance given to Malays by the British officials that, as the indigenous group, they were politically paramount over the immigrant groups, compensated to some degree for Malay economic backwardness but never fully removed their sense of loss in the land which they considered theirs.

The colonial officers, in resorting to potent images to account for the performance of the various ethnic groups in the competitive economy, only reinforced—in Horowitz's terms—the economically backward group's sense of unworthiness and weakness. For example, the colonial officer Frank Swettenham (1920: 232–3), had this to say of the Chinese:

Their energy and enterprise have made the Malay States what they are to-day, and it would be impossible to overstate the obligation which the Malay Government and people are under to these hard-working, capable, and law-abiding aliens. . . .

They brought all the capital when Europeans feared to take the risk. . . . The reader should understand at once what is due Chinese labour and enterprise in the evolution of the Federated Malay States. The part played by the Malay has already been told; it was mainly negative. . . .

British officials frequently mentioned many good Malay characteristics—such as their loyalty, generosity, and hospitality—but thought little of the Malay capability 'for really hard and continuous work, either of the brain or the hands' (Swettenham, 1920: 137). Swettenham (quoted in Rabushka, 1973: 65) said of the Malay:

. . . he is . . . lazy to a degree, is without method or order of any kind, knows no regularity even in the hours of his meals, and considers time of no importance. His house is untidy, even dirty, but he bathes twice a day, and is very fond of personal adornment in the shape of smart clothes.

These ethnic images became a salient part of inter-ethnic evaluations, persisting even today. In Rabushka's study of Malaysian ethnic stereotypes in the early 1970s, he found a high degree of consensus about stereotypes among the races (Rabushka, 1973: 66). Malays, for example, regarded the Chinese as very intelligent, very ambitious, and quite active, which was close to the Chinese self-portrait. Chinese, on the other hand, most consistently cited cleanliness and lack of ambition as the Malays' chief qualities, giving low marks for intelligence, thrift, and honesty. Such group evaluations became a powerful part of the Malay subconscious.

For much of the colonial era, Malays were basically resigned to their fate. Some turned to British paternalism to protect their rights and welfare while reformist groups turned introspective, searching for those aspects of Malay culture and religion that stood in the way of progress (Roff, 1967: 254-7). But as the immigrant groups, particularly the Chinese, became larger and got involved in their own political movements, they 'transformed Malay attitudes towards the Chinese from one of envy but toleration, to distrust' (Andaya and Andaya, 1982: 253).

The Making of Ethnic Political Structures

The uneven economic development of the ethnic groups alone would have constituted a strong basis for ethnic ill-feeling. But there were several factors which tended to preserve and harden ethnic divisions in the society. First, the British colonial government did not establish structures that would bring the ethnic groups together. In the nineteenth and early twentieth centuries, colonial administrators used existing ethnic structures and ties to rule over the respective communities. Colonial political rule over the Malays was facilitated by preserving their social structure as much as possible and using the co-opted Malay élite as a buffer between the government and the rest of the society.

The British also used existing Chinese leaders and notables, who were given the epithet 'Kapitan China', to help them keep social control over the Chinese community. In the nineteenth century, leaders of secret societies—before the societies were controlled and weakened by the government—were frequently appointed to state councils in recognition of their role in maintaining law and order. A separate Chinese Protectorate was established in 1877 in Singapore and in 1884 in Malaya by the colonial government to combat the more excessive social problems of the Chinese community, such as opium smoking, gambling, extortion, prostitution, and gang robberies (Means, 1976: 28). The use of an alternative governmental structure to oversee the Chinese lessened the need for close association between the Malays and the Chinese.

In education, too, only a tiny number of people from each ethnic group were provided with an English education in the urban centres, mainly for the purposes of working in the government as lower level administrators and technicians. The rest of the population only received a rudimentary education in the mother tongue, sponsored in a paternalistic fashion by the employers (for the immigrant groups) and by the government for the Malays. Chinese businessmen funded Chinese schools, European plantation owners provided funds for a Tamil education on estate premises, and the government helped run Malay village schools (see Loh, 1975).

One should not conclude that the separate development of the ethnic groups was a deliberate product of a British colonial policy of 'divide and rule'. Obviously the British did not see their role as the crucible of Malayan nationalism, and never encouraged it. As late as the 1930s the colonial officials continued to believe that the immigrant groups were transitory communities who did not intend to stay in Malaya. It was a convenient illusion which went against the facts and trends of immigration. Yet there was no need for them to divide and rule Malaya in order to maintain power for plainly the society was already a very divided one. The colonial officers merely took the most expedient and inexpensive way of controlling it.

Given the lack of a strong national basis for politics, the political activities of the ethnic groups, which fermented in the 1930s, tended to reflect political events in their homelands. In the Chinese community, the Kuomintang Malaya (formed in 1912) and the Communist Party of Malaya (1930) vied for control of Chinese guilds and associations, mirroring the Kuomintang–Communist conflict in China (Heng Pek Koon, 1983: 291–3). Inspired by the rise of Indian nationalism, the Indians also formed the Central Indian Association of Malaya (CIAM) to aid the cause of Indian independence and improve the lot of Indians in Malaya. Malays, too, formed Malay associations throughout the country, less to fight the British than to express concern that their culture and position were being eroded by new alien and materialist forces (Parmer, 1964: 286).

The Communist Party of Malaya (CPM) in particular became a potent political force in the late 1930s to late 1940s. It was essentially Chinese in leadership and membership, and sought to stimulate the class consciousness of the Chinese and Indian labour forces. The CPM provoked a large number of strikes from 1936 to 1941 among Chinese mine workers and Indian rubber tappers (Stenson, 1970). The party, however, hardly made any inroads into the largely rural Malay population. The very nature of its platform—to create a Malayan Republic based on the working class—not only failed to take cognizance of the rural nature of Malay society, but also failed to give them any special recognition of their 'indigenous' status or regard for their Islamic religion. Indeed, their activities made the Malays even more suspicious of the Chinese and their intentions.

During the Japanese Occupation (1941–5), anti-Chinese feelings among the Malays intensified. The CPM, with the departure of the British, was the only established force capable of resisting the Japanese, organizing civilians into the Malayan People's Anti-Japanese Army (MPAJA). The MCP and MPAJA became powerful foci of loyalty among the Chinese, who were brutally treated by the Japanese. In contrast, the Japanese deliberately cultivated the Malays, placing them in relatively high administrative positions (with the departure of their British superiors), and using them in para-military forces to fight Chinese resistance movements. Toward the end of the Japanese Occupation, the MPAJA began meting out summary justice to Japanese collaborators (mostly Malays) which ended in mutual killings between the two races (see Short, 1975: 301–2).

When the British reoccupied Malaya in 1945, the CPM was the single most important political force in the society. Had the CPM wrested political control, the nature of Malaysian politics and economy would most certainly have been different; the Chinese probably would have been politically stronger, albeit with a radical left-wing leadership, while private capital (particularly foreign) would have been given a highly constricted role. However, with British military intervention and an unsupportive Malay population, the CPM never had much of a chance. The British were prepared initially to incorporate the CPM as a junior partner to maintain order in the aftermath of the Japanese Occupation. However, the MCP aspired to political leadership, and sought to gain control of the trade union movement by creating an omnibus labour organization, the General Labour Union (later renamed the Pan-Malayan Federation of Trade Unions or PMFTU), to penetrate existing unions. Terrorist and intimidating tactics were used against employers, especially European planters, and rival unionists (Stenson, 1970: 61, 103). At the height of its power in 1947, the PMFTU had a membership of 50 per cent of the industrial work-force and controlled between 80 per cent and 90 per cent of all unions in Malaya (Stenson, 1970: 124).

As the PMFTU and CPM became more disruptive, the British began to impose new restrictions on union activity and disqualified federations of unions. With the PMFTU weakened, the CPM changed tactics and embarked on the revolutionary road to power in 1948. The colonial government declared a State of Emergency in 1948 to fight the insurgents. By 1953 it had the upper hand, and the Emergency (or anti-insurgency war) was officially terminated in 1960.

From the start the trade union movement which replaced the PMFTU was not destined to play a strong role as an ethnically integrating force. The new union leaders tended to be Indians who had organized plantation unions for Indian estate workers. They were non-communist unionists, and had resisted PMFTU's attempts to penetrate their unions. These unionists were actively encouraged by the pro-union but anti-communist trade union advisor to Malaya, John Brazier, to form a trade union federation, which came into being in 1950 as the Malayan Trade Union Congress (MTUC).

The Indian origins of the union leaders were not conducive to attracting Chinese members to support the trade union movement because of their reluctance to be led by other races. Malay participation in the unions was also marginal, since they were largely rural and poorly represented in the modern sectors of the economy. Politically active Malays preferred to direct their energies to party politics rather than to trade union activity (Zaidi, 1974: 90, 178). Politics promised a potentially larger Malay base and, with decolonization, direct access to power and prestige, while trade unionism offered neither in the foreseeable future.

The MTUC, because of its thin base[16] and weak resources, and the strict regulations governing union activity, recoiled from playing a strong role in politics despite some unionists pressing for a political party to represent workers of all races. The union leaders feared that involving themselves in the political issues of the day would only lead to internal divisions politically and ethnically, and invite government suspicion of trade unions, even if moderate (Zaidi, 1974: 74, 113). In addition, the burgeoning ethnic parties, such as the United Malays National Organization (UMNO) and the Malayan Chinese Association (MCA), which later formed the government, had little reason to cultivate the trade union movement, relying primarily on an ethnic base.

Despite the salient ethnic divisions, there were strong imperatives for the emerging Malayan élites to co-operate. The British, when they returned, were prepared to lay the basis for self-rule and eventual independence but the precondition was a workable formula for multiracial accommodation. They also wanted a leadership that would maintain close ties with Britain and safeguard its economic and military interests in the country.

In the mid-1940s, however, moderate Malay and Chinese leaders with broad political support had yet to develop. Only the politically unacceptable CPM was firmly implanted. In the Malay community, there were just a few radical, small Malay organizations, all with only a small following, such as the Kesatuan Melayu Muda, Kesatuan Rakyat Indonesia Semenanjung, and the Malay Nationalist Party.

Ironically, a strong, pro-British party sprang on to the political scene to oppose a British proposal for a new political order in Malaya—the Malayan Union scheme of 1946 (see Allen, J., 1967 and Mohd. Noordin Sopiee, 1974). Apart from creating a unitary state (although leaving out Singapore), the scheme provided for the extension of citizenship to all locally born residents as well as residents living locally for a specified number of years. All citizens would also enjoy equal political status irrespective of race. The sultans were to retain their positions but sovereignty was to pass to the Crown. The scheme was a marked departure from all previous assumptions of the special position of the Malays.

The Malays, already deeply insecure because of their economic position and the communist challenge, felt betrayed by the British, who were seen as the vital protectors of Malay society. The Malay battle cry was: 'We want protection, not annexation' (Simandjuntak, 1969: 48). Numerous Malay associations rapidly transcended their particularistic local village and state identities and coalesced against the Malayan Union scheme. The oppositionist movement, which culminated in the United Malays National Organization (or UMNO), was led by the élite stratum of Malay administrators. Using their links with district level Malay authorities right down to the Malay headman, the élites succeeded in mobilizing most of the Malay population and, in doing so, laid the basis for UMNO as a mass political party. The non-Malays, still preoccupied with events in their home countries, were slow to mobilize in favour of the new scheme, and quibbled about the exclusion of Singapore, which, with an overwhelming Chinese population, would have made the non-Malays the clear majority in the country.

UMNO's explosive reaction caused the authorities to back down. A new scheme far more favourable to Malay interests—the Federation of Malaya Agreement—was worked out in 1948 between the British officials, the Malay sultans, and UMNO; it upheld the sovereignty of the sultans and entrenched the 'special position' of the Malays in the country. While the Agreement did allow for non-Malay citizenship, the qualifications for citizenship were more restrictive than in the previous scheme. Non-Malay groups opposed the new arrangements, but having given lukewarm support to the Malayan Union scheme, were in a weak position to ask for a better deal.

With the emergence of politically moderate Malay leaders, the British next tried to encourage the development of a pro-British, anti-communist Chinese leadership that could incorporate the Chinese population and woo them away from the CPM (Heng Pek Koon, 1983: 294). In 1949, the Malayan Chinese Association was formed by prominent Chinese, among whom were the most successful Chinese capitalists in the society. Many of the new MCA leaders were noted members of important Chinese organizations such as the Straits Chinese British Association (for example, Tan Cheng Lock and his son, Tan Siew Sin), the Kuomintang Malaya (KMT), the Chinese Chambers of Commerce, and other major *huay kuan* or clan associations (for example, H. S. Lee and Yong Shook Lin). They tended to be English speaking and solidly pro-British. Their strong assets were their ability to interact with the colonial administrators, the Malay élite, as well as Chinese apex organizations like the Chinese Chambers of Commerce. This organizational resource allowed them to co-opt lower level leaders who were more Chinese oriented culturally and socially, thereby bringing in grassroots support indirectly (Heng Pek Koon, 1983: 295–7). True to their business inclinations, the MCA operated a lottery in which only members could take part—the proceeds went toward welfare services for Chinese squatters grouped in hamlets to sever them from the communists—and gradually the ranks of the party grew.

Although moderate leaders had surfaced among the ethnic groups, the precise nature of ethnic accommodation had yet to be settled. With independence in mind, the founder of UMNO, Dato Onn Jaafar, pressed UMNO to open its doors to all races. In spite of his charisma, the UMNO rank and file completely rejected his plan, reflecting the Malay wish for their own protective organizations and fear of non-Malay dominance (Vasil, 1980: 72). Dato Onn left UMNO and was replaced by Tunku Abdul Rahman, a British-educated lawyer and a member of the Kedah royal family. Dato Onn subsequently formed a rival party, the Independence of Malaya Party (or IMP), which boldly proposed to build the party on a multiracial political base. The British responded favourably to Onn's party, expecting it to lead the way to independence. The IMP also enjoyed the tacit support of the MCA, the Malayan Indian Congress (MIC)—a weak party that sought to represent the Indians—and the MTUC, the trade union organization.

In 1952, however, a major realignment of political parties took place which fixed the nature of the governing parties in Malaya. In the Kuala Lumpur municipal elections, Sir H. S. Lee ignored the support of the MCA national leaders for Onn's party (after developing personal differences with Onn) and formed an electoral alliance with UMNO as a momentary strategy to oust the IMP. The local MCA branch agreed to provide the funds on condition that UMNO not contest the MCA candidates in straight fights. The strategy worked—UMNO and the MCA captured ten seats and the IMP only two—and spelt the end of the IMP (Vasil, 1980: 86).

This victory paved the way for a coalition party called the Alliance. In 1954, the Indian party—the MIC—also joined the Alliance. In the first general elections of 1955, the Alliance won fifty-one of the fifty-two contested seats, obtaining 81 per cent of the vote. The only other seat went to the Pan-Malayan Islamic Party (PMIP), a party that wanted Islam to serve as the foundation for a Malay-dominated society. The other parties which claimed to be non-communal, such as the Labour Party and the People's Progressive Party lost badly, managing to get some Chinese votes but hardly any Malay support. It reflected a singular and persistent fact of Malaysian politics: an alliance of ethnic élites, each with its own communal organization, proved to be more appealing to the voters than non-communal political organizations.

Having met the British criteria for stable government, and with the threat of communism neutralized, Malaya was promised independence in 1957. As a prelude to independence, a series of important bargains were made between the moderate élites of the UMNO and MCA, which were reflected in the 1957 Constitution for independent Malaya. In exchange for the relaxation of citizenship requirements and a tacit understanding that Chinese economic interests would be safeguarded, the non-Malays agreed to Malay political and symbolic paramountcy in society. The concessions included Islam as the state religion, Malay as the national language,[17] and the preservation of the Malay sultans within the framework of constitutional democracy (Milne and Mauzy, 1978: 38–90). Article 153 of the Constitution also made provisions for the 'special position of the Malays' allowing for official favouritism in the bureaucracy, education, and business. This allowance was supposed to be a compensatory measure to help them catch up economically. UMNO's economic plans for the Malays were laid out in the 1955 Alliance Manifesto. Among the objectives were to convince Malays that they had the capability to become big businessmen, to finance Malays already in business and encourage others to start businesses, to initiate joint Sino-Malay pilot businesses, and to make arrangements with industrialists and merchants to train suitable Malays (Vasil, 1980: 97).

The Malays, suffering from profound economic, political, and psychological anxieties about their place in society, entered independence with the expectation that finally, with the government in their hands, they could gradually reverse their sense of backwardness after decades of colonialism. Yet there were outstanding issues to cope with, such as the necessity of interracial accommodation for political stability and the *laissez-faire* economic system inherited from the colonial period. The next chapter, on economic development under the consociational democratic framework, examines the critical interlude before the state acted in a highly interventionist fashion in the economy.

1. Malaysia was known as the Federation of Malaya (or simply Malaya) before the Borneo states of Sarawak and Sabah joined the Federation in 1963. The larger entity was renamed Malaysia. Singapore was also a member of Malaysia from 1963 to 1965.

2. The treatment of Malay society in the nineteenth century draws heavily from Gullick's *Indigenous Political Systems of Western Malaya*, 1958.

3. One of the more unpalatable aspects of the colonial revenue system was the high dependence on taxing opium consumption (principally consumed by the Chinese working class) to finance government expenditures. In the early twentieth century, as much as 45 per cent of revenues in the Straits Settlements came from opium, declining to around 30 per cent in the mid-1920s and 12 per cent in 1928 (Li Dun Jen, 1982: 20). Even in the Federated Malay States, revenue from opium was higher than from rubber in the same period. Opium revenues were around 19 per cent of total revenues in the FMS in the early 1900s, declining to 12.3 per cent in 1928 (Li Dun Jen, 1982: 102–4).

4. Swettenham, one of the earliest and longest serving colonial official, observed (1920: 147):

[T]he Malay . . . has the strongest possible objection to a Malay marrying or living with a Chinese. . . . [I]t has happened that Malay women have preferred life with the Chinese infidel to a harder lot with a man of their own race and faith. The common result was, first a warning to the woman to leave the man of her choice, and if that failed the Chinese was killed, and sometimes the woman also. . . . Of course no one was greatly shocked if a Malay man gathered a Chinese woman into his household, but the practice, seldom resorted to, was never regarded with favour.

5. They were Chinese who had settled early on in the Straits Settlements (some as early as the sixteenth century in Melaka) and were often Malay speaking though not Muslim.

6. Francis Light, the official from the East India Company who secured Penang, remarked in 1784 that the Chinese 'are the only people in the east from whom a revenue may be raised without expense and extraordinary efforts of government. They are a valuable acquisition . . .' (quoted in Purcell, 1965: 244). The revenue to run the Straits Settlements largely came from taxing the Chinese in items such as opium, pork, pawnbroking, and spirits.

7. No wave of import-substitution took place in Malaya during the Depression, unlike the independent countries of Latin America. Government measures in Malaya during the Depression were actually aimed at supporting rubber prices; in Latin America the exporters were penalized in favour of manufacturers. Western involvement in manufacturing was few and far between and only those with a decisive margin of natural protection implanted themselves in the economy (Wheelwright, 1965: 4). The few Western firms were in tin smelting,

dredge building, rubber machinery, cement, and building materials (see Thoburn, 1977: 201; Allen and Donnithorne, 1954: 262). Small Chinese firms tended to process primary products into more transportable forms and to engage in the manufacture of simple consumer goods such as sauces, biscuits, sweets, pewter, and local medicines (Courtenay, 1972: 109). When tariffs were imposed, the idea was not to encourage local manufacture but to protect British imports from competition from other countries. For example, a stringent quota was imposed on Japanese textiles in the 1930s to protect British imports (Li Dun Jen, 1982: 57).

8. Their expertise in rubber management was demonstrated by the fact that very few rubber manufacturing giants got involved in rubber planting in Malaya. The notable exceptions were the Dunlop Rubber Company of the UK and the United States Rubber Company.

9. As time went by, the previous import trade in opium and textiles declined and was taken up by plantation-based supplies (tractors, building supplies, chemicals) and consumer products (foodstuffs, clothing) for the growing labour pool.

10. As Chinese marketing knowledge increased, they formed their own marketing networks. According to Allen and Donnithorne (1954: 245–6), had the agency houses not possessed vital shipping and insurance agencies, their trading role would have diminished considerably.

11. An interesting aspect of the tin industry was the early development of tin smelting within Malaya itself. Before 1890, the main smelters were the Chinese, who used simple charcoal blast furnaces in tin-mining premises. Because of monopolistic privileges given to Straits Trading and duties favouring the export of tin ore rather than smelted tin to the Straits Settlements, Straits Trading quickly became a major smelter in Malaya (Edwards, C. B., 1975: 218). A Chinese smelting company which was established in Penang in 1887 by Lee Chin Ho was bought up by Eastern Smelting, a company linked to Anglo-Oriental, in 1907 (Allen and Donnithorne, 1954: 160). A 35 per cent export duty was imposed on tin ore (as against 12 per cent on the pure metal) to prevent American dealers from buying the ore and smelting it overseas (see Thoburn, 1977: 125). By 1914, these two smelting companies were exporting 85 per cent of tin from Malaya.

12. Some of the Hokkien banks such as Ho Hong and the Overseas Chinese Bank were more aggressive and engaged in foreign exchange operations in the region and with China. An important event for Chinese banking was the merger of three Hokkien banks—Overseas Chinese Bank, Ho Hong, and Chinese Commercial Bank—in 1932 because of the business slump. The new Singapore-based Overseas Chinese Banking Corporation (OCBC) developed into a powerful and efficient bank run on Western lines.

13. There was a 0.3 per cent stamp duty on share transfers in locally incorporated companies compared to 2 per cent for companies listed in the UK (Mamajiwala, 1968: 422). Furthermore, there was more information available to prospective buyers of locally incorporated companies. The UK listed companies held the bulk of rubber and tin assets in Malaya.

14. By the late 1920s, Malaya was importing three-quarters of its rice consumption (Doering, 1973: 18). Limited measures were undertaken to irrigate more land in the early 1930s during the Depression because of fears of overdependence on imported rice and pressure put by the Malay élite to pay more attention to the rice sector (Lim Teck Ghee, 1977: 181–3).

15. Despite official penalties, peasants continued to grow rubber in firm adherence to economic rationality. A hard blow was given to them when the Stevenson Restriction Scheme (1922–8) and the International Rubber Regulation Scheme (1934–43) were implemented to support the price of rubber. Whether intentional or not, smallholder production was severely underassessed in both schemes, and smallholders ended up with a disproportionately small share of export quotas (see Bauer, 1948). As a result, smallholders suffered from a sharp decline in income, replanting rates, and acreage, only recovering in the 1950s and 1960s (Lim Chong-Yah, 1967: 124).

16. As late as 1982, only 17 per cent of Malaysia's wage earners belonged to unions (Ministry of Labour, 1984: 173).

17. In ten years thenceforth the medium of instruction in the schools and universities was to switch to Malay from English.

3 The Restrained Role of the State, 1957–1969

Introduction

THIS chapter, on economic development and management from independence to 1969, examines how the multi-ethnic political coalition dealt with three pressing objectives: diversifying the national economy, maintaining political stability, and meeting pressures from the emerging Malay middle class for a greater economic stake. The key feature of the period was the state's relatively *laissez-faire* approach, which approximated the neo-classical economist's view of economic rationality to a greater degree than the economic arrangements after 1970. While the economy departed successfully from the colonial economic framework and was able to generate moderately high growth rates, it was difficult for the Malay political leaders to sustain. Economic development brought greater benefits to the large foreign sector and the domestic Chinese business class than to the Malays, who made little commercial advance. As a result, the Malay sense of political vulnerability and economic weakness increased, leading to diminished support for the UMNO party in 1969, and to a new politically motivated programme to buttress the Malays' economic base through strong state economic intervention.

Departing from the Colonial Framework

In order to maintain power in the new competitive electoral system, the Alliance leaders had to quickly think of solutions to the emerging problems of the nation. The population was growing at 3.3 per cent per annum and, although unemployment was relatively low at 6 per cent, there was substantial underemployment of the population (*FEER*, 21 March 1961: 544). The prospects for further employment in the rubber and tin sectors, the twin pillars of the economy—accounting for 25 per cent and 5 per cent of the GDP respectively—did not look promising. The Malay smallholder, comprising 74 per cent of the Malay electorate, was suffering from low productivity and diminishing plot size.[1] This situation was particularly worrisome for UMNO because its chief rival, the radical Malay nationalist party, the Pan-Malayan Islamic Party or PMIP (now called PAS) was trying hard to court the rural Malay voter. In short, in spite of the conservative

nature of the leaders and their open attitude to foreign capital and the
international economy, the government could not afford to be 'neo-colonial'
in any simple sense of the word.[2]

The government's economic programme was to embark on a more concerted programme of industrialization and rural development. However,
to make any headway in its development policies, changes were needed in
the administrative style of the colonial period. Colonial economic practice
had centred on minimal taxation, the strict avoidance of deficits, and an
essentially unprotected market. These assumptions had to be changed to
accommodate the government's new spending needs and desire to see
more industrial development. But it meant overcoming the preferences of
the foreign business sector, the lingering influence of a few remaining
colonial officers, and ingrained bureaucratic attitudes of the colonial era.

In wanting to institute tariff protection to make possible industrial
development, the government had to contend with strong commercial
interests that benefited from cheap imports. Spokesmen for rubber and
tin argued that the country's development depended on labour-intensive
production for export and any system of tariffs would raise the cost of living,
bid up wages, and hurt the mainstay sectors of the economy (Wheelwright,
1965: 97). The big British importing houses, such as Guthrie, Boustead,
and Harper Gilfillan, were also lukewarm to the idea of manufacturing
because of their traditional role of marketing imported goods.

However, while these interests were powerful in the past, their views
did not hold sway. A World Bank report made in 1955 provided the intellectual legitimacy for the inexperienced government to embark on tariff
protection and local manufacturing (IBRD, 1955). This report highlighted
Malaysia's potential unemployment problem if nothing was done shortly
to diversify the economy, and advocated tariff protection to compensate for
Malaysia's lack of comparative advantage in many aspects of manufacturing.
In particular, the country's relatively high wages compared to potential
competitors in the region and its lack of expertise were cited as obstacles to
export-oriented manufacturing.[3]

The government was open to the recommendations of the World Bank
policy-makers because of its concern about the political implications of a
growing population not able to find jobs. In addition, the fact that Malaysia
hoped to get substantial funds from the World Bank, especially in land
development schemes, added force to the Bank's position. In 1959, the
government eliminated the preferential minimal tariff rate enjoyed by the
British Commonwealth, raising it to the full rate (Wheelwright, 1965: 92).
This measure, affecting about 40 per cent of the country's imports, mostly
of British origin, erased the comfortable price advantages British exporters
had so long enjoyed.

The other area in which the government discarded the practices of the
colonial government was in public finance. Colonial bureaucrats had aimed
to achieve budget surpluses and strictly avoid deficit financing in deference
to the Colonial Office's stand that colonies should not look to Britain for
financial assistance (Edwards, C. T., 1970: 260). These procedures had
kept the role of the government to a minimum but the independent govern-

ment was not prepared to abide by this principle so closely, particularly after the 1959 elections when UMNO's hegemonic grip over the Malay voters seemed to be threatened by the PMIP. The Malay leaders, therefore, felt compelled to resort to some form of deficit financing to speed up development.

When a small deficit was registered in 1957, British commercial interests again spoke out strongly against the abandonment of the principle of balanced budgets. They were against the growing role of the state and the enlargement of the public sector, warning the government that going in such a leftist direction would inhibit the flow of foreign investment and reinvestment in Malaysia (Rudner, 1975: 39). In fact, the government did heed the call of the British commercial sector for a while, when the conservative Finance Minister, Sir H. S. Lee, a tin magnate and co-founder of the Alliance party, cut down development spending at the end of 1957, especially on the social sector. It was only when Tun Tan Siew Sin, the Vice-President of the MCA party, took over as Finance Minister in 1959 that the government distanced itself from direct business pressures.[4] Tun Tan was more attuned to national politics and Malay pressures on the government, and was thus more willing to see a moderate amount of deficit financing if funds were used properly to increase production and establish viable projects.

The Alliance government, by breaking away from colonial economic practices, was able to mobilize far greater resources than before for its development projects. It contracted a modest degree of public debt, chiefly from the government-run pension plan—the Employees Provident Fund (EPF)—to finance its plans. As the number of workers in the labour force increased, the resources of the EPF grew, and the government was able to draw as much as 50 per cent of its borrowings from it, with the rest coming from the domestic banking sector (Edwards, C. T., 1970: 259; Bank Negara, 1979: 19).

Furthermore, as the government became less susceptible to foreign business pressures, it became more willing to tax businesses, especially in the primary exporting sector. For example, export duties on rubber and tin were increased in the early 1960s to extract more revenue (Rudner, 1975: 68). The tin sector, after 1964, was also made to pay an excess profit tax of 10 per cent above the regular company tax of 40 per cent whenever the price of tin exceeded a certain base price. And in 1967 all firms had to pay a 5 per cent development tax on profits (Edwards, C. T., 1970: 68). As a relatively efficient world producer of rubber and tin by then, Malaysia had much leeway in taxing these sectors without hurting world demand through overpricing. The government was in the fortunate position of being able to collect high revenues without relying on economically distorting measures such as overvaluation, exchange controls, and state purchasing monopolies practised by many other Third World countries (Golay, 1969: 353). Because of these measures, the percentage of government revenue to national income was the highest in South-East Asia, averaging 23.6 per cent between 1963 and 1965, and it was achieved without recourse to inflationary financing (Golay, 1969: 353).[5]

The state's increasing fiscal capacity was reflected in its development plans. In the First Five Year Plan (1956–60), development spending was $1 billion, in the Second Five Year Plan (1961–5) $2.7 billion, and in the First Malaysia Plan (1966–70), $3.6 billion. As a percentage of GNP, public investment was 2.7 per cent, 7.3 per cent, and 6.0 per cent respectively.

The important result of increasing state capacity was that public authorities could manage the economy in ways less subject to purely external factors. Past colonial policies, reflected in the workings of the Currency Board System, merely exacerbated the fluctuations of the external environment in the domestic economy. During boom times, when foreign exchange increased, the local money supply was increased accordingly, spurring high demand and economic activity, but during recessionary times just the opposite occurred, aggravating the downturn (Drake, 1969: Chaps. 2, 3). Now, although Malaysia continued to be a highly open economy—exports constituted around 50 per cent of GNP—and suffered intermittently from bouts of export stagnation, the country managed to sustain economic growth at just above 5 per cent in the 1960s. Statistical evidence revealed no conclusive relationship between income growth and export instability, indicating that the government was effective in managing counter-cyclical spending (Bank Negara, 1979: 10).

Increased fiscal capacity also allowed the government to better shape development in response to internal political priorities. In the First Five Year Plan (1956–60), most of the emphasis was on urban infrastructural development, which amounted to 52 per cent of the budget (see Table 3.1). The heavy bias toward urban infrastructure reflected the predominant type of government spending during colonialism. The economic model was simply seen as the dynamic urban sector eventually inducing rural development via a trickle-down process whereby urban growth would gradually generate demand for rural products. Public spending in the social (education, health, housing) and rural sectors had low priority. The social sector in the First Five Year Plan received only 14 per cent of the funds and the large indigenous sector rural sector only 7 per cent (Rudner, 1975: 36). The high allocation to agriculture as shown in the Plan was deceptive because most of the spending went to replanting schemes in rubber benefiting the private estates (Toh Kin Woon and Sundaram, 1983: 35).

However, as internal politics became more competitive, state spending changed direction. In the Second Five Year Plan (1961–5), nearly half of the planned investments went to agriculture. Not only did the allocation for agriculture double, but a higher percentage of the funds for infrastructure and social services went to the rural sector. The orientation had now switched to raising rural incomes so that the domestic market could be enlarged and thus help in industrial development.

To stimulate rural incomes and productivity, the government made a concerted effort to promote land development schemes in rubber and oil palm for settlers, and subsidized the replanting of higher yielding varieties by smallholders. Large irrigation projects were also started in rice-growing areas after many decades of neglect, and an impressive effort was made to extend roads, public utilities, and social services to the rural sector. The

TABLE 3.1
Public Development Spending, 1956–1970
(current M$ in million; percentage in parentheses)

	First Five Year Plan, 1956–1960	Second Five Year Plan, 1961–1965	First Malaysia Plan, 1966–1970
Economic Sector	759.9	1,763.7	2,210.8
	(75.5)	(66.5)	(61.2)
Agriculture	227.5	467.9	911.2
	(22.6)	(17.3)	(25.2)
Infrastructure	520.3	1,236.7	1,162.6
	(51.7)	(46.6)	(32.2)
Commerce and industry	12.1	59.1	137.0
	(1.2)	(2.2)	(3.8)
Social Sector	138.8	413.6	644.7
	(13.8)	(15.6)	(17.9)
Education	60.9	236.5	286.9
	(6.0)	(8.9)	(7.9)
Health	12.7	101.9	114.2
	(1.3)	(3.8)	(3.2)
Housing	65.2	69.4	188.0
	(6.5)	(2.6)	(5.2)
General	108.0	474.4	754.7
	(10.8)	(17.9)	(20.9)
Administration	65.0	167.1	109.0
	(6.5)	(6.3)	(3.0)
Security	43.0	307.3	645.7
	(4.3)	(11.6)	(17.9)
Total Public Investment	1,006.7	2,651.7	3,610.2
	(100.0)	(100.0)	(100.0)

Source: Rudner, 1980: 57–8, Table 1.

First Malaysia Plan (1966–70) continued broadly with the principles of expanded government and rural development. By the end of the decade, the Federal Land Development Authority (Felda), had developed 308,400 acres and settled 20,700 families on ninety schemes (*SMP*, 1971: 125).

An important departure took place in the government's role in the economy in the mid-1960s. It modified its previous policy of not engaging in direct commercial and industrial activities in the modern sector because of urban Malay pressures for greater Malay progress in business. The Malay middle class, comprising aspiring businessmen, politicians, and administrators, wanted parity with rich Chinese entrepreneurs. Lacking capital and expertise, these groups turned to the state for help. As a result, the government made a special allocation of $124 million for the specific promotion of Malay economic development in the First Malaysia Plan (1966–70). The projects to be set up were a Malay bank (Bank Bumiputra) and the establishment of Majlis Amanah Rakyat or MARA (Council of

Trust for the Indigenous People), a body that was to provide commercial loans to existing and aspiring Malay entrepreneurs, and to engage in commercial and industrial projects on its own.

In hindsight, the government's effort in Malay economic development was no more than modest—the $124 million was a mere 3.8 per cent of the Plan's expenditure. Considering the backward state of the Malay economy, the deep cultural and personal desires of many Malays to expand their economic power and influence, and the backing provided by the Constitution for state favouritism of Malays, the government was surprisingly restrained in its vanguard ethnic role. This role was essentially kept within a *laissez-faire* framework; that is, the state restrained itself from going much beyond the provision of public goods. It made little effort to compete against the dominant foreign and Chinese economic groups. Although the government increasingly imposed its priorities over the direction of economic development, and public spending was very high, especially in the rural sector, the high expectations the Malays had of 'their' government helping them vigorously failed to be realized.

Constraints to State Expansion

As a latecomer to commercial enterprise, the sectors in which the state or individual Malays could enter into had more or less been pre-empted by foreign and Chinese enterprise. Any sizeable state commercial involvement would have necessitated mobilizing large resources and acting more aggressively toward the existing economic groups. This did not happen and the reasons had to do very much with the top leadership's sense of the economic constraints they operated within as well as the nature of existing internal and external political arrangements.

One of the first nationalistic acts pursued by many newly independent countries is to nationalize or gradually take over plantation and mining concerns from previous foreign owners. Such acts are politically useful in mobilizing support for the regimes. Also, the sectors targeted for take-over are not particularly demanding technologically and are relatively easy for locals to manage. However, the Malaysian leaders, in pursuing wider geo-political and economic goals, chose not to take any strong measures against these mainly British enterprises or even push them toward giving greater local control and ownership.

Malaysia, in the 1960s, was heavily dependent on Britain for its military defence. Moreover, it was Malaysia which sought such a role for Britain. The country's chief vulnerabilities then were the lingering communist-led movement and Indonesia's 'confrontation' with Malaysia. The new Prime Minister, Tunku Abdul Rahman, played a key role in persuading the Malaysian parliament to ratify the Anglo-Malayan Defence Agreement allowing Britain to keep its forces in the country, and later in 1961, in convincing a reluctant Britain to stay on (Hawkins, 1972: 18).[6] He stressed the positive economic aspects of Britain's military presence and argued that the cost of replacing a British pull-out would be exorbitantly high and an enormous drain on resources which could otherwise be used for development. Britain was spending £200 million annually maintaining its forces in the region (Hawkins, 1969: 549–59). Clearly, with Britain not enthusiastic about its costly role as a military protector, Malaysia was not in a favourable position to risk attacking local British commercial interests.

In the economic sphere, Malaysia was trying to diversify its economic base away from over-reliance on primary commodities. Since it possessed only a rudimentary industrial capacity, the government welcomed any kind of foreign investment and felt obliged to give much leeway to the foreign sector. Tun Tan Siew Sin said plainly in 1958, when he was the Minister of Commerce, that 'Malaya needs foreign capital far more than foreign capital needs the Federation of Malaya' (in Morais, 1972: 126). Tun Abdul Razak, the Deputy Prime Minister and UMNO Deputy President, also defended the free enterprise system against occasional Malay critics who did not see how it benefited the Malays: 'The Alliance Government feels that as a young and developing nation, it is necessary to keep the economic field open to encourage foreign investment here not only to provide employment for the people but also raise the per capita income' (ST, 10 September 1968).

The government, in bestowing such high priority on foreign investment, worked under the assumption that old investments had to be protected in order to project an image of Malaysia as a responsible host country. No effort was therefore made to test the idea of whether changing the terms of participation in one sector would actually lead to declining investments in other sectors.

If perceptions of national economic vulnerability helped to prop up the free enterprise system, existing political arrangements certainly under-pinned it. The 'independence pact' of 1957, which the UMNO and the MCA parties had bargained over, managed to remain intact during the 1960s. This bargain had allowed for Malay cultural and political dominance in return for the safeguarding of the Chinese economic position. Tunku Abdul Rahman's priority was to lay the basis for political stability in a potentially divisive multi-ethnic society. Pushing vigorously for Malay commercial development was a secondary concern. He did not show much confidence in Malay business capabilities and in his view the life of 'easy abundance' had created an adverse outlook in the indigenous people. His claim was that the land in Malaysia was so fertile that the Malays never had to strive for a living (ST, 4 June 1965). The MCA, for its part, by taking a conciliatory stance toward Malay cultural and political predominance, enjoyed strong influence in government and high access to the Prime Minister.

The MCA's position in the Alliance coalition was further strengthened by its strong financial resources. Chinese businessmen almost exclusively made contributions to the MCA since it was the party most favouring free enterprise in the political spectrum. It was thus able to contribute a larger than proportionate share to the Alliance party's coffers for electioneering and organizational purposes, compensating to some extent its weaker vote-pulling capacity in comparison to UMNO (Milne and Ratnam, 1965: 196). As long as the MCA could mobilize the majority of Chinese voters to support the government, which it was able to do for most of the 1960s, its voice in government was secure (see Table 3.5).

The MCA's influence in preserving the free enterprise system was brought to bear in several ways. Consistent with the political bargain it had made with UMNO, it was given control of the important economic ministries of Finance, and Commerce and Industry. This placed MCA ministers in a powerful position to influence the relative balance between the public and private sectors.[7] Tun Tan Siew Sin, as the Minister of Finance, was concerned to limit domestic borrowing to levels that would leave ample funds for the private sector. The level of foreign debt was also carefully contained—the First Malaysia Plan (1966–70) aimed for annual repayments to be around 4 per cent of government revenue and 2 per cent of export earnings so as not to strain future budgets (see *First MP*, 1965: 72–6).[8] This prudent approach automatically limited the amount of funds that could go to special Malay programmes.

Tun Tan also exerted his influence in specific instances when Chinese commercial interests were potentially threatened. For example, Abdul Aziz Ishak, the Minister of Agriculture in the early 1960s, complained several times that the Treasury blocked monies for his rural co-operative projects even though Parliament had passed his projects (Abdul Aziz Ishak, 1977: 34). Many of Abdul Aziz's projects aimed to rid the rural sector of Chinese middlemen services and dependence on extra-village Chinese suppliers. In denying the funds, Tun Tan said he was sceptical of the success and profitability of the projects (Abdul Aziz Ishak, 1977: 39).

Having an MCA politician as the Minister of Commerce and Industry was also important in keeping state bureaucratic intervention within limits. The Malay Deputy Minister, Haji Khalid, was an active and outspoken advocate of Malay business, frequently exhorting Malay individuals and organizations to pool their capital to compete with non-Malays, while warning non-Malays of the necessity of helping Malays in business (*ST*, 25 April, 10 June 1963). Both Malay officials in the Ministry and Malay business leaders were beginning to take the view that Malay business failures were the result of non-Malay economic strangulation rather than of their own shortcomings (*ST*, 1 January 1964).[9] However, bureaucratic controls to deal with this interpretation of business problems did not take place. Most of the pro-Malay activities of the Ministry in the 1960s were confined largely to data collection, the sponsorship of a few joint ventures between Malays and foreign companies, and helping aspiring and existing Malay businessmen pool organizational and financial resources. There were few direct controls and regulations on firms. An informal policy requiring manufacturing firms with pioneer status to put aside 10 per cent of their equity for Malay interests was not even applied seriously (Lindenberg, 1973: 256).

Our treatment of how economic dependence and political compromises shaped the *laissez-faire* policies of the government cannot be complete without appreciating the Prime Minister's attitudes and his position in the party. While structural constraints do indeed shape policy outcomes, it is also necessary to take into account the values and mind-set of power-holders to understand their decisions. Tunku Abdul Rahman came from the royal household of Kedah, giving him a strong sense of upper-class aristocratic identity and status, which distanced him from the status problems of middle-class Malays. He did not view with great urgency the growing desire of urban Malays for business success as a way to gain wealth and respect for themselves and their ethnic group. The Tunku's personal desire to see a workable multiracial society led him to work closely with the MCA and make major concessions to its leadership, although on purely technical grounds UMNO had enough seats to rule government alone (see Table 3.5).

The concessions the Tunku made to Chinese business interests often went against populist UMNO leaders and the sentiments of the rank and file. One instance was in 1962 when Abdul Aziz Ishak, the Minister of Agriculture, threatened to transform Chinese-owned rice mills in Perak and Province Wellesley into farmer-run co-operatives (Lim, D., 1973: 191, fn. 3). The MCA threatened to leave the Alliance over this issue. Tunku Abdul Rahman sided with the MCA and Abdul Aziz was removed from his post for unconstitutional practices. Later, the energetic Assistant Minister of Commerce and Industry, Haji Khalid, was also removed for being a militant advocate of Malay commerce (Funston, 1980: 13).

The Tunku was able to act as the ultimate guarantor of the *laissez-faire* approach and the consociational political scheme because of his autonomous and strong position within the UMNO. His colleagues never challenged his position and dissenting voices from the rank and file never really came into the open. The charisma which he enjoyed as the leader of independence made it difficult to criticize him. But a deeper reason resided within the nature of Malay society. Malays were still quite traditional in their attitudes, harboured deep respect for social hierarchy, and regarded the open challenge of a leader's position and authority as highly improper and in bad taste, even if they had fundamental disagreements with the leader. These attitudes insulated the Tunku from open challenge. Malay nationalists within and outside UMNO who were critical of some of the leadership's policies were never in a position to mount a serious organizational and political challenge to the Prime Minister (see Funston, 1980: 175–83).

Tunku Abdul Rahman's position in UMNO was not invulnerable but as long as the party and he did well in national elections, his tenure as head of the party was secure. The basic parameters within which the Tunku and the other UMNO ministers operated was to do what was necessary to get the support of the majority of the Malay voters.[10] The Malay leadership certainly wished to see greater Malay commercial progress, but their time horizon was long term. The leadership's approach was to quell the criticisms and pressures mounted by aspiring Malay businessmen by coming up with *ad hoc* economic programmes. Working on the assumption that such programmes would ensure sufficient support from the Malay middle class and broad electorate, the leadership turned its attention to political accommodation between the ethnic groups and to diversifying the economy. Here the government turned to private economic actors who seemed most capable of carrying out economic development.

We next examine the development of foreign, Chinese, and Malay business during the *laissez-faire* period of the 1960s, as a useful backdrop to the development of these groups after 1970.

Preserving the Foreigners' Role

Malaysia was among the relatively few newly independent countries to keep intact the large Western stake in the economy and to solicit foreign capital to enter into the anticipated growth sector, manufacturing. Interestingly, very few sectors of society spoke out against the favourable treatment of foreign capital. Sporadic calls by Malays like Tan Sri Ja'afa Albar, a businessman and high UMNO official, to modify the free enterprise system were not so much anti-foreign capital in thrust or ideology as an appeal to ease the rules for the Malays (*ST*, 9 September 1986). The Chinese domestic business class, in general, did not press the government for preferential treatment of local entrepreneurship. Only in one instance in 1958 did the newly created Malayan Manufacturers' Association, established by a small group of Chinese manufacturers, call for the restriction of foreign capital in manufacturing until its members were in a stronger position to benefit from the government's Pioneer Industrial Scheme. This request was rejected wholesale by Tun Tan Siew Sin when he was Minister of Commerce. He excoriated the association for its 'dog in the manger' attitude and for failing to understand the pressing need for industrial development (see Morais, 1972: 122). Chinese leaders in business and in politics seemed to have taken the position that, in the long run, a liberal and open economy, even one with strong foreign participation, was in the best interests of the Chinese. They probably reasoned that Chinese business had done relatively well under the free market policies of the colonial era and any change in the rules and regulations to favour Chinese business now could easily set an undesirable precedent for similar claims by the Malays against the Chinese.[11]

Some scholars have interpreted the government's highly favourable treatment of foreigners in the 1960s as arising from Malay insecurity about Chinese economic power (Golay, 1969: 387; Snodgrass, 1980: 210). They argue that foreign control was preferable to heavier reliance on the Chinese because it was more manageable politically. Such a view does have the merit of explaining why economic nationalism did not make sense for the Malays if they did not expect to benefit from it. Yet the argument cannot be stretched too far since in some instances, like in banking, the government put Chinese interests ahead of foreign banks because it thought that local banks would be more willing to hold government securities and bonds.

Foreign capital expansion was most pronounced in the manufacturing sector. The government did all it could to attract foreign investment by providing the right climate and generous incentives. The Pioneer Ordinance of 1958 exempted manufacturing firms producing a 'pioneer product' (generously interpreted) from the 40 per cent company tax anywhere from two to five years, depending on the amount of capital invested. Import tariffs were also liberally given to firms. In the area of labour control, weak as the trade union movement was—union membership never exceeded 13 per cent of the work-force in the 1960s—the government came up with policies to ensure that it would not get strong. For example, it instituted a system of compulsory arbitration in 1967 in a wide range of 'essential services', even seeing fit to include the pineapple, coconut, and palm oil industries (Mohd. Raza Ali, 1969: 363).[12]

Many companies got involved in Malaysia's import-substitution programme with the advent of the new tariffs and incentives. Initially Britain was the leading investor, followed by Malaysian and Singaporean capital. By the end of the 1960s, the US had become a major investor, comparable in size to UK investment commitments. Japan and Hong Kong companies were also beginning to make their presence felt (see Table 3.2).

British agency houses, who were previously responsible for importing foreign goods, were an important conduit for bringing British capital to Malaysia (Junid Saham, 1980: 140). They were goaded by the tariffs and the potential entry of new foreign companies in manufacturing. Sometimes forming partnerships with their former suppliers, agency houses like Sime Darby entered into security equipment (Chubb Malaysia), paints (Par Paints), agricultural equipment (Tractors Malaysia), and bituminous products (Malaysian Bitumen) among others.

British multinationals also entered Malaysia independently of the agency houses. Some of the companies were Shell (with Dutch capital), Castrol, and British Petroleum (petroleum refining and associated products), Dunlop and Wilkenson Process (rubber products), ICI, Glaxo–Allenburys, and British Oxygen (chemicals and pharmaceuticals), and Rothmans, British–American Tobacco, and Guinness (tobacco and beverages). These firms managed to capture a dominant share of their respective markets because of their technological superiority (Junid Saham, 1980: 240).

US firms made a later appearance. They tended to be highly capital intensive—their capital commitments nearly equalled Britain's but had half the number of firms—and were concentrated in the petro-chemical and chemical industries. The main firms were Esso Standard (ammonia

TABLE 3.2
Ownership of Pioneer Companies, 1962 and 1969 (in M$ million)

Country	1962	1969
Malaysia (West)	13.0	67.8
Singapore	19.6	86.5
UK	16.0	79.8
US	3.6	67.5
Japan	1.3	38.4
Hong Kong	4.3	33.5
Others	11.2	39.0
Total	69.0	413.4

Source: Tan Boon Kean, 1980: 10.

and sulphur), Esso Refinery (petro-chemicals), Union Carbide (dry cells), Colgate Palmolive Far East (toothpaste), and Ansul (herbicides).

Japanese manufacturing investment was relatively modest then compared to its enormous scale today, as the country's shortage of foreign exchange limited investment abroad (Ozawa, 1979: 14). Japanese products tended to rely on mature technologies in which they had developed a lower cost competitive advantage. Most of the firms produced for the domestic market, and only in wood products did the Japanese invest in order to get access to local raw materials and upgrade them for the Japanese market. Some of the firms that went to Malaysia were Matsushita Electric (electrical and home appliances), Ajinomoto (chemical seasonings), Daishowa Paper Manufacturing (lumber chips), Lion Corporation (dentifrices, toiletries), and Nissin and Mitsui (sugar refining). The interesting characteristic of Japanese investors, in contrast to British and US ones, was their tendency to enter into the joint venture form of organization, often as minority partners. They typically chose Chinese businessmen and sometimes the agency houses as partners. Both provided important distribution networks which were vital for the Japanese because they were newcomers and specialized in consumer goods.

Investments by Singaporean nationals were not as large as suggested by official figures because some of the investments coming from Singapore were made by Singapore-based foreign companies expanding into Malaysia.[13] Nonetheless, local Singaporean investments were sizeable. Singaporean and Malaysian businessmen tended to treat the two countries as basically one, given the close historical and cultural ties between them. Singaporeans were typically involved in the production of lower quality and less sophisticated products, such as mosquito repellent coils, paper cartons, polythene sheets, household utensils, and asbestos cement sheets. Partnerships with Malaysian Chinese were common, again reflecting the intimate ties between the overseas Chinese from the two countries.

The Pioneer Programme, by bringing in significant foreign investment, helped to increase manufacturing's share of the GDP from 8.5 per cent in 1960 to 13.5 per cent in 1970. By 1967, local production was meeting two-thirds of domestic demand in beverages, rubber products, chemicals, and non-metallic products, and even higher proportions in tobacco and wood products (Rao, 1980: 124). However, only 23,000 jobs were created because of the relatively high capital intensity of the Pioneer Programme, which failed to narrow the gap between the 3 per cent growth in the labour force and the 2.5 per cent growth in job creation (ST, 26 October 1970). One consolation was that the pioneer firms roughly met the expectation that they hire Malays in proportion to population ratios; Malays constituted 42 per cent of the labour force in pioneer firms but only 24 per cent for the manufacturing sector as a whole.

Foreign ownership in many of the other sectors of the economy continued to be high, as shown in Table 3.3.

In cash crop production, the private estates did not expand much because state governments, which had jurisdiction over land, were reluctant to alienate land to foreigners and Chinese. The plantation companies,

TABLE 3.3

Foreign Ownership in the Malaysian Economy, 1970
(percentage of total share ownership and fixed capital)

Sector	Share Capital (Per Cent)	Value of Fixed Assets (Per Cent)
Agriculture	75.4*	25.4*
Mining (tin)	71.5	55.1
Manufacturing	59.6	51.0
Construction	34.1	5.9
Transport	12.0	n.a.
Trade	63.6*	n.a.
Wholesale	70.1	n.a.
Retail	44.5	n.a.
Financial Sector		
Banks	35.2	n.a.
Insurance	55.3	n.a.
Total	60.7	27.6*

Source: Hoffman and Tan Siew Ee, 1980: 215, Table 7.1.
Notes: *Estimated; share capital ownership stands for ownership of the corporate sector while fixed investments represents every type of business organization, from small-holdings and sole proprietorships to public companies.
n.a. = Not available.

instead, intensified their production by planting higher yielding varieties and diversifying into palm oil, which offered better price prospects and needed less labour. Important rationalizations were also carried out by the big rubber companies such as Guthrie, Consolidated Plantations, and Harrisons. They exchanged dispersed estates to centralize operations and carried out mergers and amalgamations under larger holding companies. J. Puthucheary (1977) has argued that these strategies were made to buttress the acreage and capital of the plantation companies to discourage local Chinese businessmen from conducting take-over operations. Except for the local rubber baron, Lee Loy Seng, very few locals made much headway in acquiring large plantation companies (Tan Tat Wai, 1982: 150).[14]

The tin-mining sector remained very much the same as in the colonial period. The thirty odd dredging companies and two tin-smelting companies remained under strong foreign control and ownership. With the exception of Selangor Dredging, a company established by Chinese interests in 1963, no other tin-dredging company was formed in the 1960s. Both the high costs and uncertain demand for tin discouraged further investment in this sector. London Tin, Charter Consolidated, and the Singapore-based Straits Trading Company, continued to control most of the tin-dredging companies, which were responsible for 75 per cent of the output of the tin-dredging sector. In companies which were publicly listed in the Malaysian stock market, locals were able to invest in them, but overall, foreigners held about two-thirds of the capital of the dredging sector (Thoburn, 1977: 89).

The high level of foreign dominance in the primary sector allowed foreign plantation and mining agencies to retain a predominant role in the nation's exporting business as well. Where British traders suffered a relative decline in business was in the import of manufactured consumer goods. Competitors from East Asia and the US were more willing to choose locals as agents for their products; even British manufacturers sometimes shied away from the old agency houses because they had so many product lines and were therefore too spread out to be effective marketers of the new products (Junid Saham, 1980: 121).

The other area where foreigners lost some ground was in banking. Because local banks were considered more amenable to holding Malaysian government and treasury bills, the Central Bank (Bank Negara) showed a liberal attitude toward local bank formation and expansion. Existing foreign banks such as the Chartered Bank and the Hong Kong and Shanghai Bank were not permitted to expand their branch network and only a handful of new foreign banks (for example, Chase Manhattan, the Bank of Tokyo, and Citibank) were given entry for the purpose of servicing manufacturing investment from the US and Japan. Directives were also issued to non-resident companies to borrow a portion of their funds from local banks. These measures helped to spur local banks but it was only in the latter part of the 1970s, with active state participation, that nationals were able to displace the dominant position of foreign banks (Chin, P. Y., 1984: 196).

The Spread of Chinese Business

Chinese businesses were able to make impressive gains in the 1960s by taking advantage of the loss of the foreigner's favourable political position in the colonial era and the government's greater national orientation in its development programmes. Some Chinese businesses succeeded in becoming large conglomerates, involved in nearly every kind of business. Even Chinese small businessmen found many opportunities for growth because of good growth rates and the MCA's role in preventing excessive bureaucratic interference in private business. The greatest expansion was probably in property development and banking. Small strides were also made in manufacturing, especially in the lower technology and less capital-intensive industries, in which foreign companies showed little interest. Chinese businesses did face some constraints imposed by the state, particularly in the marketing of peasant rice and smallholder rubber. Here, the government attempted to provide an alternative to the Chinese marketing and credit system, which it considered exploitative.[15]

An interesting feature of the larger Chinese businesses was the diversified nature of their expansion. They successfully expanded from their past trading and, to some extent, primary product activities into new activities made possible by the growth of the middle class and the expanded public spending programme. Tan Tat Wai (1982: 294) has hypothesized the path of development of the big Chinese businessmen in the following way: '. . . the initial activity was usually retailing evolving into wholesaling, importing, or exporting. With larger surpluses accumulated and the development of broader experience and outlook, the traders could then move into resource-based activities related to their trading and/or some manufacturing.'

Tan's scenario epitomizes Chinese business expansion from the colonial era to independence, but in the independence era the pattern became a little less sharp and, in addition, diversifying into property development became almost a ritual for the bigger Chinese businesses.

One of the largest, if not the largest, trading and industrial group to emerge in the 1960s was the business empire of Robert Kuok and his brothers. Their expansion followed quite closely the pattern suggested by Tan. Robert Kuok's Fukienese forebears had built up a comfortable sugar and rice trading business in Johor before the Second World War (Verchere, *Insight*, August 1978). Kuok joined his family business after studying in Raffles College, Singapore, where he made important links with the future independence leaders of Malaysia and Singapore. In the 1950s he set up Rickwood and Company in Singapore to deal with general merchandising, ship brokering, and adhesive manufacturing. Across the causeway, in Malaysia, he established Kuok Brothers Sdn Bhd in Johor to trade in rice, sugar, and wheat. After a stint in London studying the workings of the London Commodity Exchanges, Kuok got deeply involved in sugar trading and soon established himself as a leading sugar broker. This line of business got him into manufacturing, and in 1959, Kuok established Malaysia's first and largest sugar refinery, Malayan Sugar, in partnership with the government agency, Felda, and Japan's Nissin Sugar Manufacturing. It processed sugar from Kuok's mills in Thailand and then re-exported much of the refined sugar to Indonesia. The business connection with the government was quite unique for Chinese business at that time, probably stemming from his close relationship with the Deputy Prime Minister, Tun Abdul Razak, whom he had met at Raffles College.

In the 1960s, Kuok diversified further into manufacturing by establishing forward and backward linkages from his existing interests, setting up Federal Flour Mills, Johor Flour Mills and, with the Perlis state government, Perlis Plantations. He was also a partner in Malayan Veneer, the region's foremost producer of blockboard, which was exported widely through his trading firm in Singapore. At the end of the 1960s and early 1970s, Kuok went into shipping, a logical extension of his vast trading interests. He helped set up, again with the government, the nation's first shipping line in 1971, taking a minority interest of 10 per cent. Kuok also became a major figure in property development, building luxury hotels in Malaysia, Singapore, Hong Kong and Fiji, and developing private residential housing estates in Malaysia.

Other Chinese businessmen who entered manufacturing lacked the scope of Kuok; nonetheless, they were making an important beginning. Some Chinese businessmen entered manufacturing as an investment outlet from money accumulated elsewhere, such as in rubber speculation. One prominent example was Loy Hean Heong of Central Securities. He initially accumulated capital from holding a Caltex petrol franchise, and then proceeded to speculate in the buying and selling of rubber estates. He bought over the smaller European estates that were divesting from Malaysia, subdivided them, and then sold them off to smallholders (*MB*, June 1974). When the government stopped this practice because it was displacing labourers and jeopardizing productivity, Loy ran the estates himself. Attracted by the incentives provided under the Pioneer Scheme, he next entered manufacturing by taking over a fledgling carbide company. From this footing in manufacturing, Loy went on to other non-related projects, such as adhesive tapes, rubber bands, and threads in a joint venture with Japanese interests, and aluminum foil lamination.

The other interesting form of entry into manufacturing was undertaken by former distributors of imported products taking advantage of tax incentives and tariff protection. The people involved were usually distributors of Japanese products; two prominent examples were Eric Chia and Loh Boon Siew of Kah Motors. Chia started selling vehicle parts in the 1950s and moved into selling heavy equipment spare parts when he realized that the government's development projects created a lucrative market for heavy equipment (*MB*, January 1973). Soon he was selling tractors for Mitsubishi of Japan and after 1965, Komatsu tractors. In the late 1960s, Chia set up a factory to manufacture certain parts for his tractor bodies and engines. He has concentrated on engineering works since then, such as reconditioning diesel engines and engine crankshafts bought second-hand from the US, and manufacturing oil and air filters. Loh Boon Siew persuaded Honda to let him sell their motor-bikes in the late 1950s. It was then a bold move because, according to Loh, 'people did not trust Japanese goods and some dealers of established British and American makes were openly critical of the Hondas. They said even their bicycles would last longer than our motor-bikes' (quoted in *MB*, January 1974). Loh's venture paid dividends because rapidly the Hondas captured 60 per cent of the market, and in 1969 the market was large enough for him to start the local assembly of Hondas in Malaysia.

On the whole, however, there were many obstacles for large-scale Chinese participation in manufacturing. Many could not so easily diversify from their base in raw materials (primarily rubber and tin) and trading. The final products made from rubber and tin, such as tin plate and rubber tyres, contained only very small proportions of the raw material in terms of volume, weight, or cost (Tan Tat Wai, 1982: 291). This militated against local production because of high transport costs in importing needed inputs and then shipping out the final product. The other problem was the relative lack of know-how among local manufacturers, which made it difficult for them to compete with foreign manufacturers. While there were many cases of small family businesses which made products such as joss sticks and paper, fish balls and sausages, fire clay bricks, roofing tiles, and steel tubes, these were all in the lower technology and less capital-intensive industries. Only in the simpler sectors fabricating plastic products, clothing, wood products, and paper and printing were Chinese investment commitments higher than foreign (see FIDA, *Annual Report*, 1971: Appendix 11). In all other sectors, the foreigners were more dominant, especially in chemicals, petroleum products, beverages, and rubber products.

It was in the construction and property development sectors that Chinese business expansion was most noticeable. Chinese business could thrive in these sectors because technological requirements were not demanding and familiarity with local conditions was a definite advantage. With urbanization and the growth of the professional and bureaucratic middle class, the demand for middle-class housing, shopping complexes, and other amenities increased. Government projects in land development, public buildings and schools, irrigation works, and general infrastructure also opened up many opportunities for the construction sector. In the absence of strongly applied directives to channel construction projects to nascent Malay firms, nearly all the government and private construction tenders went to Chinese contractors and sub-contractors. In 1970, 85 per cent of the construction work exceeding $100,000 in value went to Chinese firms, and only 11.6 per cent to foreign firms, and a meagre 2.5 per cent to Malay firms (Tan Boon Kean, 1982: Table 6). Even small Chinese businessmen found many opportunities in the construction sector. For them, MCA patronage played an important role in securing tenders and contracts at both the state and federal levels.

The large-scale property developers were usually traders who had bought choice urban land for later development. Robert Kuok was one of them. The Teo family, who were in the rice trading business, also diversified into housing development in Petaling Jaya, a satellite town of Kuala Lumpur, and in Singapore (AF, May/June 1977). The other major housing developer was Lee Yan Lian, who played an active role in the Associated Chinese Chambers of Commerce, and whose family business diversified from rubber and general trading into developing extensive housing estates in Petaling Jaya.

Having contacts with top political leaders was pivotal for some property developers. Lim Goh Tong was a case in point. He specialized in major government infrastructural projects in the 1950s and 1960s. In 1965, he conceived the idea of building a hill resort and casino complex in the mountainous jungles of Pahang. His friendship with Mohd. Noah, the Speaker of the Senate and Tun Abdul Razak's father-in-law, greatly facilitated negotiations with federal and state governments. A large tract of 12,000 acres was approved for the project and among the minority shareholders were Mohd. Noah and the Sultans of Pahang and Kedah (Gill, 1980: 22).

Banking was the other sector in which Chinese business made substantial progress in the 1960s, aided by the government's open policy of supporting the development of home-grown banks. In Tan Tat Wai's study of the banking sector (1982: 159), he found that '[m]ost of the twelve new local banks established after 1957 were incorporated in the sixties by businessmen who made their money in the rubber and tin sectors and were then diversifying into the financial sector for security, fame (as a banker), and to facilitate further industrial and property development activates'.[16] Chinese involvement in banking proved to be highly lucrative. In 1959 there were eight local banks with twelve branches. In 1970 the numbers had increased to sixteen and 177 respectively, and all of them, with the exception of the state-controlled Bank Bumiputra, were substantially controlled by local Chinese (Bank Negara, 1979: 142).

In the relatively congenial climate of the 1960s, the Chinese expanded their role as the domestic bourgeoisie. To be sure, they did not acquire the industrial skills of their counterparts in Taiwan, South Korea, and Hong Kong; the presence of many other lucrative sectors, superior foreign technology, and the lack of vigorous state backing contributed to their lack of industrial strength. Yet, as a whole, even in industry, they were making progress.

However, Chinese businesses were in a politically sensitive position. Very few Chinese firms incorporated Malay partners or hired many Malays. The few exceptions were large firms bringing in Malay directors as 'influence brokers' to facilitate dealings with the government (see Lim Mah Hui, 1981: Chap. 3). The family basis of Chinese establishments, even among large ones, inhibited their ability and willingness to absorb outsiders. In addition, many Chinese regarded Malays as lacking in enterprise, discipline, and ingenuity. In such circumstances, it was very easy for Malays to regard Chinese business development as an obstacle to their economic advancement and a potential political threat.

Malay Business Developments

From the previous chapter we saw how feeble the level of Malay business development was at the time of independence. Most Malay businesses were small and concentrated in traditional cottage industries, such as batik cloth-making, rattan products, and ornaments. The ratio of business units to the population was 1 : 623 for the Malays compared to 1 : 40 for the Chinese population (Goh Joon Hai, 1962: 84). Given this weakness, it was not surprising that business development during the 1960s was closely linked to state support.

The bureaucracy was involved in various ways in trying to bring about greater Malay progress, even undertaking the elementary task of organizing Malay businessmen and aspiring businessmen into associations. Combination was seen as the only way to compete against the more powerful non-Malay economic groups. In 1963, the Ministry of Commerce and Industry initiated the formation of an association of timber contractors, even providing the name 'National Timber Industry' for them (*ST*, 6 July 1963). Later in the year it sponsored a joint venture between the association and an Australian company to manufacture timber products. The Ministry also sponsored a $5 million joint venture between the United Malay Contractors and another Australian company.

The other major attempt to pool Malay resources in the early 1960s was the setting up of the National Investment Company by the government in 1961. The company was supposed to buy shares allocated to Malays in pioneer manufacturing companies and engage in business projects on its own. All 50,000 or so Malay civil servants were allowed to buy up to

$10,000 each in the shares of the company. By the end of 1964, the company held $3.2 million worth of shares in pioneer companies out of the Malay total of $3.8 million. Both figures were far short of the $15.1 million allotted to Malays, reflecting the plain fact that even among the privileged stratum of Malay civil servants, the savings capacity of Malay society was paltry (*ST*, 17 October 1964).

Perhaps the most politically visible programme to promote Malay commercial development was the Rural and Industrial Development Authority (RIDA). It was established prior to independence in 1953, and was a direct outgrowth of the political bargain to grant easier rules for non-Malays to become citizens in exchange for a programme of Malay economic upliftment. In the 1950s the agency concentrated on providing small loans to the rural sector for agricultural enterprises. When the Ministry of National Development took over these functions in 1959, RIDA turned to more urban-based activities (Beaglehole, 1969: 222). Its chief activities were providing loans to Malay contractors and taxi-drivers, and conducting business training courses. Unfortunately, RIDA, which was scuttled in 1966, failed to make a strong impact on Malay commercial development during its existence, suffering chronically from poor funding, bad management, and high losses in the enterprises it ran directly.

The nascent Malay business community, which had come into being from some of these government programmes, began to exert pressure on the government for a more concerted economic programme for the Malays. The President of the Associated Malay Chambers called on the government to 'prove its good intentions with deeds and not just lip service' and 'give serious attention to prevailing economic strangulation and discrimination now being expressed by Malay businessmen' (*ST*, 5 October 1964). The Malay business leaders had much leverage with government officials because many of them were either at present or in the past high UMNO officials and top civil servants (Popenoe, 1970: 221). The politico-administrative élite were the only stratum in Malay society with the political influence and economic means to think about business. These business spokesmen, enjoying close ties with the government and as potentially important opinion makers, found a receptive ear among politicians and bureaucrats.

The government's response was to summon two congresses, one in 1965 and the other in 1968, to deliberate, review, and recommend policies on all aspects of the Malay economy, concentrating especially on the urban sector. Both congresses were sponsored by the Ministry of National and Rural Development, showing the strong role played by its Minister, Tun Abdul Razak.[17] In the First Bumiputra Economic Congress, sixty-nine recommendations were made on nearly every type of governmental action that ought to be taken to benefit the Malays, ranging from tackling rural indebtedness to suggesting that the government emulate Meiji Japan in setting up state enterprises and selling them off cheaply to private capitalists (*Konggeres Ekonomi Bumiputra Malaysia*, 1965). The second congress not only made a greater number of recommendations but these were also much bolder than the first, especially in advocating a greater role for the state.

The outcome of both congresses was a slightly more active role for the state in promoting Malay commerce. The first Malay commercial bank, Bank Bumiputra, was established in 1965 by the government to provide Malay individuals and companies with easier access to credit facilities. MARA, a revamped and expanded version of RIDA, was set up in 1966 as a statutory board under the Ministry of National and Rural Development—it received a $51 million allocation under the First Malaysia Plan, a rather large increase from the $10 million RIDA received between 1961 and 1965. Finally, toward the end of the First Malaysia Plan, a state-owned trading enterprise was set up to engage in import–export trade and raw material exploitation.

These measures were a departure from the pre-1965 pattern, but it was obvious that they were not meant to make a major onslaught on the existing pattern of wealth ownership. As a result, Malay participation was still weak in 1970. Malays and state agencies acting on their behalf together had only 2.2 per cent of the total share ownership in manufacturing, 1.4 per cent in trade and commerce, and 2.4 per cent in mining. Less than 6 per cent of the larger Class A and B contractors registered with the government were Malays (Mohd. Jali Tajuddin, 1974: Appendix 2). Their strongest participation was in the transport industry, where the Malay share was 13.3 per cent of the share capital of limited companies (*MTR SMP*, 1973: 86–7, Table 4-9).

No solid class of Malay entrepreneurs could thus be properly regarded as having emerged in the 1960s. In Popenoe's study of 140 leading Malay entrepreneurs (1970: 354) he found that their scale of activities was relatively small. About 75 per cent of them had made investments of less than $250,000 and about 70 per cent had a turnover of less than $500,000 (Popenoe, 1970: 354). They were concentrated in the timber industry, mining, transportation, and contracting (Popenoe, 1970: 418–50). These were sectors where the federal and state governments had a strong say over entry through such instruments as the control over licences and permits, and could therefore favour Malay applicants, especially their friends and kin. Many of the Malays who entered these sectors were encouraged by their good access to government officials and enticed by the quick money to be made. For example, one member of a royal family who went into timber gave the following reason: 'I saw people make money. Timber is the quickest way. You cut in the morning and you get your money in the afternoon' (quoted in Popenoe, 1970: 418).

Thus, the early independence period provided more chances for the Malays to participate in business than in the colonial era. However, given the fact that most sectors of the economy had been taken over by more skilful and experienced groups, it was only through extraordinary efforts, either by the state or individuals, that Malays could hope to catch up economically with the others. The state lacked the political imperative for this effort and its actions strove to pacify overt Malay demands through a gradualistic approach. Malay individuals, for their part, vacillated between defeatism and wanting to get rich quickly, between a secure government career and the titillation of business, and never approached business with the necessary single-mindedness.

The Breakdown of the *Laissez-faire* Framework

The state's relatively restrained role in the economy underwent a major change after 1970. The state thereafter began to intervene strongly in the economy, introducing a battery of controls over the activities of the private sector, and expanding the state enterprise sector. The immediate precipitating factor was the crumbling of the political basis of rule of the Alliance party. In the May 1969 elections, Malay and Chinese electoral support for the UMNO and MCA parties weakened visibly, and there were bloody racial riots immediately following the elections. For nearly two years, the country was governed by emergency rule, and during this period UMNO's leadership changed in a more Malay nationalist direction.

The *laissez-faire* model was based on the two main ethnic groups respecting their particular 'resource monopolies' (that is to say, Malay political predominance and Chinese economic power) and not making sharp inroads into each other's sphere of influence. It was critical in this arrangement for both groups of voters to give strong support to their moderate ethnic leaders who were willing to abide broadly by this principle. There were, however, underlying forces which made it difficult for the leaders to sustain the *laissez-faire* framework.

Economic factors certainly played a role in weakening the consociational framework. Manufacturing employment and land development did not keep pace with the growth in the labour force, so unemployment increased for all the ethnic groups in the 1960s.[18] Equally disappointing was an 11 per cent decline in the mean household income of the bottom 40 per cent of the population (Snodgrass, 1980: 81). This bottom group consisted of Malay farmers and smallholders as well as the urban unskilled of all the ethnic groups. The government's frequent claim that it was carrying out a successful developmentalist drive seemed less than convincing to significant sectors of society. From field reports, many rural Malays felt that the government, while having good intentions, was not doing enough for them and was too friendly to non-Malay interests (Rogers, 1975: 222).

It was the urbanized Malays in particular who, in frequently coming into contact with the Chinese in the towns, felt the gap between themselves and the Chinese to be growing. Many middle-class and aspiring businessmen resented the difficulty of getting high-level company jobs and becoming successful entrepreneurs, occupations which increasingly conferred status in the modernizing society. The type of economic development that was occurring hardly gave ownership opportunities to Malays in the modern sector. In addition, they were under-represented in most white collar jobs in the private sector. As shown in Table 3.4, Malays were poorly represented in most sectors of the modern economy, from executive positions to urban workers. Only in the lower categories of professional and technical jobs such as nursing and teaching (mainly government jobs) and

TABLE 3.4

Employment by Occupation and Ethnic Group, 1970
(percentage of ethnic representation in occupation)

Sector	Malay	Chinese	Indian
Professional and technical	47.2	37.7	12.7
Administrative and managerial	22.4	65.7	7.5
Clerical workers	33.4	51.0	14.3
Sales workers	23.9	64.7	11.0
Production workers	31.3	59.9	8.6
Service workers	42.9	42.5	13.4
Agricultural workers	68.7	20.8	9.6
Total	51.4	37.0	10.7

Source: TMP, 1976: 82, Table 4-15.

high-level administrative positions were Malays well represented or over-represented.

Too much emphasis, however, cannot be placed on economic factors alone. In the 1960s, there was also an increasing struggle over each group's place in and power to determine the nature of the society. With the spread of communication—via newspapers, radio, television, and transport networks—and political mobilization, the ethnic groups became increasingly aware of their relative standing vis-à-vis each other. Indeed, whatever underlying economic grievances there were, especially on the part of the Malays, took the form of, to use Horowitz's terms, the struggle over relative group worth and capacity in society (Horowitz, 1985). Past compromises made by the political leadership came to be seen less as wise government and more as leadership sell-outs of the interest of the ethnic group. Two trends were encouraging this tendency—the emergence of a younger generation who did not feel obliged to honour past compromises, and a greater willingness on the part of Malay and Chinese opposition parties to appeal along particularistic lines in trying to gain influence.

Non-Malay opposition parties began to question the special rights provisions in the Constitution for the Malays and called for political equality in Malaysia. The entry of Lee Kuan Yew's People's Action Party (PAP) into Malaysia from Singapore between 1963 and 1965 was a major factor in politicizing the non-Malay population; its banner 'Towards a Malaysian Malaysia' implicitly criticized Malay political hegemony and contributed to ethnic polarization.[19] The Chinese population began to see themselves as second-class citizens and came to resent a number of specific issues, such as the high quotas allocated to Malays in the administrative service, the preponderance of Malays in the army and police, their inability to get Chinese listed as an official language and to obtain greater assistance for Chinese education.

The Malays, for their part, became anxious—from the campaigns of the opposition parties—that the Chinese wanted to challenge Malay political supremacy and privileges. All Malays, including Malay villagers, saw their political supremacy as the only guarantee of their stake in the country and their economic survival (Rogers, 1975: 210). The Malays considered the more favourable economic position of the Chinese bad enough, but now it seemed the Chinese wanted to extend their economic power into the political sphere. This view came out clearly in the present Prime Minister's controversial book (Mahathir bin Mohamad, 1970: 54):

Time and again they (viz Chinese chambers of commerce) have taken the role of, and have been accepted as the spokesman for, the Chinese community on matters other than business. Their racialist role often exceeds their commercial role. They have branched off into politics, and they have stood up for Chinese culture and language. It is to be expected that these organizations should also promote and sustain extreme racial exclusiveness in business. Covert Chinese chauvinism is in fact their *raison d'etre*. The stress is more on Chinese than on commerce.

Evidently each ethnic group was beginning to perceive its situation as unjust while taking for granted its particular sphere of influence in society.

These centrifugal forces formed the background to the 1969 elections. The Alliance party lost its two-thirds majority in parliament and suffered a major erosion of electoral support, although it did not lose the elections (see Table 3.5). The MCA, in particular, was hit by a dramatic loss of seats. Although UMNO did not lose as many seats as the MCA, the Malay voter abandoned the Alliance coalition (and UMNO) even more than the Chinese. About 67 per cent of Malays voted for the Alliance in 1964 but only 54 per cent did so in 1969; in contrast, 43 per cent of the non-Malays voted for the Alliance in 1969 when 48 per cent had done so in 1964 (Drummond and Hawkins, 1970: 333; Ratnam and Milne, 1967: 374–6). In the forty-three constituencies where UMNO and its rival, PAS, were involved in straight fights, PAS polled more votes than UMNO. It was at the state-level elections that the Alliance lost the most ground as shown in Table 3.6. The Gerakan Party won the Penang state, PAS retained

TABLE 3.5
Parliamentary Election Results, Peninsular Malaysia, 1959–1969

Parties	1959		1964		1969	
	Won	Contested	Won	Contested	Won	Contested
Alliance	74	104	89	104	66	103
UMNO	52	70	59	68	51	67
MCA	19	31	27	33	13	33
MIC	3	3	3	3	2	3
Opposition						
PAS	13	58	9	52	12	59
DAP	—		1[1]	11[1]	13	23
Gerakan	—		—		8	14
Others	17		5		4	
Total	104		104		103[2]	

Source: Vasil, 1972: 85.
Notes: [1]Contested by PAP.
　　　[2]Election in one constituency postponed.

TABLE 3.6
State Election Results, Peninsular Malaysia, 1959–1969

Parties	Seats Won			Votes Polled (Percentage of Total)		
	1959	1964	1969	1959	1964	1969
Alliance	206	241	162	55.5	57.6	47.9
UMNO	140	164	133	37.0	37.7	33.5
MCA	59	67	26	16.3	17.4	12.7
MIC	7	10	3	2.3	2.5	1.7
Opposition						
PAS	43	25	40	20.8	15.3	22.8
DAP	—	—	31	—	0.9	11.8
Gerakan	—	—	26	—	—	8.8
Others	33	16	18	23.7	26.2	8.7
Total	282	282	277	100.0	100.0	100.0

Source: Vasil, 1972: 73.

Kelantan, and there were electoral deadlocks in Selangor and Perak.

In another society the ruling government would probably have been disappointed by the election results but still found them acceptable. In Malaysia, the government acted as though it had lost the elections and the opposition parties, particularly the non-Malay ones, acted as though they had won. The opposition parties had weakened the centrist position of the Alliance party in the political system, and with that, the existing principles of racial accommodation in the society.

Chinese opposition parties held 'victory' processions and openly taunted Malay passers-by. The Malays had meanwhile become agitated because of the electoral deadlock in the state of Selangor, giving rise to the possibility of a non-Malay opposition coalition taking over power in the state. The capital, Kuala Lumpur, was in Selangor and it represented to the Malays the symbolic seat of Malay power. Malays responded with their own processions, and in this atmosphere of political confusion and heightened racial feelings, the races clashed (see Slimming, 1969; Reid, 1969; Von Vorys, 1975; Comber, 1983). There were bloody racial riots for about two months, concentrated in the capital city, but occasional flare-ups also occurred in other parts of the country. For the first time in decades, the main ethnic groups collided directly and bitterly, breaking all assumptions about the underlying stability of Malaysian society.

The society was put under a state of emergency on 14 May 1969, and a crisis management body, the National Operations Council (NOC) was created under the leadership of Tun Abdul Razak, the Deputy Prime Minister. This body was heavily Malay in composition and consisted of high-ranking personnel from the civil service, military, and police (Funston, 1980: 231). Tunku Abdul Rahman remained as Prime Minister but he had lost much credibility with the Malays and executive functions lay largely with the NOC. Social calm was restored by July 1969, but the NOC ruled until February 1971, when parliament was restored under new constitutional rules.

The existing leaders of UMNO, even without the social crisis and the period of NOC rule, would probably have instituted more pro-Malay policies following the elections to regain their Malay base. The MCA had been badly damaged and its capacity to lobby for Chinese business interests and free enterprise weakened accordingly. But during the period of the NOC, new pro-Malay economic policies began to be explicitly laid out as a younger group of Malay nationalists made their impact in national politics. The NOC, by providing an alternative power structure, gave space for the critics of the Tunku to emerge. Among them was Dr Mahathir Mohamad (the present Prime Minister) and Musa Hitam (Deputy Prime Minister from 1981 to 1986). These nationalist elements attacked the Tunku for his allegedly pro-Chinese policies, contending that they were ultimately responsible for the racial riots. Malay academics and tertiary students rallied strongly behind the emerging leaders, leading to Tunku Abdul Rahman's resignation in September 1970. By 1971, Tun Abdul Razak had built up a team of leaders more willing to impose UMNO's preferences and interests as a party on the functioning of government.

The new leaders wanted to change not just the employment pattern of society but also the whole ownership structure of the economy. The architects of the new policies argued that such a transformation was necessary for national unity and for assuaging the psychological anxieties of the Malays. Ghazali Shafie, a major figure in the NOC and Minister with Special Functions and Information, argued that it 'would not be conducive to national unity to have the urban–rural split replaced by an employer–employee split' (ST, 6 March 1971). The worry was that if the Malays remained merely employees even as they moved into the urban economy, racial and class cleavages would overlap and threaten political stability once again.

Quite apart from this concern with laying the groundwork for political stability, it was also apparent that the new leaders wanted greater control over the economy. They sought to lessen dependence on the Chinese for economic development as well as to strengthen UMNO by giving the party greater resources to expand and provide selective benefits to its base. Many of the new leaders also personally wanted to see, and perhaps hoped to benefit from, the creation of a new class of Malay businessmen co-equal with the Chinese and the foreigners.

A new economic strategy, paving the way for a vastly expanded economic role for the state, was officially promulgated in 1971 in the Second Malaysia Plan (1971–5). The policy, called the New Economic Policy (NEP), was an ambitious twenty-year plan, extending from 1971 to 1990, whose goals were: (1) to accelerate the process of restructuring Malaysian society to correct economic imbalance, so as to reduce and eventually eliminate the identification of race with economic function, and (2) to eradicate poverty by raising income levels and increasing employment opportunities for all Malaysians, irrespective of race (MTR SMP, 1973: 1).

The most salient aspect of the plan was the restructuring of wealth ownership. Malays and Malay interests (that is, government trust agencies and state enterprises) were targeted to own at least 30 per cent of the share

TABLE 3.7

Ownership of Shares in Limited Companies, 1970 and 1990 Targets
(in percentage and absolute value in M$ million in parentheses)

Sector	Malays		Non-Malays		Foreigners	
	1970	1990	1970	1990	1970	1990
Agriculture	1.0	30.0	23.7	40.0	75.3	30.0
	(14)	(628)	(339)	(837)	(1,080)	(627)
Mining	0.7	30.0	26.8	35.0	72.5	35.0
	(4)	(829)	(146)	(967)	(394)	(967)
Manufacturing	2.5	30.0	37.9	40.0	59.6	30.0
	(34)	(9,709)	(510)	(12,945)	(804)	(9,709)
Construction	2.2	30.0	63.7	45.0	34.1	25.0
	(1)	(221)	(37)	(331)	(20)	(184)
Transport	13.3	40.0	74.7	50.0	12.0	10.0
	(11)	(117)	(61)	(146)	(10)	(29)
Commerce	0.8	30.0	35.7	40.0	63.5	30.0
	(5)	(769)	(216)	(1,024)	(386)	(769)
Banking and insurance	3.3	30.0	44.4	40.0	52.3	30.0
	(21)	(963)	(283)	(1,284)	(333)	(963)
Total	1.9	30.1	37.4	40.1	60.7	29.8
	(103)	(14,076)	(1,979)	(18,767)	(3,207)	(13,949)

Source: MTR SMP, 1973: 86–7, Table 4-9.

capital of the corporate sector by 1990, starting from a base of less than 2 per cent in 1970. Table 3.7 provides detailed sectoral targets which the government hoped to achieve.

The NEP as initially conceived did not plan to forcibly make existing firms divest their equity for the sake of Malay accumulation. Malay capital expansion would take place only in the context of growth and voluntary divestment. As Table 3.7 indicates, all the groups would experience an increase in their capital holdings, except for foreign plantation companies.

Since the attainment of these targets was simply beyond the capacity of the Malay business class, state enterprises were designated as the chief vehicles for asset acquisition. The assets were 'to be held in trust for the Malays and other indigenous groups until such time as they [were] in a position to acquire these shares on their own' (MTR SMP, 1973: 14). The high burden to be shouldered by state enterprises and agencies was apparent in plan estimates that targeted 22.6 per cent of the 30 per cent goal to be held by the public sector and only 7.4 per cent by individuals (TMP, 1976: 86).

The transition from the 'laissez-faire state' to the 'interventionist state' has been analysed primarily in terms of the Malay leaders' twin desires to expand their political base and to increase the economic capacity of the Malay group. Although the new Malay leaders' preoccupation with ownership questions had an element of self-interest, the NEP cannot be so easily reduced to narrow class interests. An influential view amongst some scholars has been that the NEP represented a naked strategy directed by the 'bureaucratic class' to transform itself into a new 'bureaucratic capitalist class' (see Sundaram, 1977; Lim Mah Hui and Canak, 1981; Toh Kin Woon, 1982).[20] The bureaucratic class was a catch-all term which included politicians, bureaucrats, and royal members—indeed, anyone remotely connected with the state. Because of the relatively powerful position of the state in post-colonial societies in relation to the capitalist classes, the bureaucratic class, the argument goes, has the ability to make a strong bid for personal wealth aggrandizement through the state. State enterprises, in particular, allow this class to appropriate wealth for itself through high director fees, bloated salaries, and corruption. There is much that rings true in this approach, but its weakness lies in obliterating the ethnic dimension of the society and its politics. Ethnic groups and sub-groups are reduced to class factions contending for greater wealth. The imperatives of political mobilization and building a political base for the party and state are slighted; instead, parties are tools for class factions to advance their own interests while ethnic appeals are merely forms of ideological manipulation.

Because this view neglects ethnic structures and political competition, it is ultimately too narrow and one-sided. In many societies, particularly in the more homogenous ones such as Taiwan, Singapore, and South Korea, powerful bureaucrats derive much prestige and reward from successfully promoting existing entrepreneurial groups (whether domestic or foreign) toward high national growth. It is difficult to argue that the bureaucratic classes in these countries have used the state to become a bourgeoisie in pursuit of narrow economic interests. We have to ask if bureaucrats and politicians in strong states universally desire such a status. Secondly, considering Malaysia in particular, this view fails to investigate if non-élite Malays have provided support for the regime. If they have, it becomes difficult to see the whole NEP strategy as simply one of a small élite seeking to maximize its wealth.

Clearly the NEP contained many benefits for the politico-bureaucratic Malay élite, but we have to also consider the policy as a wider political strategy to provide a 'new deal' for the Malays, which was vital for party power and for remedying their widespread and historical sense of economic and group weakness. By getting greater control of society's resources, and thereby helping to shape the rate of Malay mobility and wealth expansion, the government could, under the right conditions, create a positive sum situation for the Malays as a whole.

Conclusion

The *laissez-faire* system was underpinned by the Alliance leaders, personified by the Prime Minister, Tunku Abdul Rahman, opting for multi-ethnic political compromise rather than Malay ethnic particularism in structuring the political basis of the state. The compromise route was an important factor in keeping the economic field open because the MCA leaders and their key Chinese supporters regarded the preservation of the Chinese economic stake as the party's central goal. The Malay leaders, for their part, also seem to have believed that the economic and political benefits of the *laissez-faire* system outweighed its costs. The one potential political cost, the disaffection of the Malays, was to be countered by the government's gradualistic approach to Malay commerce and high spending in the rural sector.

On purely macro-economic terms, the *laissez-faire* system was relatively successful in generating national income and diversifying the economy, although employment creation was less than satisfactory. However, its Achilles' heel was political, because it contributed to the process of ethnic polarization in the society. Each ethnic group began to take its own 'resource monopoly' for granted and saw itself, in what it lacked, as relatively deprived in comparison to the other group. The Malays did not see any benefit in the existing economic arrangements and began to harbour fears of marginality and weakness in their own society. These feelings of exclusion contributed to the breakdown of political order in May 1969, spelling the political exhaustion of the economic system. The Malays, who were numerically superior and in control of the state, had the upper hand in determining the future of the economy.

In the post-Tunku era, the Malay leaders altered the state's role in the economy in a much more pro-Malay direction, aimed at increasing Malay control of the economy and strengthening the political base of the UMNO party. The New Economic Policy (1970–90) geared the state to counter-balance foreign and Chinese dominance in the economy. The central question was, given the past economic dominance of these two groups, how would the state achieve its economic and political goals? How easily would the private sector accommodate to the state's objectives? What were the economic and political outcomes of the new strategy? These issues are the subject of the chapters to come.

1. In the late 1950s, there were 116,000 applicants for land entitlements, representing, according to the author's rough calculation, as much as 20 per cent of Malay rural households (*MB*, July 1977: 7).

2. Neo-colonialism was a disparaging term used by left-wing scholars and statesmen to depict regimes which had nominally acquired formal independence but were still subservient to metropolitan interests (see Nkrumah, 1966; Mohamed Amin and Caldwell, 1977).

3. In hindsight, this policy appears to have been mistaken. In the 1970s, Malaysia embarked on a relatively successful policy of manufacturing for export using multinationals after realizing the constraints of import-substitution industrialization in a limited domestic market.

4. Tun Tan Siew Sin was Minister of Commerce and Industry from 1957 to 1959, Minister of Finance from 1961 to 1974, and President of the MCA from 1961 to 1974.

5. The rate of growth of consumer prices averaged only 0.8 per cent from 1956 to 1970 (Bank Negara, 1979: 20).

6. Britain wanted to pull out in 1961 because of domestic economic difficulties. It finally disengaged its forces in 1967 when it could no longer afford the heavy financial commitment (Hawkins, 1972: 18).

7. The other Ministry the MCA controlled was the less important one of Housing and Local Development.

8. Tun Tan's powerful role in the Ministry of Finance and in national spending in the 1960s was conveyed to the author in an interview (January 1985) by a top official in the present Ministry.

9. For example, a prominent Malay businessman and secretary of the Associated Malay Chambers of Commerce, Raja Nasron Ishak, attacked the Minister of Commerce and Industry for saying that Malay weakness in business resulted from a civil service mentality, discouragement from past bankruptcies, and lack of capital. In his view, Malays suffered because they had been boycotted by long-established organizations (*ST*, 2 January 1964).

10. In particular, Tun Abdul Razak, the Deputy Prime Minister, who perhaps had a better sense of UMNO's standing with the Malays, provided the main impetus behind policies to uplift the Malays economically, such as the rural development effort and the special programmes to promote Malay commerce.

11. The Malaysian Trade Union Congress was also in favour of foreign investment. One of its leaders in the 1960 annual conference assured the government that the MTUC would do 'its utmost to help maintain stable labour conditions so the Government could attract industrial investment' (in Zaidi, 1974: 130).

12. Mohd. Raza Ali (1969: 363) has argued that the old voluntary system permitting the more liberal use of the strike weapon was not so threatening when the unions were weak, but the new system of compulsory arbitration was better suited to deal with the possible rise of strong unions.

13. Malaysian statistical accounting classifies the nationality of the investments according to the geographical source of fixed capital and loans.

14. Only in Sime Darby's case was there sizeable ownership of the parent company by local and regional interests, especially the OCBC group of Singapore. Sime Darby from the beginning had close connections with Chinese businessmen in Singapore and Malaysia.

15. It turned out that the 'exploitative role' of the traders was exaggerated because state organizations did not necessarily offer better prices or services than private marketing systems (Vokes, 1978: 106–19).

16. Details of the original founders and shareholders of the major domestic banks can be found in Tan Tat Wai (1982: 196, fn. 62). For example the fastest growing local bank, Malayan Banking, was founded by Khoo Teck Puat, formerly an executive in Singapore's Overseas Chinese Banking Corporation. Among his associates were Goh Tjooi Kok, a Singaporean estate owner and industrialist, Loke Wan Tho, the heir of tin miner Loke Yew, Oei Tjong Ie, son of Indonesia's sugar king, Oei Tiong Ham, and Wang Teng Kiat, a financier. The next largest local bank, United Malayan Banking Corporation, was formed by Chang Min Thien, and the other shareholders were Yeoh Chin Hin (tin miner), Tee Teh (rubber trader/planter), Datuk Saw Choo Teng (estate owner and co-founder of Southern Banking) and Ong Chin Chion (Singapore rubber trader).

17. Ironically, while both the Bumiputra (indigenous) Economic Congresses were meant to get feedback from the Malay business community, it was the political and bureaucratic élites that played a strong role in running and providing ideas for the congresses (Tham Seong Chee, 1977: 244). Tun Abdul Razak himself lamented the fact that the various Malay Chambers did not take more initiative in running and giving feedback to the Second Congress (*ST*, 10 September 1968). The essential problem was the Malay business community's weakness and high dependence on the state for its development.

18. In 1970 the unemployment figures were 8.0 per cent for the Malays, 7.4 per cent for the Chinese, and 11.0 per cent for the Indians (*MTR SMP*, 1973: 77). A 1962 survey revealed that the unemployment rate for each ethnic group was 6.0 per cent (see Snodgrass, 1970: Appendix A).

19. Singapore joined Malaysia in 1963 when it was granted independence. The PAP initially sought to replace the MCA as UMNO's partner by appealing to the Chinese population on a social democratic platform (see Mohd. Noordin Sopiee, 1974). UMNO, however, was solidly behind the MCA. Thereafter the PAP changed tactics by trying to unite the non-Malay opposition parties under the banner 'Towards a Malaysian Malaysia'. Many Malays were incensed by Lee Kuan Yew, and the situation became so racially divisive that Singapore was asked to leave Malaysia. But the PAP's interlude had roused the non-Malay opposition parties, including its progenitor, the Democratic Action Party (DAP) to defend Chinese rights and language more forcefully (Vasil, 1980: 158).

20. A related view of small cliques of Malay organizations attempting to maximize wealth for themselves can be found in a recent book by Ozay Mehmet, 1986.

4 The Enlarged State

Introduction

THIS chapter examines the capacity of the state to transform the ethnic pattern of economic ownership that existed in 1970 and evaluates the economic and political outcomes of the state's expanded role. It shows that the state élites were able to mobilize large resources toward meeting their goals; however, the key components of the NEP—the vast expansion of the state enterprise sector and the vigorous attempt to breed Malay capitalists—brought few national benefits. The economic inefficiencies and the high opportunity costs of the state's policies were underwritten by an extremely favourable external sector in the 1970s and early 1980s. However, the sharp fall in commodity prices in the mid-1980s exposed the weaknesses of the economy, and left the state in a serious financial position. However, the regime was able to enjoy strong electoral support because the state's vanguard ethnic role allowed the leaders to broaden their Malay political base.

Gearing for State Expansion

To make headway with the NEP, the state had to have a number of important political and economic prerequisites. Since the Malay leaders wanted to compete against, control, and sometimes reduce the role of existing foreign and Chinese economic interests, they needed sufficient economic and political leverage over the private sector. They also had to contend with the opposition of the non-Malay middle class, whose desire for easy access to tertiary education and meritocratic recruitment into universities and corporations was endangered by the new, drastic system of positive discrimination in educational and job recruitment in favour of the Malays.[1] One pre-condition, therefore, was to restrict the range of demands and political issues that existed under the previous system of quasi-pluralist political decision-making.

The other prerequisites were the same as those required by any state that wished to control the economic élites, whether foreign or domestic. Stepan (1978: 237–43), in his analysis of economic bargaining between the state and foreign capital, lists a number of factors affecting state control capacities. Two in particular are relevant here: (1) the state élite's internal strength and commitment to control and (2) state/national savings and investment capacity.

State power is increased when the state élite has sufficient internal strength to impose a consistent strategy of control and a high degree of ideological and programmatic unity about why such control has priority. National and state financial capacities are also crucial because they allow the leaders to pursue their goals without high dependence on foreign capital or domestic capitalists, who might try to frustrate those goals. Another factor, advanced by Hamilton (1982: 281) in her historical study of state autonomy in Mexico, is that state élites are more successful in confronting the dominant economic élites if they have the support of subordinate groups and classes. The equivalent in Malaysia was getting the support of a wide section of the Malay population.

Let us turn to the changes the Malay political leaders made in the state's political, bureaucratic, and economic functioning in pursuit of the NEP.

One of the UMNO leaders' first undertakings was to change the previous system of interest representation in society. Both the nature of the issues that could be brought up in the political system and the structure of the party system were modified in order to increase UMNO's hegemony in politics. In 1971, the Constitution was amended to make it a seditious act to question both within and outside Parliament the 'special position' of the Malays. This provision in the Constitution legitimized government favouritism of Malays in education, business, and bureaucratic recruitment, among other guarantees (see Mohamed Suffian, 1972: 192–201), and effectively made direct criticism of the NEP and its rationale difficult. Discussion and debate could only be directed at the way the NEP was being *implemented*. Limiting debate in this way took away the mobilizing potential of the government's adversaries and insulated state policy-makers from criticism.

The UMNO leadership, however, did not want a political system that was too exclusionary, fearing that a high degree of political and racial disaffection could jeopardize political stability. When he was Prime Minister, Tun Abdul Razak (1971–6) embarked on an innovative strategy of incorporating a greater number of political parties in the old Alliance framework. The idea was to pluralize the role of the MCA in galvanizing the Chinese vote. All opposition parties were invited to join the ruling party, now called the Barisan Nasional or National Front. This political strategy, which we shall call 'ethnic corporatism', approximates Schmitter's idea of 'corporatism', by which he means a highly centralized system of interest representation controlled strongly by the state (Schmitter, 1974). The choice for the leaders of opposition parties was to either join the ruling party and have a small amount of influence and prestige, or remain as opposition parties with their hands tied. Many former opposition leaders joined the broad coalition, including UMNO's chief rival, PAS, between 1973 and 1976.[2]

This arrangement suited UMNO well because it could be the commanding party in the National Front at little cost. In exchange for giving relatively unimportant ministerial portfolios to leaders of the component parties, UMNO could get their grudging agreement by exercising the National Front whip—essentially enforcing UMNO's preferences—on them. UMNO's position was further strengthened by frequent infighting amongst component parties, especially between the MCA and Gerakan, over seat allocations in elections as well as cross-overs by party cadres from one party to another (Lee Kam Hing, 1980: 186–93). An MCA party activist (quoted in H'ng Hung Yong, 1979: 35) captured the role of the MCA in the National Front very well:

> . . . the MCA and the other parties have severely limited influence. While they are able to bring their influence to bear in some cases, more often than not this influence is of an indirect nature. The MCA may be able to prevent changes of policies which are likely to adversely affect its constituents, but rarely can it initiate changes to improve the welfare of the community it represents.

As UMNO accumulated greater system-wide power, its leaders were able to influence the behaviour of the bureaucratic and technocratic organs of the state. As a prelude, only trusted personnel were put in key planning and decision-making positions. Early in 1971, the Trade and Industry ministerial portfolio was taken away from traditional MCA control and given to UMNO. Tun Tan Siew Sin, the cautious Finance Minister, remained in his Ministry until 1974 (when he retired from politics) but already in 1970, his power to control expenditure had been taken away from him (*FEER*, 3 October 1970: 7). When Tun Abdul Razak took over the Finance portfolio in 1974, it marked the end of MCA's strong influence over national economic management.

In the other organs of the state, including the technocratic ones, persons who were politically loyal and committed to the leadership's world view were given authoritative positions rather than those who were merely technically competent. For example, in the 1960s and early 1970s, the nation's foremost planning agency, the Economic Planning Unit (EPU), was headed by a Chinese economist. It also had a lot of foreign technical input, especially from Harvard University. Since then, the level of foreign personnel has fallen and the last few director-generals have not even been economists.[3]

The next step involved changing the power balance in technocratic agencies in favour of those more solidly behind the state's goals. The Economic Planning Unit in the Prime Minister's Department was considerably strengthened while the Treasury in the Finance Ministry suffered a secular decline in influence.[4] In the past, the EPU worked in tandem with the Treasury and Bank Negara (Central Bank) on macro-economic planning, including selecting and prioritizing development projects submitted by all government departments. The Treasury was very influential in setting limits to public spending in order to keep within the bounds of national fiscal and financial balance. It routinely discarded projects it deemed to be wasteful and questionable. Inherently conservative and oriented toward preserving the nation's resources, the Treasury was given powerful backing by the strong-minded fiscal conservative, Tun Tan.

With the NEP, not only was the urge to spend far greater, but also political criteria became more important in spending decisions. As an agency basically geared to spending, the EPU was highly suited to act as the custodian of the NEP, enjoying the firm backing of prime ministers[5] committed to NEP goals. This power shift gave the EPU far greater say over the selection of projects as well as the power to 'call the shots' in pressing for greater straining of the nation's resources in spite of the reservations of the Treasury and the Central Bank.

To increase its control over the private sector, the government also instituted many new regulations on the terms of economic participation of non-Malay firms, creating new bodies to monitor and influence the behaviour of the private actors. The desire for greater control increased toward the mid-1970s when state officials realized that merely requiring new and expanding firms to restructure their ownership would be unlikely to achieve its targets. It now wanted existing firms, especially large ones, to restructure whether they were growing or not. The guidelines were that local non-Malay firms had to have at least 30 per cent Malay ownership. Foreign firms could only have 30 per cent equity, unless they were predominantly exporters of manufactured products.

Many of the policies, such as the Industrial Coordination Act of 1975 will be discussed later. But two in particular are relevant here. One was the Foreign Investment Committee (FIC), created in 1974 and composed of high-ranking administrators from the Ministries of Finance, Trade and Industry, the EPU, and the Registrar of Companies. Set up originally to monitor foreign acquisitions of Malaysian companies, the FIC in practice became an important instrument for enforcing the NEP, especially in getting large public and non-public corporations to restructure their equity. Relying on back-up services provided by the EPU, the FIC applied constant but subtle pressure on firms to draw up their restructuring plans. Because of its high-powered bureaucratic membership, it enjoyed strong leverage. Firms which ignored the Committee risked developing a strained relationship with the general bureaucracy; this could spell potential trouble for their businesses when it came to getting approvals for machinery imports and other permits.

The other body, the Capital Issues Committee (or CIC), originally formed in 1968 to supervise the capital market, worked with the FIC to set the price of shares issued to Malay interests (including government enterprises) by private Chinese and foreign companies. It was a bureaucratic intervention into a market-determined transaction. The prices were usually set below market price.[6] The official justification was that the prices of the small stock market were so subject to market manipulation that it did not reflect the 'real' value of a company (see *Insight*, June 1983). Instead, a price-setting formula was used based on a company's profits, assets, and the growth potential of the sector it belonged to.[7]

These political and bureaucratic transformations gave the state élite new powers to influence and shape the economy, but the critical question was whether they could sustain their goals over the longer term. Could the Malay leaders be co-opted by the dominant foreign and Chinese economic groups or could splits occur amongst them over the desirability and feasibility of the NEP?

In Malaysia, there were a number of important factors, arising chiefly from the country's ethnically segmented character, which supported élite agreement and purpose over the pursuit of the NEP. At the ideological level, the combination of potent ethnic sentiments and economic inferiority, gave the Malay leaders a ready-made framework to assert a strong sense of right in their policies. Dr Mahathir Mohamad, when he was Deputy Prime Minister in 1979, made the point sharply in an interview (*FEER*, 13 April 1979: 42):

We are the Negroes in this country. . . . Here the Blacks are in charge. What is a fact is that because of their struggle the Blacks in America are able to get to places they never got to before. This is what we are trying to do here—not by taking what belongs to others, but by securing a place for us here. No other country has tried this kind of experiment. We are doing it very nicely, very slowly. I am not anti-Chinese in any way, but I feel Malays must have a place in the sun, otherwise there is going to be bitterness, which is no good for anybody.

As the goals of the NEP became internalized throughout Malay society, the Malay leaders found themselves bound by the expectations that their very policies had engendered. Various 'opinion rings', such as the UMNO Youth, comprising ambitious lower-echelon leaders, and the various Malay chambers of commerce and trade associations continually brought up the progress of the NEP in party assemblies, economic forums, and congresses. Indeed, when the top leaders themselves competed for party posts, a common tactic was to hint that their rivals were sympathetic to Chinese economic interests in the quest for party votes.

Clearly, it was not going to be the lack of élite unity that would potentially derail the state's economic objectives. Rather, it was the other critical pillar of state functioning: its fiscal and financial capacities.[8] The state's financial position was especially important because the NEP was highly ambitious and dependent on the state for its success. Malay share ownership in limited companies was to grow from less than 2 per cent to 30 per cent between 1970 and 1990. This meant much faster growth in absolute terms in comparison to the other economic groups.

State finances, therefore, could not just rely on taxing the private sector in the normal way. Otherwise state expenditure would be pegged to private sector growth, slowing down the achievement of NEP targets. Were the state élites able to find the extraordinary resources they needed?

A cursory examination of Table 4.1 shows that development expenditure, a form of public investment, more than doubled in real terms from plan period to plan period, starting from the First Malaysia Plan (1966–70), the baseline period before the NEP was introduced. As a percentage of GNP, public sector development expenditure averaged around 8 per cent annually in the First Malaysia Plan, 11 per cent in the Second, 16.3 per cent in the Third, and 25.6 per cent in the Fourth. This enormous increase in public investment resulted in a decline of real private investment from

TABLE 4.1
Public Sector Financing and Expenditure, 1966–1985
(First to Fourth Malaysia Plans, in M$ million)

	First Malaysia Plan, 1966–1970	Second Malaysia Plan, 1971–1975	Third Malaysia Plan, 1976–1980	Fourth Malaysia Plan, 1981–1985
Government Financing				
Government revenue	11,656	21,700	54,706	93,770
(in 1970 $)	(11,656)	(18,706)	(35,756)	(45,742)
Public authorities current surplus (oil profits)	340	800	1,853	29,442
Foreign borrowing	458	2,300	3,907	26,163
Net domestic borrowing	1,864	4,650	9,610	24,263
Use of accumulated reserves	−53	1,170	3,584	468
Government Expenditure				
Current expenditure	10,266	20,800	48,723	91,890
Development expenditure	4,242	9,820	24,937	80,331
(in 1970 $)	(4,242)	(8,644)	(16,299)	(39,185)
Overall Deficit	2,512	8,120	17,101	50,889
Deficit/GNP (annual average) (percentage)	3.9	10.9	9.3	16.3
Deficit/revenue (percentage)	22.0	37.0	31.0	54.3
Foreign borrowing/ deficit (percentage)	18.0	28.0	23.0	51.4

Source: Compiled from Second, Third, Fourth, and Fifth Malaysia Plans.

70 per cent in 1970 to 50 per cent in 1985 (*Fifth MP*, 1986: 13). The sources of finance varied from plan to plan. The common pattern was the progressive willingness of the planners to rely on domestic and foreign debt, and to maximize revenues from offshore petroleum which was discovered in 1973. In the Second Malaysia Plan, before petroleum became a factor, the government depended on a stronger tax effort to collect more revenue; it levied a sales tax in 1972 and made improvements in its tax machinery. Already the planners had shown a greater appetite for going into debt, principally borrowing domestically from the Employees Provident Fund, although foreign borrowing also increased compared to the First Malaysia Plan. The planners in the EPU, reflecting the changing nature of technocratic influence, considered Malaysia's public and foreign debt to be very low by international standards and saw greater scope for borrowing. When the foreign debt servicing ratio increased from 2.2 per cent in 1970 to 4 per cent in 1975, the planners did not show much concern because they considered it well within the means of Malaysia's diversified commodity export structure to finance (see *SPM*, 1971: 80; *TMP*, 1976: 46).

However, at the onset of the Third Plan, before knowing how much oil revenue Malaysia would get, the planners began to show concern that future government finances might be slow to expand. Malaysia's taxation rate was already high by international standards, and without the prospect of a large boost in export earnings and national income both domestic and foreign borrowing could not grow much further (see *TMP*, 1976: 243). The very real question of how constrained government finances would have affected the course of the NEP became largely academic, however, with the new-found oil wealth. Although Malaysia's oil and natural gas reserves were modest by the standards of the large oil-producing states, they changed the whole equation of government finances and expenditure.

Malaysia's petroleum policy gradually evolved into one of intensifying petroleum extraction and revenues for its NEP objectives. In 1974 and 1975, the national leaders, spearheaded by Tengku Razaleigh Hamzah, the first chairman of the national oil company, Petronas (1974), bargained hard with the principal oil companies in Malaysia, Exxon and Shell, to gain a favourable production sharing arrangement.[9] The previous concession system, contracted when Malaysia was producing meagre amounts of petroleum, gave Malaysia a 12.5 per cent royalty of gross output and the usual company income tax. It was unilaterally terminated in 1974 and oil companies were asked to enter into a new agreement (*BT*, 19 September 1973). Although a small producer, Malaysia's bargaining power was increased by advantageous sharing arrangements established by other producing nations. It obtained a favourable after-tax oil split of 83.5 : 16.5 (after deducting for recovery costs), nearly comparable to the sharing ratios of much larger producers such as Indonesia's 85 : 15 (*NST*, 15 December 1976).

In addition to extracting more revenue from the oil companies, the volume of petroleum production was also adjusted to meet the state's spending needs. The initial plan to conserve oil reserves by limiting production to a maximum of 250,000 barrels per day (bpd) was quickly abandoned by 1980.[10] From 100,000 bpd in 1975, production of crude oil increased to 180,000 in 1977, 280,000 in 1980, 450,000 in 1984, and to around 510,000 in 1986 (Ministry of Finance, 1986: 55; *TMP*, 1976: 311). In 1980, crude petroleum exports had taken over the historical position of rubber as the chief foreign exchange earner in Malaysia.

The oil windfall made possible large increases in government revenues in the Third and Fourth Malaysia Plans. In 1980, 16 per cent of total government tax revenue came from petroleum and by 1985, the figure had reached 25 per cent, thanks to new export duties and expanded production (Ismail Muhd. Salleh, 1983; Ministry of Finance, 1985: 95). Because of petroleum revenues, expenditure in the Third Plan more than doubled over the Second Plan's but at the same time there was a relative decline in domestic and foreign borrowing. However, in the Fourth Plan, the reverse occurred. Faced with a recessionary climate because of poor prices for Malaysia's commodities, but still extremely optimistic about the future of oil prices— the Fourth Malaysia Plan projected that oil prices would reach US$73.2 per barrel—the government carried out an unprecedented amount of domestic and especially foreign borrowing. Originally, $32.8 billion had been earmarked for development expenditure but at the end of the plan period, $80.3 billion had been spent. Believing that oil would save the day, the government, which had borrowed only $309 million externally in 1980, pushed foreign borrowing to $4.7 billion in 1981, $6.7 billion in 1982, $7.3 billion in 1983, $5.2 billion in 1984, and $3.1 billion in 1985 (Ministry of Finance, 1986: xxxii). Foreign banks, mainly from the US, eagerly lent to Malaysia at excellent rates as they considered Malaysia a very good credit risk. As for the Malaysian planners, even when the nation's external debt servicing ratio had reached 16 per cent in 1985, they continued to rationalize that 'the external debt service ratio [was] relatively low compared with some other developing countries and within the ability of the nation to service the external debt' (Ministry of Finance, 1985: 104).

The new oil wealth had all the dangers, as in so many other oil-producing

TABLE 4.2

Sectoral Breakdown of Development Expenditure, 1966–1985

(in M$ million; percentage in parentheses)

Sector	First Malaysia Plan, 1966–1970	Second Malaysia Plan, 1971–1975	Third Malaysia Plan, 1976–1980	Fourth Malaysia Plan, 1981–1985
Economic	2,210 (61.2)	7,349 (71.9)	13,570 (54.4)	55,777 (75.3)
Agriculture and rural development	911 (25.2)	2,368 (23.2)	4,672 (18.7)	8,714 (11.8)
Commerce and industry	137 (3.8)	1,608 (15.7)	3,246 (13.0)	20,211 (27.3)
Transport	355 (9.9)	1,687 (16.5)	2,842 (11.4)	12,966 (17.5)
Communications	159 (4.4)	640 (6.3)	1,152 (4.6)	5,033 (6.8)
Energy and utilities	646 (17.9)	999 (9.8)	1,582 (6.3)	8,644 (11.7)
Social	644 (17.9)	1,431 (14.0)	1,431 (14.6)	9,980 (13.5)
Education	289 (7.9)	763 (7.5)	1,548 (6.2)	4,687 (6.3)
Health	114 (3.2)	226 (2.2)	307 (1.2)	736 (1.0)
Housing, social services (including government officers housing loan scheme)	243 (6.7)	440 (4.3)	1,780 (6.8)	4,470 (6.0)
General administration	109 (3.0)	369 (3.6)	465 (1.9)	810 (1.0)
Security	645 (17.4)	1,104 (10.8)	3,529 (14.2)	7,495 (10.1)
Total	3,610	10,225	24,937	80,331

Source: Compiled from Second, Third, Fourth, and Fifth Malaysia Plans.

countries, of being a short-term boon but a long-run curse. Malaysia's recourse to foreign borrowing was a high-risk act, and any prolonged recessionary climate would have adverse consequences for the economy and the financial position of the state. Throughout the 1970s and early 1980s, however, the state was in a strong financial position. This made several objectives possible. First, it allowed enormous resources to be used for the state's direct and indirect role of spearheading Malay capital accumulation. Table 4.2 shows the large increases in the allocations made to Commerce and Industry, which represented monies for the state enterprise sector and schemes to create a Malay bourgeoisie. From just 3.8 per cent of development allocations in the First Malaysia Plan (1966–70), Commerce and Industry claimed 27.3 per cent of the Fourth Malaysia Plan (1981–5). Secondly, the state's large resources during the Second, Third, and Fourth Plans also allowed for absolute increases to be spent in agriculture. By being able to provide agricultural subsidies (for example, fertilizers and price supports), infrastructure, and land replanting schemes to its still critical rural political base, the government could ensure that political support from Malay farmers would remain strong while carrying out its urban policies.

The State as Entrepreneur

For the new wave of dependency theorists, the state provides the critical counterweight to the economic and social distortions caused by multinational activity in the economy (Moran, 1974; Evans, 1979; Bennett and Sharpe, 1985). Multinational participation, it is argued, exacts a high cost by displacing local entrepreneurs and removing national surplus. Only if the state actively regulates, bargains, and participates directly in the economy might some of the more injurious effects of multinational participation be checked.

These assumptions about multinationals are not very convincing, but the main problem of the dependency theorists is their failure to see the state's economic role as originating from political concerns. The Malay leaders sometimes collided and bargained strongly with foreign companies (and local Chinese companies) as they increased state economic power. But the broader logic was to use the state as a lever to advance capital accumulation for Malay interests. Both the nature of state accumulation and its results were an offshoot of this goal.

State enterprise expansion, at best, was an enormous exchange of assets in which the state paid out cash for existing assets built up by the foreign and Chinese sectors. There was little net increase in production and employment, although it met the ethnic goal of having greater control of the economy. More problematic, many state companies hardly reached the point of commercial viability. The success rate per dollar spent was very low but state authorities were slow to undertake corrective action because of the high priority given to these state enterprises.

Before 1969, the state's main experience in running commercial corporations was in a few key natural monopolies, such as railways, utilities, and telecommunications (see Raja Mohammed Affandi, 1978). The public sector had little experience in running enterprises which directly competed with the private sector. Other than very good research and operational capabilities in plantation crops, the state did not have a storehouse of technical and managerial expertise.

Tugwell (1975) has linked state economic participation with bureaucratic learning and skill accumulation. He argues, from his study of Venezuela, that the state's direct participation in the petroleum industry resulted from its earlier role of monitoring the activities of the international and private oil companies. In Malaysia it worked in the opposite direction—the politicians first defined the political desirability of state intervention and then hoped that the necessary technical expertise would develop from experience. Their critical leverage was the financial resources of the state, backed by a battery of state regulations and controls. Table 4.3 shows the large amount of public funds in the form of grants and loans, excluding government-backed commercial loans, made available to the key state enterprises.

Perbadanan Nasional (National Corporation) or Pernas, Permodalan Nasional Berhad (National Equity Corporation) or PNB, and the State Development Corporations (SEDCs) were established mainly to accumulate corporate assets directly, while MARA and the Urban Development Authority (UDA) were supposed to focus on promoting private Malay entrepreneurship.

This section examines three state enterprises in particular: Pernas, PNB, and the SEDCs.[11] In the 1970s, Pernas was the vanguard of state

TABLE 4.3
Public Allocations to Selected State Corporations, 1971–1985
(in M$ million)

Corporations	Year of Operation	Second Malaysia Plan, 1971–1975	Third Malaysia Plan, 1976–1980	Fourth Malaysia Plan, 1981–1985
Pernas (National Corporation)	1970	150.0	382.0	233.9
State Economic Development Corporations (SEDCs)	mostly early 1970s	200.0	493.2	525.3
Permodalan Nasional (PNB)	1978	—	500.0	2,922.9
MARA	1966	252.2	231.9	303.9
Urban Development Authority (UDA)	1971	169.0	300.0	691.4
Heavy Industry Corporation of Malaysia (HICOM)	1981	—	—	330.6

Sources: TMP, 1976: 240; FoMP, 1981: 120; MTR FMP, 1984: 295; Fifth MP, 1986: 360, 374.

capitalism while in the 1980s, the baton was passed to PNB. Both organizations have been commended by the national leaders for carrying out their
functions in the expected manner. The SEDCs, in contrast, have generally
failed to meet the minimal standards of the leaders and bureaucrats. They
provide a good illustration of the economic costs the leaders were willing
to tolerate in pursuing their objectives. We will consider the mode of accumulation of the enterprises and the tensions between economic rationality and ethnic priorities in their development. In a later section, we will
evaluate the ethnic and political benefits state economic intervention
brought for the Malays and their leaders.

Pernas and PNB

Both these corporations were set up with the highest backing of the
top leadership. Pernas was established in November 1969 just after the
May 1969 ethnic riots, and put under the charge of the Prime Minister's
Department. The pivotal and ambitious role assigned to it can be gauged
from its corporate structure, which had by 1971 spawned six main subsidiaries specializing in most of the sectors of the economy: Pernas Construction, Pernas Engineering, Pernas Properties, Pernas Securities, Pernas
Trading, and Malaysia National Insurance (AF, April/May 1977: 64).

PNB was established in 1978 to speed up the acquisition of corporate
assets on behalf of the Malays. In 1975, Malay (individual and state) corporate ownership fell short of targets—it was 7.8 per cent instead of 9 per
cent. A serious shortfall of the 16 per cent target set for 1980 seemed imminent if the same rate continued. The government therefore provided
enormous funds to PNB (see Table 4.3) to accelerate the purchase of shares
in non-Malay and foreign companies.

From its inception, PNB was supposed to buy shares of established
companies with a good track record, including the shares of other state
companies which performed well. Pernas, in contrast, was supposed to be
more risk taking and establish wholly owned and joint venture companies.

In keeping with their central role in state capital accumulation, both
corporations recruited their top executives from the uppermost corps of
Malay bureaucrats and technocrats. These state bureaucrats-turned-state
corporate managers had little experience in business but they were the
most technically able Malay professionals with broad knowledge of the
national economy. Their other important asset was their strong identification with the goals of the political élite.

Pernas's first chairman, Tengku Razaleigh Hamzah (1970–4), was
formerly the Chairman of Bank Bumiputra, the state-owned bank, and a
close confidante of Prime Minister Tun Abdul Razak.[12] His successor,
Tunku Shahriman Sulaiman, was formerly the Director-General of the
Implementation and Coordination Unit (ICU) of the Prime Minister's
Department (see Who's Who in Malaysia and Singapore, 1983). Pernas's
other top executives were heavily recruited from either the EPU, the ICU,
or the ministries overseeing the economy.

The Chairman of PNB, Tun Ismail Ali, credited with having the best
knowledge of the corporate sector in the country, was a Cambridge-

educated economist who had a distinguished career as Chairman of Bank Negara (Central Bank) from its establishment in 1959 to his retirement in 1978 (*MB*, January 1982: 18). PNB's chief executive, Haji Desa Pachik, was unusual in not having served in government. An accountant by training, he was a company secretary of the Shell oil group in Malaysia and later worked as a top executive in Fleet Group, the investment arm of the UMNO party. In 1978, he joined PNB at the urging of Tun Ismail to help establish the corporation (*MB*, February 1981: 6).

Any discussion of the two companies cannot be neatly compartmentalized. Not only have they shown interest in similar sectors of the economy but, furthermore, Pernas transferred eleven of its most profitable companies, amounting to around $1 billion in assets to PNB in 1981 at the request of the government and PNB (*SP*, 1981: 8(1)).[13] We shall therefore focus on how the original assets were accumulated rather than on which company owns what at present.

Challenging the Commodity Sector. Pernas initially vacillated between acting as a purely commercial organization and performing the social role of aiding individual Malay businessmen, for example, by giving them sub-contracts and dealerships in its burgeoning industrial and trading concerns (see *SP*, 1973: 1(1); 1976: 4(1)). Its early involvement in industrial projects was a series of joint ventures with foreign interests, usually on a minority shareholding basis.

However, because of its bitter experiences as a minority partner, and the issue of achieving NEP targets becoming more pressing, Pernas soon shifted its policy toward acquiring large-scale, established companies (*SP*, 1974: 2(2)). The Chairman, Tengku Razaleigh Hamzah, who was instrumental in the shift, gave these reasons (quoted in *MB*, July 1976: 14):

Number one, we are sure of the returns on our investments. Number two, it lends creditability so that we can perform bigger things in the future for the Malays. Even if the Malays we are trying to bring up now fail to do what we expect of them to do, say in the next 20 years, at least the Malays will have, in trust, big, big investments which are held through Pernas.

To maintain political credibility, Pernas's subsidiaries, Pernas Trading and Pernas Edar, continued to provide distribution rights and an alternative wholesaling network to Chinese wholesalers for its Malay clientele. But its priority became the Malaysianization of the plantation and tin-mining sectors.

In the 'Outline Perspective Plan, 1970–1990' (*MTR SMP*, 1973) there was no indication that the government's objective was to make foreign resource companies divest their interests in the country. Foreign asset holding was expected to decline from voluntary divestment while the growth of Malay equity, it appeared, would come from new state or private Malay entry into these sectors. However, with the rising influence of Malay nationalists and concern with finding the quickest way to accumulate assets, it became desirable to control and own plantations and tin-mining companies.

These sectors were most amenable to the realization of NEP goals because the foreign companies did not have strong leverage over national actors; they were not providing technological expertise or new foreign markets for industrial diversification (Bowring, 1978). Plantation companies in particular did not possess significant advantage over locals in production technology or in international marketing. Malaysia possessed world-class capabilities in plantation technology and research while the complex world-wide marketing network was not under the control of plantation companies.[14] In tin-mining, there had been few technological changes in dredging since 1917 and it was quite easy for nationals to hire a broker to sit on the London Metal Exchange for marketing purposes.[15]

Furthermore, state officials were becoming increasingly vexed by the behaviour of big tin-mining companies and plantation houses. Profits made were not being ploughed back locally. They were either paid out entirely in dividends to foreign shareholders or utilized for subsidizing struggling subsidiaries in other parts of the world (ST, 5 November 1974).

Thus, as the economic benefits provided by the resource-based companies decreased and the economic costs increased, the state technocrats and public enterprises managers were ready to act against them. The FIC began to pressure the companies to outline their restructuring plans for reducing their equity to 30 per cent by 1990.

The Malaysian International Chamber of Commerce and Industry, representing the foreign sector, contended that plantation and mining companies were not growing in physical assets and in paid-up capital, therefore they did not come under the NEP net, which was supposed to be based on growth (MICCI, Yearbook 1977/78; FEER, 13 January 1978: 48). The government, however, chose to define 'growth' on a broad basis, including growth in output; in essence it wanted to act as it saw fit (TMP, 1976: para. 870).

Although the executives of Pernas concluded that the acquisition route would be the fastest and easiest way of getting well-managed and profitable companies, they still had to master the intricacies of the corporate take-over process and the codes governing them in the stock markets of London and Singapore, where many foreign companies were listed. Lacking this expertise, Pernas's first move to Malaysianize the resource sector ended in failure. Pernas wished to gain control of London Tin, the largest tin group in the world, which produced 10 per cent of the world's tin and had over $1 billion in assets. About 75 per cent of its assets were in Malaysia, distributed among twenty-five dredging companies. London Tin's added attraction was that its shareholding structure was loosely held by institutions and individuals, and many of the companies it owned in Malaysia had large cash resources.[16] From normal share market purchases in London, Pernas had come to own about 20 per cent of London Tin in 1975 (FEER, 13 June 1975: 13). Haw Par Brothers International, a Singapore-based company, had also acquired a 30 per cent stake in London Tin. Pernas's plan was to merge with Haw Par, which would give it 51 per cent control of London Tin and majority ownership in the new company.

Unfortunately, difficulties with Singaporean authorities scuttled the transaction. The Singaporeans insisted that Pernas was in fact taking over Haw Par and, according to the rules, would have to make a general offer for Haw Par. It was an expensive proposition (amounting to $258.5 million) which Pernas was not willing to undertake (*FEER*, 4 July 1975). Pernas's executives insisted in vain that they were merely a willing buyer to Haw Par's offer and were not engaging in a take-over; they merely wished to control London Tin and not buy Singaporean companies (Gale, 1981b: 119).[17] Pernas had miscalculated badly, and in thinking that Singapore would bend its rules to allow for Pernas's nationalistic mission, neglected to learn the complex rules and procedures its corporate strategies required.

Coming to terms with its shortcomings, Pernas next employed Rothschilds and Sons of London, an English merchant bank, as its financial adviser. Davenport described the relationship as bringing to bear 'some of the most ruthless takeover tactics perfected in the City of London to advance the cause of Malay economic nationalism' (Davenport, *FEER*, 3 December 1976: 39). British capitalism had lost its cultural close-knittedness so that it was quite respectable for a British institution to work against the interests of its own community on behalf of a former colony.

Through complex manoeuvring, Rothschilds succeeded in giving Pernas control of London Tin. The strategy it worked out was to merge London Tin's assets with those of the second biggest tin group in Malaysia, Charter Consolidated, to form a new company which would be 71 per cent owned by Pernas and 29 per cent owned by Charter. The company, presently called Malaysian Mining Corporation, is the largest tin company in the world and is owned by PNB.[18] The partnership with Charter was a marriage of convenience: Pernas was uncertain of its expertise in running such a large tin-mining operation[19] and Charter needed a Malaysian partner to facilitate the critical task of getting licence renewals.

The relative ease with which London Tin was acquired was mainly due to the fact that the twenty-five-year leases of many of the companies were expiring soon; the prospects that they would be renewed without substantial Malaysian participation were remote. Since Pernas was willing to pay slightly above market rates for the company, the case for shareholders selling off was compelling (*FEER*, 1 April 1977: 36). Also critical to the transaction was the co-operative attitude of the British regulatory authorities, who had even changed the rules to facilitate London Tin's transfer of domicile to Malaysia. The law as it stood did not permit a transfer when a company's management and cash reserves were in Britain. This flexible attitude grew out of concern in British financial circles[20] that Malaysia appeared ready to take the nationalization route. Therefore, the British tried to place as few obstacles as possible in Malaysia's path; the cost of carrying out Malaysia's wishes was small while non-agreement could result in much higher potential costs for remaining British shareholders holding Malaysian assets.

Pernas sought next, in 1976, to get control of Sime Darby, the largest foreign-owned company in Malaysia. The company was peculiar in that it was incorporated in London, owned substantially by Singaporeans and Malaysians, and managed in Singapore by mostly British executives. It was listed in Kuala Lumpur, Singapore, and London, and had 50 per cent of its gross assets in Malaysia, primarily in rubber and oil palm but also in trading houses, shipping, factories, and insurance institutions (*NST*, 22 November 1976).

The policies of Sime Darby increasingly annoyed Malaysian authorities. Its directors used the company's profits for expansion outside Malaysia, and began to raise capital in the form of special shares on the Singapore exchange in order to make it harder for Malaysian authorities to have a grip on the company (*FEER*, 21 May 1976). When the CIC asked it to submit plans for restructuring, Sime Darby claimed that as a foreign-incorporated body it was under no obligation to comply with the wishes of the CIC.

Controlling Sime Darby became a desirable goal, and Pernas embarked on a plan to oust some of the existing Sime Darby executives. From market purchases, it had accumulated a 9.9 per cent stake in the company. Because some of the other shareholders were Malay-based institutions such as MARA and the Pilgrims Fund, Pernas could count on about 25 per cent out of the 36 per cent Malaysian stake in the company (*FEER*, 3 December 1976). Singaporeans held 46 per cent, including 11.4 per cent by Sime's single largest shareholder, the Overseas Chinese Banking Corporation of Singapore, while Hong Kong and British interests held 16 per cent. Rather than make a bid for the corporation, which would have cost at least $500 million, Pernas sought to replace four of the eight British expatriates with three of its own nominees in the 1976 annual general meeting, thus leaving the company with four British executives and seven locals on the board (*NST*, 1 December 1976).

The Sime Darby Chairman, Dr Keith Bright, accused the Malaysian government and Pernas of 'backdoor nationalization'. Bright appealed to the general shareholders for support and pressed the London City Takeover Panel to rule that Pernas was breaking the take-over code, arguing that if Pernas got its way, Malaysians would control three other companies listed in the UK through Sime Darby (*NST*, 8 December 1976).

The Chairman's position was seriously weakened, however, when the City Panel ruled that Pernas had not broken any rule. In addition, OCBC, although sympathetic to the present board, decided, after enormous lobbying by Pernas representatives, to stay neutral.[21] Rather than engage in a bitter and divisive proxy war, the Chairman resigned as the tide turned against him along with two other British directors. Pernas was thus able to place its own nominees on the board. Tun Tan Siew Sin, Malaysia's former Finance Minister and a previous non-executive board member, became the new Chairman with strong support from OCBC. Pernas was hence able to control and influence Malaysia's largest company with very little outlay in cash because of strong purposeful behaviour on the part of state authorities and managers, and close co-ordination amongst Malay institutional holders.

In the early 1980s, PNB joined Pernas in controlling the foreign plantation sector. Cash rich and charged with speeding up Malay accumulation, PNB sought control as well as ownership in foreign and local companies. Many plantation companies, instead of accommodating state interests, were still dragging their feet about divesting and were carrying out strategies to foil the government's attempt to control them. This set the stage for PNB to engage in a dramatic corporate coup: a dawn raid on Guthrie Corporation Ltd of London. The company controlled about 200,000 acres of rubber and oil palm plantations in Malaysia as well as trading operations in numerous countries. Unlike Sime Darby, Guthrie's owners were primarily British—institutional and family trusts held about 40 per cent of the company.

In 1980, PNB purchased 25 per cent of Guthrie shares from Sime Darby after the latter narrowly failed in a take-over attempt of the plantation company (*FEER*, 6 April 1979). Fearing a hostile move by PNB, the executives of Guthrie embarked on an international diversification programme, buying far-flung assets in the US and UK without consulting PNB as a shareholder. It also offended the political sensitivities of PNB executives by selling off its trading company in Singapore to Malaysian Chinese interests after PNB had shown interest in the company.

PNB, aided by Rothschilds and Sons and the British stockbroking firm of Rowe and Pitman, decided to take over the whole company in 1981. Willing to pay a good price, PNB managed to induce the major institutional holders of Guthrie to sell one early morning in 1981 just when the London Exchange opened for trading. Through careful co-ordination with other confederates, PNB managed to reach the trigger point for a general take-over without the knowledge of Guthrie's management, who were left 'caught with their trousers down around the ankles' and in no position to counter-mobilize (Smith, P., 1981).[22] PNB had spent a colossal $932.8 million for its take-over.

The lesson of Guthrie induced the other plantation companies, such as Harrisons and Crosfield, Dunlop Holdings, and Barlow Holdings, to sell off the majority of their assets to state corporations, especially to PNB. Participation as minority partners was preferable to being taken over since it offered growth possibilities both inside and outside the plantation sector.[23]

By 1982, the process of Malaysianization of the primary sector was nearly complete. Although very little information is made public on the ethnic ownership of economic sectors, occasional statements made in parliament by ministers revealed that Malays, through their state enterprises, controlled about 60 per cent of the corporate shares in the mining and plantation sectors in 1981 (*BT* (S), 26 November 1981). These figures were far beyond the original target of 30 per cent set for both sectors in 1973 in the 'Outline Perspective Plan' in the Mid-Term Review of the Second Malaysia Plan (1971–5). Up to 1985, PNB alone had spent $2.6 billion for restructuring the primary sector (*Fifth MP*, 1986: 113, Table 3.10).

The Other Sectors. State penetration into the other sectors of the economy was not as spectacular as the primary sector, but it was quite extensive. The government used the stick and the carrot approach. The Industrial Coordination Act of 1975, which instituted an industrial licensing system, gave the state the power to control, revoke, and impose whatever conditions it saw fit in the 'national interest' (see Chapter 5 for an extensive discussion). The Act was pivotal for Malay entry and for inducing joint ventures with the state. There was also the carrot. With public consumption and investment totalling around 30 per cent of GDP, the government constituted the largest single domestic buyer of products and inputs. The public sector, therefore, provided a ready-made market for state firms, inducing private companies, especially multinationals, to be a partner in state corporations (*FoMP*, 1981: 17, Table 2-2).

Since Pernas lacked essential manufacturing skills, it depended greatly on foreign multinationals to supply the basic know-how. Being in a hurry to expand, it was not interested in gradually building up an indigenous technological capacity either on its own or in partnership with other domestic manufacturers. Easy access to foreign partners and technology made it less compelling to ally with the lesser skilled and politically problematic Chinese business sector. Nearly all of Pernas's partners in joint ventures were foreign companies.

Some examples of foreign companies allying with Pernas to gain access to the government market were the joint ventures between Nippon Electric Company (NEC) and Pernas Engineering, and KH Consolidated Pty Ltd of Australia and Pernas Sime Darby. The NEC–Pernas joint venture was established in 1973 to produce sophisticated multiplex equipment for the Malaysian Telecoms Department. In 1981, the joint venture company won a ten-year contract worth $1 billion to supply Stored Programme Control (SPC) electronics switching equipment for Telecoms. The lucrative contract resulted in the Japanese agreeing to renew the original agreement and to reduce their 40 per cent equity holding to 30 per cent in 1986. It also Malaysianized the management subtantially except for a few advisers (*SP*, 1981, 8(2)). The joint venture with the Australian company was started in 1983 to manufacture lightweight, aluminium-coated steel roofing sheets in response to the Fourth Plan's aim of speeding up the building of low-cost housing (*SP*, 1983, 9(3)).

In construction, trading, and insurance, Pernas's close links with the state provided substantial business for the corporation. Although Pernas did not go too deeply into construction for fear of competing with individual Malay businessmen, whatever major contracts it won were awarded by the government. For example, Pernas Construction (Percon) partnered Sambu Corporation of South Korea in 1981 to undertake a $300 million contract on the Kuala Lumpur Traffic Scheme (*SP*, 1981: 8(3)). Percon, in partnership with Ballast Nedam Groep of Amsterdam, also won a $40 million project from the National Electricity Board to reclaim land and undertake civil engineering works for a power station.

Pernas's insurance wing, Malaysia National Insurance, which was set up in the early 1970s, emerged rapidly to become a major life and general insurance company in an industry previously dominated by foreign firms. In 1981, it was the top mortgage insurance company in the country, getting its main business from civil servants obtaining mortgage cover for their housing loans contracted from the Treasury. It also insured the big government companies such as Malaysia Airlines, Malaysian International Shipping

Corporation, Petronas, and the National Electricity Board.

Pernas's special status with the government also gave it many trading opportunities. Pernas Trading was appointed in 1971 as the sole agent to deal with communist and socialist countries.[24] Some foreign manufacturers such as OTIS Elevators and Sperry Univac Systems, chose Pernas Trading as the sole distributor of their products. The company rapidly became a major supplier of computer facilities as well as office and building supplies to the government. Various government departments and agencies also turned to Pernas to import industrial chemicals and fertilizers that were used for land development schemes, public works projects, and for providing fertilizer subsidies to farmers.

Other trading opportunities have come from Pernas's equity participation in a number of manufacturing companies, which gave the company the leverage to gain a foothold in wholesaling activities. For example, Pernas's 46 per cent ownership in Malayawata, a Japanese–Malaysian joint venture in steel, allowed Pernas to supply the company with steel billets and to distribute the company's steel products. Indeed, trading became Pernas's main source of revenue after 1984 when it transferred its most profitable companies to PNB (Pernas, 1984).

Finally, Pernas also played an important role in strengthening the government's control of the banking sector. The government desired greater control and ownership of the commercial banks in order to influence lending patterns, particularly in ensuring compliance with the targets set by Bank Negara (Central Bank) for lending to the Malay community. The opportunity to add another bank, in addition to the two large banks already controlled by the government,[25] came in 1976 when the directors of the nation's fourth largest bank, United Malayan Banking Corporation (UMBC)—owned by a syndicate led by a Singaporean—were suspected of diverting internal bank funds for themselves (*FEER*, 10 September 1976: 54). The Central Bank intervened to restructure the management and ownership of the bank, and brought in Pernas as a 30 per cent shareholder. Through a series of highly controversial transactions, its share increased to 41 per cent in the early 1980s and in 1986 Pernas became the sole owner. As a result of the government's increasing dominance of the commercial banking sector, the percentage of outstanding commercial bank loans to Malay interests has not just met the Central Bank's target of 20 per cent but has also been considerably over-achieved. At the end of 1984, outstanding loans to Malay-based interests was 32.7 per cent (Bank Negara Malaysia, 1986: 89).

In 1984, Pernas had $1.9 billion worth of assets distributed among fifty-five subsidiaries and seven associate companies across all sectors of the economy (see Pernas, 1984: Table 4.4). The corporation was responsible for 13 per cent of the total investment made by government trust agencies at the end of 1982 (*MTR FoMP*, 1984: 103). Its asset position would have been higher if $0.9 billion out of $1.7 billion worth of assets from its most profitable companies, such as Sime Darby, Malaysian Mining Corporation, Pernas–NEC, Goodyear Malaysia, Malaysia National Reinsurance, and Kontena Nasional, had not been transferred to PNB in 1981

TABLE 4.4

Pernas's Subsidiary Companies in 1984

Company	Effective Interest	Company	Effective Interest
Pernas Securities	100	Pernas Properties	100
Tradewinds (M)	100	Pernas Realty Development	60
PS Trading	100	Pernas Trading	100
Quek Shin & Sons	100	Pernas Daikin	69
Mikeng Development	100	Pernas Technical Services	100
Tamia S.B.	100	Pernas Hall Thermotank Engineering	100
Jean Simon Wigs	85	Malaysia Timber Exports	100
Pernas International Hotel and Properties	61	Pernas Aviation Sales	100
		Sincere Leasing	51
Pernas Sime Darby Holdings	51	Pernas Wakil	100
Pernas S.D. Trading	51	Pernas Hotel Chain Holdings	100
PSD Rent-A-Car	51	Pernas Hotel Chain (Sabah)	100
Wallock Systems	51	Pernas Hotel Chain (Sarawak)	100
Wallock Partitions (M)	51	Pernas Hotel Chain (Selangor)	90
PSD Technical Services	51	Pernas Hotel Chain (Penang)	100
PSD Shipping	51	Pernas OUE	70
Ford Concessionaires	51	Malaysia Kuwaiti Investment	52
Land Rover (M)	51	MKIC Securities	52
Zees Motors	51	MKIC Amlak	
Kubota Agricultural Machinery	45		

Berger Paints (M)	35
Chubb Malaysia	35
Vera (M)	35
Steelform Industries (M)	35
IT International	35
PSD–OTS	26
Pernas Construction	100
Percon–Syabina	51
Percon–Putra	51
Pernas Engineering	100
Pernas Malaysia Engineers	100
Pernas Electronics	70
Robert Newton Lumber	70
Malaysia International	
Palm Oil Industries	51
Pernas Mining	100
Malaysia Offshore Supplies	100
Pernas Okanagan	
Helicopter Supplies	75
Avlau Engineering	100

MKIC Enterprises	52
MKZ Bina	52
Pernas Shipping Line	100
Malaysian Dredging Corporation	60
Parcel Tankers Malaysia	60
ASSOCIATED COMPANIES	
PBS–MKIC	50
Malayawata Steel	46
United Malayan Banking	41
Beriaya Kawat	38
Beriaya Mesh	44
Malaysia National Insurance	30
Central Sugars Refinery	47
TRANSFERRED TO PNB (1981)	
(approx. M$ 1 billion)	
Sime Darby	
Malaysian Mining Corporation	
Goodyear Malaysia	
Pernas–NEC	
Island and Peninsula Development	
Malaysia National Reinsurance	

Source: Pernas, 1984: 82–3.

(*SP*, 1981: 8(1)). Through share acquisitions in property development and manufacturing companies, Pernas managed to recover its former asset position by 1984.

Pernas's profits in 1984 stood at $60.9 million, or around 3 per cent of its assets (Pernas, 1984). The company's long-term loans were $798 million or 40 per cent of its assets. Some 70 per cent of the loans came from the government of which 85 per cent was interest free. Considering that the capital costs of Pernas were heavily subsidized and it enjoyed captive state markets, its financial performance could hardly be described as impressive if compared to well-managed private firms. Yet, in managing to stay in the black, the political leadership has praised the organization for its 'continuing success even after the transfer of its 11 profitable companies to PNB' (Dr Mahathir Mohamad quoted in *SP*, 1984, 10(4)). Control and ownership of assets was evidently more important than a good financial return.

Permodalan Nasional (PNB) went on to acquire assets in local companies after its spectacular take-over of Guthrie. At the end of 1985, PNB had spent a colossal $6.2 billion to acquire interests in 159 companies. Table 4.5 provides PNB's equity involvement in the various sectors of the economy.

Backed by government institutions such as the FIC and CIC, PNB has been in a unique position to pick and choose lucrative companies for ownership. The corporation has had an interest in abiding by the commercial logic of the market-place in order to maintain a good profit position for its companies, particularly since 1981 when the corporation's assets started being sold to the wider Malay community. PNB has sought board representation in companies it has a sizeable equity in, but its partners, such as foreign plantation companies, have had little to complain about in terms of PNB sacrificing commercial logic for other socio-political concerns.[26] PNB's representation in company boards has been aimed more at protecting

TABLE 4.5

National Equity Corporation (PNB) Group Shareholdings by Sector, 1985

	Quoted Companies		Unquoted Companies	
Sector	Number of Companies	Investment Cost ($ Million)	Number of Companies	Investment Cost ($ Million)
Manufacturing	62	523.0	41	291.2
Finance[1]	5	1,435.5	6	249.4
Property[2]	13	458.9	4	101.5
Plantations[3]	14	1,122.9	3	1,230.9
Mining	8	322.4	—	—
Total	102	3,862.7	54	1,873.0

Source: Fifth MP, 1986: 113, Table 3-10.
Notes: [1]Includes investment sector.
        [2]Includes hotels.
        [3]Includes rubber and oil palm industries.

its investment than at interfering with the management of its subsidiaries. At the end of 1982, the latest date in which information is available, PNB's holdings constituted 31 per cent of the investment of government trust agencies and public enterprises (*MTR FoMP*, 1984: 103).

Even though Pernas and PNB have been considered relatively successful by the political leaders, their primary function was in their ethnic and political role rather than in giving an important impetus to economic development. The major part of state resources was used for taking over and buying existing companies, some of which were in slow-growth or declining sectors like tin. This route, which involved a large exchange of assets, cannot be considered very productive in increasing national income and employment, and in promoting economic diversification. But from an ethnic point of view, it allowed for the quick control of well-managed, profitable companies and gave the Malay leaders access to surpluses which could be used to provide their Malay base with tangible and symbolic benefits.

The other important result, at least among the more successful enterprises, was the creation of a new corps of state managers who were centrally and powerfully involved in Malaysian corporate life. While their numbers were probably no more than a few hundred, these Malay managers have helped spread the Malay élite from its sole base in the bureaucracy and in politics to the corporate economy. They could now claim equal standing with their non-Malay peers, mitigating in the process past fears of Malay economic marginality.

From a national standpoint, two favourable outcomes might, arguably, be cited concerning the state's expanded role. One is the greater retention of profits within the domestic economy. This can be seen in the change of the total profit share between 1971 and 1983 held by locally controlled companies, where residents own 50 per cent or more of the company. For rubber companies, the share increased from 12.2 per cent to 72.5 per cent, other agriculture from 37.1 per cent to 76.5 per cent, tin from 7.8 per cent to 96.3 per cent, manufacturing from 25.2 per cent to 39.9 per cent, banks and financial institutions from 36.2 per cent to 61.1 per cent, and retail trade from 67.7 per cent to 74.3 per cent. Overall, the local profit share increased from 29.9 per cent to 66.0 per cent. (Department of Statistics, 1975 and 1985). Without the state's strong role, it was most unlikely that domestic, private businessmen on their own would have had the resources, power, or even inclination to effect this vast change.

Greater state control has also made, if ever so slightly, former foreign resource companies diversify locally. Malaysian Mining Corporation has been exploring for base metals such as copper and gold in Malaysia because its executives do not see good prospects for tin. Sime Darby has also been investigating the possibility of growing new plantation crops. Recently it went into partnership with a Californian biotechnology company involved in plant genetic engineering, hoping to adapt valuable semi-arid crops, such as the wing bean and jojoba plant, for tropical conditions.

Despite these side benefits, the real issue is whether, from a national point of view, resources have been used productively for increasing national competitiveness. Billions of dollars have been spent buying over essentially slow-growth sectors rather than invested in new industries that might lay the basis for a more sophisticated and dynamic economy. Furthermore, from the benefit of hindsight, the sharp fall in rubber, tin, and oil palm prices in the 1980s throws new scepticism on whether the yield on the expensive assets purchased has been worth the cost. The great hope in downstream processing of rubber and palm oil has proved more intractable than anticipated since tyre or soap production require only small amounts of primary commodity input and depend critically on establishing an international brand name. At present, further processing of rubber and tin have made marginal progress.

Yet, from an ethnic point of view, the state's activities have a rationale. Starting new enterprises from scratch in the absence of a solid corps of dedicated and experienced managers would have been hazardous. Buying existing assets at least ensured that there would be returns to the investment. The State Economic Development Corporations (SEDCs) illustrate the real problems of state entrepreneurship without the basic technical and managerial attributes.

The SEDCs

The thirteen SEDCs were formed mainly in the early 1970s to complement the NEP effort at the state level. They were nominally under the control of the Ministry of Public Enterprises, but their management boards were composed of state executive officers and one or two representatives of central co-ordinating agencies, such as the Ministry of Public Enterprises and the Implementation and Coordination Unit (ICU) of the Prime Minister's Department. When a SEDC contracted large loans from the government, a few Treasury officials also sat on the board (Puthucheary, M., 1979: 199). Until the early 1980s, the chairman of the board was the chief minister of the state, typically from the UMNO party. So as not to compromise the ethnic mission of the SEDCs, the executives were nearly always Malay. Even when experienced Malay managers were not available, SEDCs preferred to hire recent Malay graduates rather than non-Malays.

As central instruments of the NEP, SEDCs received generous funds from the central government (see Table 4.3). State governments in addition made legislative changes to existing enactments to allow them to act as guarantors to commercial loans made to SEDCs (NST, 20 April 1976). Such moves were aimed at getting further sources of funds and bypassing central government controls and scrutiny.

The SEDCs expanded rapidly because of easy access to credit and ease of getting land from their respective state governments. By 1981, they had spawned a total of 321 subsidiaries with a total investment of $564 million (NST, 20 November 1982). In their great desire to proliferate, they undertook all types of ad hoc projects in plantation agriculture, manufacturing, trade, construction, and mining.

The speed of growth, however, was at variance with their performance. In the mid-1970s, nearly all the SEDCs were making losses, and only a handful of their subsidiaries were making any money. The Perak SEDC, for example, had more than thirty subsidiaries but only one company in transport was making profits (*NST*, 21 April 1976). The picture did not alter appreciably in 1981. Except for the Johor SEDC, which had an unusually dynamic general manager, all the other SEDCs were struggling to show profits. In 1981, the Ministry of Public Enterprises revealed that out of 260 companies it had information on, ninety-four were making losses and twenty-one had yet to operate (see *MB*, December 1981).[27]

The bleak performance of the SEDCs was a direct result of their management structure and the confusion of the central authorities toward them. The people who ran the SEDCs had, in fact, very little stake in their companies doing well. The chief ministers and local politicians who sat on the SEDC boards pushed for projects that would extend their patronage and enhance their political fortunes, paying little attention to economic rationality (Thillainathan, 1976: 68). The managers, too, sometimes conspired with the non-executive members of the board. They would eagerly enter into projects because they could get remuneration from sitting on the boards of the new companies—some executives and board members held as many as twenty-eight directorships in the subsidiaries of the SEDCs (*NST*, 13 September 1981). It was also common for SEDC officers to award sub-contracts to companies that they or their relatives had started on the side (*NST*, 13 September 1981; Puthucheary, M., 1979: 201).

This form of parasitism on state resources led to a situation in which SEDC officers were highly reluctant to close down companies which were making large losses until central authorities forced them to do so.[28] Interestingly, some of the foreign companies the SEDCs formed partnerships with, particularly from India, hardly exercised any commercial discipline on the joint venture because they appeared to be more interested in making profits through selling machinery and getting management contracts. This point was demonstrated in the sugar refinery joint venture established in 1975 between Phaltan Sugar Works Ltd of Bombay and the Negeri Sembilan SEDC. The Indian partner invested $4 million in the project while the SEDC put in $29.5 million, including land worth $23 million for a sugar plantation. To get more capital, the SEDC borrowed a total of $80 million from a state agricultural bank as well as the central government (*ST* (S), 23 November 1979). Phaltan did the feasibility study, sold machinery worth $21.5 million to the joint venture, and had a management contract for seven years. Whatever the outcome of the venture, Phaltan probably made profits from the sale of the machinery alone. The project turned out to be a nightmare of bad corporate planning, and by 1979 the company had lost $30 million. Both the SEDC and the Indian partner were quite willing to go on with the project in spite of the great losses. Eventually it had to be abandoned because the federal government refused to provide any further loans (*NST*, 23 November 1979).

The central authorities were also to blame for the SEDCs' situation. Because of the cardinal priority given to the NEP, bureaucrats and ministers had a political and cognitive bias in giving the public enterprise managers the benefit of the doubt even when performance was dismal. For example, in 1976, when it was obvious that the SEDCs were losing money and managers were pursuing narrow self-interests, Hussein Onn, the Prime Minister (1975–81), who was also the Minister of Public Enterprises, could only exhort the delinquent managers (whom he called traitors) to stop their practices at once. There was no question of severe punishment: 'All these deviations will create political problems and, ultimately, the Government will have to bear the consequences' (*NST*, 23 April 1976).

Only in 1981 was a serious attempt made to reassess the SEDCs. Datuk Musa Hitam, upon becoming Deputy Prime Minister, pushed for profits to be made the sole criterion in evaluating SEDC performance, and wanted poorly performing companies closed down (*ST* (S), 7 September 1981).[29] But confusion soon set in when the Minister of Public Enterprises, Rafidah Aziz, argued that many of the SEDCs' activities were not profit based— that they were pursuing socio-economic goals—and hence performance should not be based purely on profitability (*ST* (S), 25 September 1981). The Minister's defence found many supporters in the UMNO party.

This schism reflected the basic uncertainty among the top Malay leaders and bureaucrats about how to measure the performance and rectify the problems of the state enterprise sector. In typical fashion, the compromise route was taken—non-priority projects in the pipeline were shelved but to help companies in difficulty their interest costs on accumulated government loans were waived; in 1983 the SEDCs were also made exempt from the profit tax until 1990 (*The Star*, 18 May 1983).

The most recently available data show continuing problems for the SEDCs. The aggregate losses ($360.6 million) of 125 companies exceeded the aggregate profits ($346.8 million) of 103 firms (*NST*, 4 March 1984).

The Malay leaders were prepared to pay a high economic cost to build up Malay assets and economic participation via the state enterprise programme. It was more important for them to counterbalance the economic power of the existing foreign and Chinese groups, capture further avenues for Malay mobility, and get access to national surplus than worry about enhancing overall national economic capacity and efficiency. The whole question of economic efficiency faded into the background because it was compensated by political rewards for the UMNO party and underwritten by the state's considerable economic resources.

The State and Private Malay Capitalists

Some Malaysian scholars have concluded that state enterprise expansion and private Malay capitalist development were antithetical and contradictory processes (Lim Mah Hui, 1981; Sundaram, 1986; Toh Kin Woon, 1982). From selected instances of Malay business complaints against state competition and encroachment, the claim has been advanced that the state élite's only concern is its own monetary aggrandizement. This view is an exaggerated one for, in actual fact, the Malay leaders have had strong reasons to see the development of a broader Malay business class, even at considerable economic cost to the state.

Not only did this élite lack a strong 'statist' view, seeing the state as the only rightful and progressive economic actor in society, but it also

had a strong interest in politically co-opting the incipient Malay businessmen and extending its patronage network. The Malay business class,
despite its economic weakness, was growing in organization and influence,
and its views were not only taken seriously by the leaders, but often deeply
shared by the political leaders themselves.

The state's main strategy to promote Malay businessmen was to make
even larger funds available to them and to use its administrative powers
more fully than in the 1960s. The poor record of Malay businesses did not
deter the UMNO leaders who had come to view the former's past shortcomings and failures as stemming from a lack of capital and opportunity.
As the *Second Malaysia Plan 1971–1975* proclaimed: 'Entrepreneurship
can be created by providing opportunities to develop this talent' (*SMP*,
1971: 7). Even if the political leaders secretly believed that cultural or
religious obstacles were behind Malay business development, they pinned
the solution on the provision of new opportunities.

The flow of funds to the Malay business community was increased in a
number of ways. Bank Negara set targets for bank lending to Malays.
Failure to comply resulted in punitive charges being imposed on commercial banks. New development banks were also established, such as Bank
Pembangunan Malaysia Berhad (1973), Bank Kemajuan Perusahaan
(1979), and Bank Islam (1982). As a result, bank lending to the Malay
community increased enormously, from only 4 per cent of the total amount
of loans approved in 1968 to 20.6 per cent in 1980, and to 28 per cent in
1985 (Ministry of Finance, 1975; *FoMP*, 1981: 65; *Fifth MP*, 1986: 112).
State enterprises accounted for the bulk of the loans given out but the
government also created special institutions to ensure that money flowed
to small-scale businesses as well. In 1972, the Credit Guarantee Corporation
(CGC) was established to provide guarantee cover of up to 60 per cent of
the value of the loans advanced by commercial banks to small businesses.
Interest rates were fixed at below market rates and the maximum allowable
loan was $250,000. Between 1981 and 1983, the CGC dispensed $1.34
billion in loans to 45,830 borrowers.

Outside the banking sector proper, the government also increased the
resources of specialized entrepreneurship-promoting agencies, such as
MARA and UDA. Their role was to provide credit, business premises,
business courses, and advisory services to Malay small business. MARA, for
example, gave out 27,252 loans worth $11.5 million during 1971–5, 14,211
loans worth $80 million during 1976–80, and 29,363 loans worth $163.4
million during 1981–3 (*NST*, 22 August 1980; *MTR FoMP*, 1984: 281).
Its loans usually carried less stringent conditions than regular commercial
bank loans. Those below $5,000 did not need any collateral or guarantor,
and interest rates were pegged at 2.2 per cent, below market rates of about
8–10 per cent. MARA's loans went for varied purposes such as construction,
furniture making, tailoring, restaurants, and retailing (Gale, 1981b: 67).

More funds promised that a greater number of businesses would sprout
but they did not ensure success. To increase the probability of success,
the government used its administrative powers to control the amount of
competition Malay businesses would face. The Ministry of Works and

Public Utilities, a major contractor for construction projects, reserved at least 30 per cent of its contracts for Malay firms, that is, those with at least 51 per cent Malay ownership. In 1981, 51 per cent out of $281 million worth of contracts given out by the Public Works Department in the Ministry went to Malays while in 1985, 33 per cent of $198 million went to them (*Fifth MP*, 1986: 116). The Telecommunications Department also stipulated that at least 30 per cent of its contracts would go to Malays but in fact the figure has gone much higher. In 1985, 99.9 per cent of $284.6 worth of contract work was given to Malay firms. A significant portion of contracts given out by Felda and Felcra, the government's agricultural development agencies, were also awarded to Malays. Indeed, most ministries and state governments, when they dispensed contracts and permits, heavily skewed the distribution in favour of Malays. Some ministries, like the Ministry of Works and Public Utilities, actually went as far as trying to guarantee that Malay firms would make profits. In 1983, it set up a cost-plus plan, in which a certain profit margin was ensured once material costs were taken into account, thus helping to prevent a situation in which sudden increases in material costs would destroy profits (*NST*, 5 March 1983).

It will be useful to divide the Malay business class into small-to-medium businessmen, and the large 'bourgeoisie'. There is a qualitative difference in each group's access to funds, political backing, and method of accumulation that warrants a separate treatment. Let us start with the small-to-medium scale businesses.

On the surface, the rate of Malay business development has been quite spectacular. In 1970, Malay businesses constituted only 14.2 per cent of all businesses registered in Malaysia but in 1980 the figure had increased to 24.9 per cent and in 1985 to 30.5 per cent (*FoMP*, 1981: 66; *Fifth MP*, 1986: 117). This rate was nearly twice the rate of non-Malay business expansion. The sectors which Malays entered most noticeably were construction, transport, and agricultural-based trading activities, industries which required little skill or in which the government had high control over entry and the issuance of contracts. The number of Malay contractors registered with the Public Works Department increased from 1,911 in 1970 to 7,834 in 1980, or from 30 per cent of all registered contractors to 63 per cent (*FoMP*, 1981: 66–7). Malays in the larger contractor categories—the government-registered classes of A, B, BX, and C—increased from 37 in 1970 to 321 in 1980, or from 6.2 per cent to 24.1 per cent. The greatest increase was in the smaller categories where they appeared to have increased at the expense of the Chinese, whose total numbers fell from 3,138 to 2,494 in the ten-year period (Lim Mah Hui, 1985: 51). In 1985, Malays held 73.5 per cent of the licences in logging and 63.9 per cent in road transport.

Probing behind this rosy statistical picture was a rather unhappy situation for most Malay businesses. But there have been a few success stories. From what can be made out of profiles of successful Malay businessmen reported in local journals and magazines, they seem to have come from varied backgrounds. For those with a background in government, contacts with government officials were important for their careers as businessmen.

For those without a government past, knowledge of the possibilities opened up by the NEP and a strong desire to excel in business were critical.

Abu Bakar Lajim, for example was a government survey draftsman in Singapore for eleven years, and later joined the Selangor State Development Corporation or SSDC (*MB*, February 1975: 18–19). In 1971, while still in the State Corporation, he set up a sundry shop with a colleague in response to the government's call to Malays to go into business. Abu Bakar next went into construction because of past familiarity, and contacts with the SSDC landed him his first job of building houses for the Corporation. Abu Bakar went into ever larger projects, became a Class A contractor, and got his first big break in 1974 when he was awarded a $17 million contract for shore installation work at Pasir Gudang, Malaysia's new port. Government backing was essential for Abu Bakar's rise in business, but ethnic pride and a strong desire to make it were also strong motivating forces: 'I work from seven in the morning to ten at night. I have little time with the family. The penalties are so great. If I succeed people will say I have received all kinds of assistance. If I fail people will say what can you expect from Malays' (*MB*, February 1975: 19).

An example of a businessmen who surfaced without a government background was Ismail Mydensah, who was a charge hand on the Penang waterfront until 1971 (*AB*, May 1982). When he saw the opportunities offered by the NEP to Malays, he started a stevedoring business with members of his family to service ships coming to Penang. This business was sold off in 1978 to found a bigger company, Tunas Setia, a shipping brokerage firm capitalized at $200,000. Tunas Setia served shipping interests from Japan, South Korea, and the Middle East. Through shipping, Ismail established contacts with Japanese and Korean manufacturers. These allowed him to go into the production of charcoal-related products for export back to Japan and South Korea. He became the Penang branch chairman of UMNO after his business career developed but 'unlike many other cases, there are no grounds for equating his business successes with political contacts' (*AB*, May 1982: 32).

These two cases illustrate that for some Malays, government exhortation and government financial and institutional backing were pivotal in channelling them into business careers. Unfortunately, the successes were the exception rather than the norm. In 1979, the Chairman of MARA announced that very few Malays had shown progress in their businesses, and had remained stagnant at where they started (*NST*, 19 December 1979). A more devastating picture was given in 1983 by the Minister of National and Rural Development, who pointed out that of 55,000 loans given out by MARA to Malay businesses, only 6,000 had been paid back. Most of the defaulters had either gone bankrupt or thought it was not necessary to pay back MARA's loans (*NST*, 17 February 1983).

The situation was no better in the construction sector, which was to be the seed for crystallizing Malay entrepreneurship. In 1980, the Minister of Works and Public Utilities announced that out of 5,000 Malay contractors registered with the Ministry, only about 20 per cent could be regarded as successful (*NST*, 21 July 1980). As a rough estimate, it appeared that only about 15–20 per cent of all registered Malay businesses were on a sound footing.

There are probably unique reasons for the failures of any particular business, but if one could propose two general reasons, they are: (1) the failure of Malays to develop the Weberian equivalent of a methodical, rational approach to accumulation, and (2) the very nature of state policies toward Malay business development.

Many Malay businessmen continued to approach their businesses as a quick means to a high consumption life-style. Their main interests remained achieving community status and recognition through the display of prestigious goods, such as cars and luxury houses. Business was a means to such a life rather than an activity which generated its own rewards and motivations. Such an attitude, crippling to any enterprise, was especially damaging when manifested in the infant stage of business development. The detrimental effects of such an orientation revealed themselves in several ways. Some Malay contractors used their bank loans to finance car and house purchases instead of their own projects (NST, 27 September 1979). The same 'quick rich' mentality also resulted in others pursuing over-ambitious goals, of equal detriment to their businesses. Instead of building up the businesses by slow, steady increments, some started several ventures, with none receiving adequate attention and all failing.

The government's policies did not help the situation very much. Political logic dictated extending its political patronage as widely as possible. The government was extremely generous in giving out permits and licences to Malays, resulting in over-capacity and excessive competition amongst themselves. Even a free market zealot would have flinched at the situation. In rice trading, for example, there were only four Malay retailers to one Malay wholesaler, whereas the ratio for the non-Malays was 200 : 1 (NST, 11 December 1981). There were so many Malay contractors (especially in the lower categories) that government jobs had to be allocated by ballot, leading to many contractors remaining jobless for months (MB, April 1976: 82). In film distribution and in travel agencies, the initial successes of a few businesses attracted so many others that most of the establishments failed (NST, 7 February 1977).

From the government's point of view, restricting entry probably provided fewer political benefits than appearing to openly encourage Malay business participation. Failure, in this case, could be placed on the individual businessman. Supporting this point, the Prime Minister, in October 1983, urged unsuccessful Malay businessmen not to blame the government for their failures since only in being competitive could they succeed (NST, 26 October 1983).

Because the government has found it difficult to rationalize its policies,[30] its major policy response to Malay business problems, such as excessive competition, has been to swing to extreme protectionism. For example, in late 1983, the Ministry of Trade and Industry announced a special $300 million protection programme to increase the chances of Malay success in industry (NST, 28 November 1983). Only Malays would be allowed to enter as newcomers into eighty-seven low-technology industries, such as wood and rattan products, light engineering, and construction materials. Once a sufficient number had entered, no new entrants would be permitted. The Malay firms would be monitored very closely by ministerial officials, poised to nip burgeoning problems in the bud. It is too early to evaluate this programme, though past experience provides few grounds for optimism. However, as long as there are plenty of resources available, the government is quite prepared to sacrifice national competitiveness and risk dissipating funds to see more widespread Malay entrepreneurship.

We now briefly examine the spectacular rise of the small group of extremely wealthy Malay businessmen. The present Prime Minister, Datuk Seri Dr Mahathir Mohamad, has defended this group's development more than any other Malaysian politician or intellectual. In his 1970 book, *The Malay Dilemma*, he made a psychological argument that Malay tycoons were necessary for the racial ego, that it was important for Malays to feel that they need not be chauffeurs for only the wealthy Chinese businessmen but also for Malay tycoons. At other times his reasoning has been more pragmatic: '. . . the best way to keep the shares [corporate shares] within the bumiputra [sons of the soil] hands is to hand them over to the bumiputra most capable of retaining them, which means the well-to-do' (quoted in *FEER*, 13 April 1979: 41).

Whatever the psychological mainsprings, there was obviously a strong element of naked self-interest among members of the Malay élite in desiring to be co-equal with Chinese millionaires. They were, without a doubt, the group best poised to exploit the NEP. Whether politicians, bureaucrats, members of royal families, or professionals, the members of the élite had strong access to political power, a key springboard to the accumulation of wealth.

Two mechanisms were critical for the rapid ascent of the Malay bourgeoisie. The first was its access, from strong connections and political links, to enormous funds from the banking system, especially the state-controlled and state-owned banks such as Bank Bumiputra, Malayan Banking, Bank Rakyat, and Bank Pembangunan.

The other mechanism is familiar enough—the state's regulatory power in opening up ownership opportunities for Malays in local and foreign companies. Private Malay capital has tended to buy into local Chinese firms while state enterprises have concentrated on foreign companies. The prices of company shares set by the CIC for Malays to buy into were often below market rates, which was a source of complaint among Chinese businessmen.[31] For the Malay investor, the windfall gains from buying cheap shares using borrowed money were acquired at very little risk, and were a key means of capital accumulation.

A few examples will reveal the rapid growth of élite Malay businessmen. In as little as a decade, they have become some of the richest men in the country and the region. It is hard to think of any other Third World country, or even advanced country, where the rich have burgeoned so quickly. Among the most prominent is Datuk Syed Kechik, a lawyer and son of a sundry shop owner, who in the 1960s became Deputy Speaker of Parliament. In 1967, he went to the timber-rich state of Sabah as Political

Secretary of the Ministry of Sabah Affairs. There he associated very closely with the businessman–Chief Minister, Tun Mustapha (*Insight*, August 1982: 4). In Sabah, Syed Kechik was able to use his political influence to engage in timber deals, where he made a small fortune (Lim Mah Hui, 1985: 53). When he returned to Kuala Lumpur in 1975, he benefited from the restructuring requirements on firms, using his accumulated capital and bank borrowings to build stakes in forty companies. One of his largest holdings was a 30 per cent share of the Development and Commercial Bank, the sixth largest commercial bank in Malaysia, controlled by Malaysia's first Finance Minister, Tun H. S. Lee. The fact that even the company of a former government minister had to restructure in favour of Malay interests showed the difficulty of large Chinese companies getting immunity from restructuring. As a politically influential Malay, Syed Kechik was attractive as a partner. Syed Kechik also got involved in property development, a logical area to enter because of the partiality of state governments in giving out land to Malays.

Syed Kechik's major form of accumulation has been buying already existing profitable companies. The companies which he established himself have not performed well. He has spent a colossal amount on film production and distribution—films are his passion—but the yield has been poor (*AF*, 15 September 1980: 24). According to *Business Times* (M), Syed Kechik's assets are reported to be $800 million (*BT* (M), 10 May 1982), but without knowing his debt position it is difficult to know the net value of his wealth. Syed Kechik's rise in business would not have been possible without the influence and early capital accumulation made possible by his earlier involvement in politics.

Another Malay who has risen to the apex of the business world is Datuk Azman Hashim, who once had the distinction of being the only man to have complete control of a bank. Azman has not been in politics, but has enjoyed strong links with the banking sector. Trained as an accountant, Azman joined Bank Negara in 1960 for four years. Between 1971 and 1980 he was a top executive of Malayan Banking, which was government controlled (*MB*, August 1978: 9). During his stint at Malayan Banking, Azman had broad exposure to the corporate world, sat on numerous company boards, and was involved in Pernas's complex deals, all of which gave him a taste and knowledge of rapid expansion through takeovers and borrowing (*MB*, November 1982: 7).

Azman's close links to the banking sector allowed him to borrow enormous funds, which were used to buy public corporations. In 1982, he bought a 40 per cent stake in Taiping Textiles, a publicly listed company controlled by Hong Kong interests. Azman was less interested in textiles than gaining access to a corporate vehicle, which would help his wealth accumulation. In the same year, he bought over Arab–Malaysian Development Bank, a merchant bank jointly owned by Arab interests and the Malaysian government, for $101.8 million. These expensive purchases were made by borrowing from local bank sources and secured by the company shares he was purchasing (*MB*, 5 November 1985: 5). State banks, in particular, were quite willing to take this risky form of collateral to assist the development of the Malay bourgeoisie.

In 1984, Azman used his position in Taiping Textiles to make the company buy 45 per cent of Arab–Malaysian Bank for $311 million, giving him a windfall profit. Although Taiping Textiles was doing badly, the rationale was that this expensive purchase was a necessary diversification measure. A study done by the *Singapore Monitor* rated Azman as one of the twenty richest men in Singapore and Malaysia, with an estimated net value of $525–840 million (*Sunday Monitor*, 9 September 1984). This wealth came in only five years or so, and was made possible by easy access to bank funds and the skilful use of large corporations for personal gain.

The most controversial Malay businessman at present is Datuk Paduka Daim Zainuddin, who became the Minister of Finance in July 1984 when the Prime Minister, Dr Mahathir Mohamad, a close friend, persuaded him to join the cabinet. Daim grew up in the same town as Dr Mahathir, studied law in London, joined the legal service for three years, and worked in a private law firm until 1970, when he began to concentrate on business.

In the early 1970s, Daim's business concentrated in property development. His first break came in 1972 when the influential Chief Minister of Selangor and UMNO notable, Datuk Harun Idris, helped him acquire a piece of mined-out land near Kuala Lumpur, which Daim subsequently developed into a residential and commercial area (*AF*, 15 August 1984: 16).

Daim appeared to lose interest in business in the mid-1970s and went to study urban planning in Berkeley, California. When he returned, he got actively involved in high-level business and politics. With Dr Mahathir's backing as Deputy Prime Minister, Daim headed the property and commercial arm of UDA, the state corporation, and became Chairman of Fleet Holdings, the investment arm of the UMNO party. In 1980, he was appointed a Senator and became a Member of Parliament in 1982.

Daim's business success increased greatly with his entry into politics. Most of his stakes in public companies were acquired in the 1980s.[32] His most controversial acquisition was a 40.6 per cent stake in the third largest bank, UMBC, which he bought in 1984 just before becoming Finance Minister. This share was bought from Multi-Purpose Berhad, the investment arm of the MCA, a co-owner with Pernas. The stake was increased to 50.38 per cent in 1985 only to be sold off completely to Pernas in 1986 at a good price.[33]

Daim's personal worth is not known. When a regional weekly claimed that Daim, on just becoming Finance Minister, was worth $600 million, Daim, without the slightest hint of irony said, 'If I had that kind of money, I shouldn't be here. I should be relaxing' (*ST* (S), 7 September 1984).

These illustrations reveal how state backing was critical for the development of the Malay bourgeoisie. In the 1960s, when state support was limited, Malays played the role of sleeping partners on the boards of Chinese and foreign companies. Since the mid-1970s, a few Malays have emerged to become powerful wheelers and dealers in their own right. They busily make corporate transactions and actively shape corporate policies to increase their wealth within and outside the company.

Nonetheless, the Malay bourgeoisie has a fragile existence. Because it borrows to expand, any diminution of the value of its corporate shares, through a recession or poor corporate performance, can easily result in the loss of its vital credit line, or in bankruptcy. Because the path to wealth has come so easily and without many risks, it is very tempting to over-stretch and expand at a frantic pace, piling up dangerous levels of debt. The case of Datuk Ibrahim Mohammed illustrates the point well. Until recently, he was widely regarded as one of the success stories of the NEP. Ibrahim began life as a lawyer, but by accumulating wealth through logging concessions and linking himself closely to UMNO notables such as Dr Mahathir and Tengku Razaleigh Hamzah, he managed to get director-ships and chairmanships of about twenty publicly listed companies (see *FEER*, 2 September 1977). His most prominent interest was in Promet, an offshore engineering firm founded by Brian Chang, a South African-born Chinese (see *MB*, May 1983: 17). Brought in by Brian Chang so that Promet could get a slice of the rig-building business in Malaysia, Ibrahim became Chairman of the large corporation and had 30 per cent ownership of it. Instead of consolidating his rather substantial stakes, Ibrahim and his brother, Abdullah Ibrahim, borrowed large sums of money from local and Singaporean banks during the stock market and property booms of the early 1980s. The idea was to buy land, develop property, and buy more shares (*AWSJ*, 15 January 1986). However, when the stock market hit a slump and Promet got into deep financial difficulty, the foundations of Ibrahim's empire crumbled. Ibrahim was removed as Chairman of Promet while his family-owned company, Fawanis, was $44 million in debt to Bank Bumiputra ($26 million) and to the Development and Commercial Bank. The Overseas United Bank of Singapore also filed a suit against Abdullah to recover US$18.7 million in loans (*AWSJ*, 22 January 1986).

It remains to be seen whether a self-confident Malay bourgeoisie, con-tributing productively to the nation will emerge. Thus far, its development has been rather parasitic. Strong links to political power and Malaysia's moderately high growth rates (until recently) were the essential props for the rise of this new class. Its contribution to employment generation and diversification has also been minimal, since much of its expansion has come from buying companies at good prices, and selling its shares when prices are right.

However, from anecdotal evidence, it appears that members of the Malay middle class and even lower class have not shown much overt anger and resentment toward the Malay tycoon. For example, a university lecturer spoken to said: 'People like Syed Kechik are *bona fide* businessmen. You can't accuse him of being a front man for others. His investments are world-wide.' When surprise was expressed to a Malay taxi-driver about the sudden wealth of Daim Zainuddin, he retorted: 'How do you know if he did not put in a lot of effort before he became wealthy? Everybody talks once a person becomes rich, but they forget all the work done before' (translated from the Malay). Whatever feelings might be amongst them-selves *vis-à-vis* non-Malays, Malays have a psychological and ethnic stake in defending the Malay tycoon, perhaps because it suggests that Malays can be economic achievers.

Resentment may also have been diluted by lower status individuals expecting that their chance will some day come. The economic growth of the 1970s and early 1980s would have contributed to this positive sum view of economy among the Malay community. However, the deep economic problems of the mid-1980s appear to have brought new internal conflicts. Some Malaysian observers have said that the near defeat of the Prime Minister, Dr Mahathir Mohamad, by his rival, Tengku Razaleigh Hamzah, in the April 1987 UMNO elections was the result of small Malay businessmen resenting competition from both the state and a few large Malay capitalists favoured by the regime. This has been a long-standing view, which might now have greater plausibility given the economic contraction. Whether this apparent conflict is deep or will diminish with new economic growth remains to be seen.

Group Worth and Support for the State

Measured in terms of both resources and duration, the Malay leaders' undertaking to increase their group's role and control of the 'modern economic sector' was phenomenal. From owning less than 2 per cent of the corporate sector in 1970, Malay individuals and trust agencies owned, according to official statistics,[34] about 17.8 per cent in 1985 (*Fifth MP*, 1986: 109, Table 3-9). Although planners estimate that Malays will own only 22.2 per cent of the corporate pie in 1990—the targeted 30 per cent has been curtailed by the serious economic problems of the mid-1980s—the transformation has nonetheless been remarkable (*Fifth MP*, 1986: 109, Table 3-9).

One important result of UMNO's efforts was that it was able to reverse its weakened position in the 1969 elections and re-establish itself as the hegemonic Malay party. Although the élite benefited the most, there were sufficient benefits for the poorer groups for them to support UMNO.

Tables 4.6a–c show UMNO's electoral performance from 1969 to 1986. The UMNO party won all the seats it contested in the 1974 elections. However, it was not a representative year because PAS did not challenge UMNO between 1974 and 1977 when it was a member of the National Front.

The 1978 and 1982 elections show UMNO firmly entrenched in the political system and able to win significant Malay political support. It had effectively met PAS's new challenge, whose platform shifted from strong advocacy of Malay special rights in the 1960s to the vigorous promotion of the creation of an Islamic state, mixed occasionally with strong doses of populist rhetoric. In both elections UMNO won about 36 per cent of the total vote, or about 65 per cent of the Malay vote. PAS's share of parliamentary seats fell from fourteen in 1974 to five in both 1978 and 1982.

In the 1986 elections, UMNO won all but one parliamentary seat against PAS. The Malaysian economy was at its worst level since independence: real GDP fell by 1.5 per cent in 1985 and was close to zero per cent in

TABLE 4.6(a)

Results of Parliamentary Elections, Peninsular Malaysia, 1969 and 1974

	1969			1974	
Parties	*Contested*	*Won*	*Parties*	*Contested*	*Won*
Alliance	103	66	National Front	114	104
UMNO	67	55	UMNO	61	61
MCA	33	13	MCA	23	19
MIC	3	2	MIC	4	4
			PAS*	14	14
			Gerakan	8	5
Opposition	110	37	Opposition		
PAS	59	12	DAP	46	9
DAP	24	13	Pekemas	35	1
Gerakan	14	8		63	0
PPP	6	4			
Others/Independent	7	0			

Source: Milne and Mauzy, 1978: 156–8, Table A and Table B.
Note: *PAS joined the National Front briefly from 1974 to 1977.

1986 (Ministry of Finance, 1986: vi, Table 1.2). The incomes of rural producers, comprising about 40 per cent of the work-force, were severely hit by sharp falls in the prices of Malaysia's cash crops (see Table 4.13). Yet UMNO was able to get large support. In terms of popular votes, PAS's share increased from 16.1 per cent in 1982 to 18 per cent in 1986, but it was a small increase considering the severity of the economic decline.

TABLE 4.6(b)

Results of Parliamentary Elections, Peninsular Malaysia, 1978 and 1982

	1978			1982		
Parties	*Contested*	*Won*	*Votes (Per Cent)*	*Contested*	*Won*	*Votes (Per Cent)*
National Front	113	94	57.2	114	103	61.0
UMNO	74	69	36.0	73	70	35.8
MCA	27	17	14.9	28	24	18.3
Gerakan	6	4	3.2	7	5	4.0
MIC	4	3	2.2	4	4	2.1
Others	1	0	0.2	2	0	0.8
Opposition						
DAP	51	15	21.5	56	6	20.7
PAS	87	5	17.4	82	5	16.1
Others/						
Independent	29	0	3.6	21	0	2.1
	284	114	100.0	273	114	100.0
Total No. of Voters			3,027,603			3,707,782

Source: Mauzy, 1983: 128, Table E.

TABLE 4.6(c)

Results of Parliamentary Elections, Peninsular and East Malaysia, 1986*

Parties	Contested	Won	Votes (Per Cent)
National Front	177	148	55.8
UMNO	84	83	31.1
MCA	32	17	12.4
Gerakan	9	5	n.a.
MIC	6	6	n.a.
Others (including East Malaysian parties)	n.a.	37	n.a.
Opposition			
DAP	n.a.	25	21.0
PAS	n.a.	1	18.0
Others/Independents	n.a.	4	n.a.

Source: Asiaweek, 17 August 1986: 33–5.

Note: *Not strictly comparable with preceding tables because it includes the election results in East Malaysia. More complete sources were not available at the time of writing. n.a. = Not available.

Why was UMNO able to regain and even improve its political standing with the Malay population after 1969? Horowitz's point that ethnic demands and ethnic conflicts primarily reflect struggles over relative group capacity and worth, is useful for understanding UMNO's popularity, and ultimately its development policies. UMNO's increased legitimacy with the Malay population was principally due to its success in increasing the relative group capacity of the Malay population. However, we argued that Horowitz's notion of group worth and capacity was excessively based on group psychology, pointing out that there were actually three aspects of increased group economic capacity which binds a member, even a relatively poor one, to the ethnic leaders. Two had a utilitarian basis in expanded material benefits while the third was psychologically grounded. They are (1) the actual receipt of tangible benefits, (2) the individual's expectation that greater benefits will flow to him or his family in the future, and (3) the increased sense of individual competence or worth emanating from the successes of fellow community members in arenas where the ethnic group had been backward.

The most tangible benefit of the NEP was the creation of a larger Malay middle class and the shift of the Malay population from predominantly agricultural occupations to more diversified occupational activities (see Tables 4.7 and 4.8). The expansion of the state enterprise sector, the vigorous promotion of Malay business, and the battery of regulations imposed on private firms to employ Malays in rough proportion to their population now opened up a greater number of positions in the urban sector than before. The Chinese occupational structure remained more or less constant between 1970 and 1980 while there was more mobility within the Malay group in the same period. Most of the Malay gains, however, were in the lower occupational categories of employment in the urban sector such as production workers and transport operators. Nonetheless, because these

TABLE 4.7

Employment by Occupation and Ethnic Group,
Peninsular Malaysia, 1970 and 1980
(percentage of ethnic representation; parentheses in thousands)

Occupation	Malays		Chinese		Indian	
	1970	1980	1970	1980	1970	1980
Professional	47.0	50.0	39.5	36.9	10.8	11.4
and technical[1]	(64.2)	(118.2)	(54.0)	(87.1)	(14.8)	(26.9)
Administrative	24.1	31.6	62.9	57.0	7.8	6.1
and managerial[2]	(7.4)	(16.2)	(19.3)	(29.2)	(2.4)	(3.1)
Clerical[3]	35.4	55.3	45.9	36.2	17.2	6.9
	(50.4)	(169.4)	(65.4)	(110.8)	(24.5)	(21.0)
Sales[4]	26.7	23.1	61.7	69.2	11.1	7.6
	(69.1)	(99.8)	(159.6)	(299.0)	(28.7)	(32.7)
Service[5]	44.3	47.9	39.9	39.9	14.6	11.6
	(100)	(168)	(89.5)	(140.1)	(32.9)	(40.7)
Production	34.2	45.4	55.9	42.6	9.6	11.4
and transport[6]	(266)	(640.6)	(434.5)	(601.9)	(74.4)	(160.9)
Agricultural[7]	72.0	67.7	17.3	19.3	9.7	11.9
	(920.5)	(998.9)	(221.3)	(289.9)	(123.7)	(175.4)
Total	51.8	51.9	36.6	36.5	10.6	10.8
	(1,477)	(2,211)	(1,043)	(1,558)	(301)	(460.7)

Source: *FoMP*, 1981: 59, Table 3-11.
Notes: [1]Includes architects, doctors, lawyers, teachers, and nurses (public and private).
          [2]Includes government administrators and managers.
          [3]Clerical supervisors and typists.
          [4]Managers and salesmen (retail, wholesale).
          [5]Managers in catering and lodging, and housekeeping.
          [6]Production supervisors, foremen, miners, and workers.
          [7]Plantation managers, farmers, and agricultural workers.

urban sector jobs provided better remuneration than agricultural activities
and allowed members of rural households more urban opportunities, the
average Malay household saw its income increase the most, relatively,
among all ethnic groups (see Table 4.10).

The size of the Malay élite and middle-class stratum increased both
absolutely and relatively. The Malay share of the professional and technical
stratum increased from 47 per cent to 50 per cent while its share of the
administrative and professional stratum increased from 24.1 per cent to
31.6 per cent between 1970 and 1980 (see Table 4.7). Most of the gains in
the professional category came from the lower paying professions such as
teachers and nurses, but Malays made significant gains in the share of
doctors, engineers, lawyers, and architects (see *Fifth MP*, 1986: 105,
Table 3-7). Malays continued to be under-represented in the managerial/
administrative stratum, but their share increased relative to the other ethnic
groups, while their absolute numbers doubled. The chief characteristic of
the Malay managers, especially those working in the state enterprise sector,
appears to be less their rapid growth in numbers, than the swift way they

TABLE 4.8
Malay Occupational Distribution, 1970 and 1980 (in percentage)

Occupation	1970	1980
Professional and technical	4.3	5.3
Administrative and managerial	0.5	0.7
Clerical	3.4	7.7
Sales	4.7	4.5
Service	6.8	7.6
Production and transport	18.0	28.9
Agricultural	62.3	45.1

Source: As for Table 4.7.
Note: Please refer to notes in Table 4.7.

have come to control a sizeable portion of the nation's corporate assets.

Education was another benefit which the NEP conferred on the Malays. The government used education to shape the recruitment process into professional positions. Six tertiary institutions were established after 1970 and the three existing ones vastly expanded in order to boost the intake of Malay students into local tertiary institutions (see Table 4.9). The Chinese intake fell in percentage terms, and many had to go overseas to secure an education. In 1985, there were more Chinese students overseas than in Malaysian tertiary institutions. In order to increase the intake and provide a tertiary education to a greater cross-section of Malay students, educational requirements for entry were lowered and the government gave out scholarships to nearly every Malay, rich or poor, entering university.[35] Even though the wealthier sections of the Malay population obtained the majority of university

TABLE 4.9
Enrolment in Tertiary Institutions, 1970 and 1985 (local and overseas)

Local Institutions	Malays		Chinese		Indians	
	1970	1985	1970	1985	1970	1985
TAR College	—	3	—	2,099	—	42
MARA Institute of Technology	—	1,560	—	0	—	0
University of Malaya	2,843	5,041	3,622	3,374	525	841
University of Science	67	3,996	126	2,509	33	657
National University	174	6,454	4	1,914	1	468
Agricultural University	—	3,652	—	603	—	253
University of Technology	—	2,284	—	567	—	154
International Islamic University	—	363	—	14	—	14
Northern University	—	488	—	161	—	44
Local enrolment	3,084	23,841	3,752	11,241	559	2,473
(percentage for each group)	40.2	63.0	48.9	29.7	7.3	6.5
Overseas enrolment	n.a.	6,034	n.a.	13,406	n.a.	3,108
(percentage for each group)	n.a.	26.8	n.a.	59.5	n.a.	13.8
Total enrolment (per cent)	n.a.	49.4	n.a.	40.7	n.a.	9.2

Sources: FoMP, 1981: 352, Table 21-3; Fifth MP, 1986: 490–1, Table 19.3.

TABLE 4.10
Household Income by Ethnic Group, 1970, 1979, and 1984
(in constant 1970 M$)

Category	1970	1979	1984	Average Annual Growth Rate (Per Cent)
Malays				
mean	172	296	384	8.8
median	120	197	262	8.4
mean/median	1.43	1.50	1.47	
Chinese				
mean	394	565	678	5.1
median	268	373	462	5.2
mean/median	1.47	1.51	1.47	
Malay mean/				
Chinese mean	0.44	0.52	0.57	
Malay median/				
Chinese median	0.45	0.53	0.57	
Indian				
mean	304	455	494	4.5
median	194	314	347	5.6
mean/median	1.57	1.45	1.42	
All ethnic groups				
mean	264	417	494	6.2
median	166	263	326	6.9
mean/median	1.59	1.59	1.51	
Urban				
mean	428	587	695	4.5
median	265	361	463	5.3
mean/median	1.61	1.62	1.50	
Rural				
mean	200	331	372	6.1
median	139	222	269	6.7
mean/median	1.44	1.49	1.38	
Urban mean/				
rural mean	2.14	1.77	1.87	

Sources: *FoMP*, 1981: 56, Table 3-9; *Fifth MP*, 1986: 99, Table 3.4.

places and scholarships, students from poorer families also managed to enter university in greater numbers than before.[36]

Most of the benefits of the NEP clearly went to the élite and middle-class Malays. Table 4.10 shows that the ratio of the mean to median income for Malays increased between 1970 and 1984, although the peak was reached in 1979.[37] The NEP has been unequal in outcome, but there has been enough of a positive sum situation to allow for large numbers of Malay households to enjoy real increases in income from 1970 to 1984. The ratio of the Malay to the Chinese median household income increased from 0.44 in 1970, to 0.52 in 1979, and to 0.57 in 1984. Government figures show the incidence of poverty falling from 49.3 per cent in 1970 to 39.6 per cent

TABLE 4.11
Incidence of Poverty,* 1970–1984 (in percentage of households)

	1970	1976	1984
Total	49.3	39.6	18.4
Urban	21.3	17.9	8.2
Rural	58.7	47.8	24.7

Source: Fifth MP, 1986: 86, Table 3.1.
Note: *Criteria for poverty line not specified.

in 1976, and to 18.4 per cent in 1984 (see Table 4.11). However, the lowering of the poverty rate and income increases among the poor were only partly the product of the state's ethnic policies. Good commodity prices in the 1970s and early 1980s, generous state subsidies in fertilizer and credit, and agricultural price supports, especially in rice, were also important factors (see Scott, 1985: Chap. 4). Any drastic and sustained decreases in the above, especially in commodity prices, could easily wipe out the gains of the rural sector.

The Malay leaders, conscious of the political need to make the benefits of the NEP positive within the Malay community, embarked on an innovative strategy to channel the surpluses of the well-performing state-controlled companies to the larger Malay community in 1981. The framers of the NEP had left open the question of when and to whom the government's assets would be imparted. From the mid-1970s, Malay business groups, chambers, and associations began pressing the government to sell them at cost the profitable assets held by the state (see NST, 12 March 1979). This demand was firmly articulated by Malay businessmen during the Third Bumiputra Economic Congress in June 1980 (NST, 2 June 1980). Under the weight of these pressures, the Malay political leaders turned these demands into a broader strategy of political gain by launching the Amanah Saham Nasional (ASN) or National Unit Trust Scheme in 1981. ASN's mandate was to buy at cost PNB's assets and sell them to the wider Malay community. It was a brilliant strategy that simultaneously kept the state managerial stratum in control of the companies, spread the profits to the wider community, and kept the shares in Malay hands, since an individual could only buy and sell through ASN. The maximum an individual could purchase was $50,000 while the minimum could be as small as $10 (FEER, 23 January 1981). To make the scheme attractive, a minimum of 10 per cent return was guaranteed, and banks were instructed to lend for buying these shares.[38] By 1985, a total of 2 million or 43 per cent of total eligible Malays held ASN shares, investing a total of $1.9 billion, or an average of $950 per person (Fifth MP, 1986: 111).

Of all the government's policies of ethnic redistribution, the ASN scheme was the fairest—85 per cent or 1.7 million of the trust holders, many farmers, labourers, and housewives, had shares of less than $500 each. While many left-wing intellectual critics of the government were right in saying that ASN benefited the poor Malays only marginally, they failed to understand the cleverness of the government's broader political strategy. The government leaders, through a mix of symbolic appeal and actual benefits, could claim that their efforts not only gave Malays greater control of the economy, but that tangible benefits for individuals, previously unavailable, resulted in the process.

These immediate rewards were an important by-product of increased Malay economic capacity, and a vital cornerstone of support for the UMNO party. However, it would be wrong to view UMNO's success as merely a direct, exchange relationship or a product of simple patronage. Many supporters of UMNO probably benefited little from the NEP. Roughly 5 per cent of poor families (those with less than $300 in monthly income) had a son or daughter in the university. More than 50 per cent of eligible Malays did not or could not participate in the ASN scheme. Hence, what was equally important was the role of future expectations in binding political support. Individuals not benefiting presently could hope that sometime in the future, either they or members of their families would get their due share. The role of expectations, especially when individuals think they are dealing with an ultimately responsive government, is not as nebulous as one might think. For example, Hansen (1971) explains the rather paradoxical behaviour of Mexican peasants who benefited very little from Mexican development but who strongly supported the PRI party, by the peasant's hope, based on occasional government land redistribution schemes, that one day he will get land too.

UMNO had demonstrated that it had the intent and ability to give poor Malays a better livelihood. A Malay government controlling more of the economy was, from the Malay point of view, far better than control by either foreigners or Chinese, if only because there was a greater chance that a Malay would get the benefits. Thus, even if a particular individual did not personally expect to benefit materially from the government, he or she could at least hope that a child or close relative might get a better education, a business licence, or a high corporate job in the future, a hope underpinned by visible evidence of the increase in the Malay middle, professional, and business classes.

Enhanced economic capacity also contributed psychologically toward augmenting group worth. The term as it is used here refers to the sense of individual empowerment that is shared by all members of an ethnic group by the economic or cultural achievements of the few. The success of a few ethnic members, especially in an activity the ethnic group was regarded as not capable of achieving, is important for the ethnic group because it changes the status of the group in the eyes of ethnic members as well as outsiders. The case of lower status individuals defending the new Malay bourgeoisie illustrates the point well. When an ethnic member becomes a big businessman or attains some other desired status, the rest of the members can say that the ethnic group, and therefore any particular member, has the potential to be successful. This renewed faith can perhaps reach unrealistic levels, as reflected in the eagerness of many Malays to rush into business without the proper grounding. The question of whether an enhanced sense of ethnic group worth can persist in individuals who do not enjoy real benefits cannot easily be answered. One suspects that both are somewhat independent, although as time passes ethnic members will probably expect some correspondence between the two.

In conclusion, the state élite managed to reap significant electoral rewards by their attempt to buttress the group economic capacity of the Malays.[39] Such a capacity provided greater material benefits to the Malays as well as an enhanced sense of group worth. The political success of the leaders' economic policies, therefore, compensated amply for any misgivings about the high national economic costs of the policies. The process of capital accumulation was channelled to serve political and ethnic imperatives, and indeed the political élites were rewarded precisely for breaking the rules of market rationality.

The Over-burdened State

The state's considerable financial resources were the most critical lever for realizing the politico-cultural goals of the leadership. Neither the protests of the Chinese business sector nor internal divisions within the UMNO élite threatened to derail the NEP. The whole policy was instead premised on having the necessary resources for Malay-based efforts to substitute the entrepreneurial function of the Chinese and foreign sectors, and to provide a sufficient flow of benefits to UMNO's other critical base, the rural farmers.

High commodity prices in the 1970s and revenue contributions from new commodities, such as petroleum and liquified natural gas, were crucial both in camouflaging the many inefficiencies and long-term opportunity costs[40] of the state economic programme, as well as in maintaining the relatively high growth rates from 1970 to 1984. Real national income grew at 8.5 per cent from 1971 to 1980, and at a respectable 5.7 per cent between 1981 and 1984 (*FoMP*, 1981: 24; Ministry of Finance, 1986: xi).

However, there were strong underlying internal and external forces that worked to undermine this fortunate state of affairs. Internally, the NEP brought in its wake an enormous concentration of power in the hands of the top political executive and a few key technocratic agencies. Parliament weakened in its role as a watchdog of the government. The reasons included the reduced role of opposition parties, UMNO's hegemony in the National Front, and the general cramping of debate by constitutional restrictions. The earlier more pluralized set-up of economic decision-making gave way to a few decision centres having a large say over national economic management. And as power agglomerated at the top, it meant that even politically trusted economic agencies such as the EPU could lose power and influence quite easily *vis-à-vis* the executive. Thus, when a strong-minded leader like Dr Mahathir Mohamad took over as Prime Minister in 1981, he was able to impose his own views on economic policies.[41] The NEP had sanctioned a high level of politically warranted inefficiency in the economy, but now the particular economic wishes of the top leaders strained state and national resources even further.

Externally, the international economy, which had so long supported the state's programme, changed drastically in the early 1980s. Nearly all the prices of Malaysia's commodities weakened in the 1980s, and when the price of petroleum fell precipitously in 1986, the rug was pulled from under the government's feet (see Table 4.12). The state's new schemes were already beginning to hurt public finances and the nation's external balance but the decline of commodity products highlighted the problems and vulnerability of the economy. Part of the problem lay in the nature of national economic management. In the 1960s, the government avoided excessive domestic and foreign borrowing, adjusting public expenditure according to the resources available, and amassed reserves to be spent during a bad economic patch. The new approach was to spend resources as they were available, accumulating debt and drawing down on reserves in the process. The change in the external sector produced problems, but internal economic management made the economy even more vulnerable. Thus, with the collapse of commodity prices, Malaysia was left in its worst crisis since independence. In 1985, GDP growth was −1.5 per cent and near zero per cent in 1986, and the state was financially strapped, with little prospect of an imminent recovery (Ministry of Finance, 1986: xi).

We now examine further the internally generated causes of the state's financial problems. Three important cases stand out. The first was the move to heavy industrialization in 1980. The impetus came from Dr Mahathir, especially after he became Prime Minister. He was concerned that the country was too dependent on primary commodities, and had made little progress in industry. Part of the problem lay in state regulations impeding Chinese investments in manufacturing and the enclave nature of foreign investment. Rather than solve the political impediments to deeper industrial development, the government decided to go into heavy industry on its own, establishing the Heavy Industry Corporation of Malaysia (HICOM) in 1980, capitalized at $500 million. By the end of 1984, HICOM had a cement plant ($510 million), a hot briquetted iron and steel plant ($990 million), a car manufacturing plant ($553 million), a small engines manufacturing project ($165 million), and industrial estates (*MB*, 6 December 1984). Almost from the beginning, academic economists and some government officials took issue with the move to heavy industry, arguing that Malaysia neither had the market, skilled manpower nor technology for it, and it would be better off to start in small, purposeful steps rather than make a quantum leap. The Prime Minister was unimpressed, and stuck to his course (*FEER*, 14 February 1985: 80):

Apart from a close circle of advisers—only a few of whom are in the cabinet—Mahathir keeps his own counsel. He has not consulted many within his own party, let alone outside it, about his decisions. . . . Top level advice from the Treasury and Primary Industries Ministry sometimes takes issue with the prevailing orthodoxy, using balance-of-payments or indigenous resource development arguments (the HICOM projects mean merchandise-account drains and much less money for traditional resource development). But the HICOM strategy is set in concrete—one official close to Mahathir explained by using an old proverb: 'The dogs bark but the caravan moves on.'

HICOM's projects have been shrouded in secrecy but its most celebrated project, the National Car Project, demonstrated the problems of heavy industrialization without a sound ancillary industry and adequate market. HICOM joined with Mitsubishi Corporation and Mitsubishi Motor Company (30 per cent stake) to manufacture a car for the domestic market. The project effectively displaced the existing local assembly industry which was manufacturing numerous models and makes from imported kits. Mitsubishi was falling behind in the Malaysian car market—in 1980 it had only an 8 per cent share—and going into partnership with the Malaysians promised a bigger market as well as the opportunity to sell equipment and know-how (*FEER*, 24 December 1982: 33). Unfortunately, with the recession and the appreciation of the yen, the middle-class market shrank drastically and the plant began to operate from 1986 onwards, a year after the project came on-stream, on a three-day week. Only exports might possibly save the project.[42]

The government also made large losses in another scheme to corner the world tin market.[43] It turned out to be a sorry lesson in the folly of over-stepping the bounds of dependency. Dr Mahathir, as an exponent of Malaysia's belated economic nationalism, often expressed the view that commodity-producing countries were not fairly rewarded for their products in international markets, which were controlled by the advanced countries for their own advantage. The opportunity to increase the price of tin came when David Zaidner, a tin trader with a tainted financial past but 'obsessed with the idea of cornering the [tin] market' approached Malaysia's top leaders with his grand plan in 1981 (Pura, *AWSJ*, 22 September 1986a). The plan was to secretly buy tin in the market and jack up prices. This would lead to traders in the London Metal Exchange either defaulting on their forward contracts or being forced to meet their contracts by buying tin at a much higher price from Malaysia.

The whole scheme had little economic merit. At the time, the demand for tin was steadily declining. There were also other producers, so any marked increase in prices would only bring in new entrants. In other words, if the price went up from the tin buying operation, it was only because Malaysia was subsidizing the whole purchase. As it turned out, not only did new-comers enter—including releases of the US tin stockpile, which angered the Malaysians—but also the London Metal Exchange changed its rules to allow traders to pay a fine instead of defaulting on their contracts.

The Malaysian government managed to temporarily increase the price of tin in 1981 and 1982 through its own purchases. However, when the government decided not to commit further resources to the scheme because it was obviously failing, the tin price collapsed in the mid-1980s to half its value in 1981. The total losses to the government are not known, but the government had borrowed about $1.5 billion from Bank Bumiputra alone. At the current price of tin, the loss from the loan would have amounted to about $500–600 million (*AWSJ*, 22 September 1986).

Besides the economic folly of the scheme itself, the gamble reflected the economic groove the leaders had got themselves into: risking enormous resources for short-term gains (in a declining industry) rather than seeking ways to employ capital more productively and judiciously.

Finally, as decision-making became more and more concentrated in the executive, the scope for abuse magnified enormously. Again, the result was the loss of billions of dollars. Not surprisingly, the site of the greatest corruption was in the banking system, especially in the state-owned banks where state managers oversaw enormous funds and could hide behind secrecy laws protecting depositors and borrowers. The first large-scale case of financial abuse took place in the mid-1970s involving Bank Rakyat, a co-operative bank for farmers and fishermen (see Mehmet, 1986: 147–50). More than $100 million was lost in fraud and embezzlement; the culprits, who were imprisoned for a short while, included the Chief Minister of Selangor, who was the chairman of the board, and the managing director. Only a few years later, in what must be one of the greatest banking disasters ever, Bank Bumiputra Finance, a subsidiary of Bank Bumiputra, lost a total of $2.5 billion in bad loans made to a Hong Kong property company, Carrian, between 1979 and 1983. The scandal hit Malaysia only in 1983 through the foreign press, most notably the *Asian Wall Street Journal*, and to this day the full details are not known. The government's initial explanation was that the top officials in Bank Bumiputra and the Bank Bumiputra Finance subsidiary in Hong Kong gave out these massive loans to Carrian and related companies in exchange for special consultancy fees and other forms of graft payment. When the property market collapsed, Carrian went under, and Bank Bumiputra was not able to recover even a small portion of its loans.

Another view which casts more doubt on the role of the top leaders emerged with the BMF Inquiry Committee Report in 1986, a report of eighteen volumes and 6,000 pages. The Inquiry Committee (which could not obtain evidence under the force of law) was an attenuated version of a Royal Commission of Inquiry that political interest groups clamoured for, but which the government of Dr Mahathir refused to grant (see *NST*, 12 October 1983). The Committee hinted that top leaders such as Tengku Razaleigh Hamzah and Dr Mahathir were more aware of the transactions between Bank Bumiputra and Carrian than previously thought (see Lim Kit Siang, 1986). No one has been punished for the scandal, leaving plenty of room for speculation about leadership intrigue and corruption. The DAP opposition leader has hinted that perhaps the funds went into the UMNO party's coffers (see Lim Kit Siang, 1986: 46). Whoever the culprits, the national loss was truly staggering.

Regardless of the international environment, the losses and economic costs of these three cases alone would have put real strains on the national budget. As much as $6 billion might have dissipated. Thus, it was not surprising that when the international environment turned sour, the economy reached crisis proportions. Table 4.12 shows the fall in prices and export value of Malaysia's key commodity exports.[44] The poor export earnings have been even more serious when considered in the light of the planners' fundamental assumptions that Malaysia's diversified commodity economy would go on enjoying high export revenues. The enormous increase in export earnings from 1975 to 1980 led planners to forecast in 1981 that export earnings would be $63.1 billion in 1985; the actual figure was merely $37.6 billion, and has not increased much since (*FoMP*, 1981: 204).

TABLE 4.12
Exports and Prices of Major Primary Commodities,
1975–1987 (selected years)

Commodity	1975	1980	1982	1984	1986	1987*
Crude Petroleum						
Volume ('ooo tonnes)	3 240	11 822	11 973	16 497	18 792	17 573
(US$/barrel)	12.4	36.5	36.3	29.3	14.7	18
Value $ (million)	727	6,709	7,694	8,783	5,408	6,223
Palm Oil						
Volume ('ooo tonnes)	1 161	2 260	2 700	2 959	4 305	4 050
($/tonne)	1 055	1 140	829	1 583	579	720
Value ($ million)	1,320	2,576	2,656	4,531	3,010	3,038
Rubber						
Volume ('ooo tonnes)	1 460	1 620	1 378	1 591	1 516	1 570
(ct./kg.)	137	300	201	231	208	245
Value ($ million)	2,026	4,860	2,655	3,672	3,138	3,784
Sawlogs						
Volume ('ooo cu.m.)	8 477	13 900	19 297	16 939	19 116	19 500
($/cu.m.)	71	62	175	166	150	165
Value ($ million)	670	669	3,382	2,808	2,876	3,217
Liquified Natural Gas (LNG)						
Volume (tonnes)	nil	nil	nil	3 458	5 265	5 800
($/tonne)	—	—	—	513	360	294
Value ($ million)	—	—	—	1,775	1,895	1,705
Tin						
Volume ('ooo tonnes)	80.0	70.0	48.6	41.3	29.1	32.0
($/kg.)	9.6	36.0	30.2	29.2	15.2	16.8
Value ($ million)	1,206	2,504	1,484	1,162	650	857
Total Exports (fob) (M$ billion)	9.2	28.0	27.9	38.5	35.4	40.6

Sources: FoMP, 1981: 18–19; xxiv–xxv, Table 3-2; Ministry of Finance, 1986: xv, Table 2.3;
and 1987: xxiv–xxv, Table 3-2.
Note: *Estimated.

That enormous optimism probably gave ministers and bureaucrats the confidence to carry out one of the largest deficit-spending binges in the world (averaging 16.3 per cent of GNP between 1981 and 1985) in pursuit of their economic projects and dismissing the early signs of recession as only temporary.

The problems of the export sector have put a deep squeeze on the state's fiscal position, and therefore on the NEP. Lower revenues and the spectre of large interest payments as a result of enormous borrowing in the past, have put the state in a dilemma.[45] Public debt service charges (for domestic and foreign debt) have increased from 18.8 per cent of operating expenditure in 1983 to 28.7 per cent in 1987 (Ministry of Finance, 1987: 70). Table 4.13 shows the dilemma of public finance. Operating expenditure (mainly emoluments and debt charges) has remained stubbornly high in spite of falling revenues, leaving the overall deficit still very high despite

TABLE 4.13

Public Sector Revenue and Financing, 1981–1987

(in M$ billion, current prices)

	1981	1983	1985	1986[1]	1987[2]
Revenue	18,295	21,605	26,317	24,731	22,353
Operating expenditure	17,266	19,939	24,094	24,320	26,118
Non-financial public enterprise surplus	2,826	4,306	5,749	2,447	2,972
Total current surplus	3,855	5,972	7,972	2,858	−793
Development expenditure	15,214	17,048	13,589	12,210	11,572
Overall Surplus	−11,359	−11,076	−5,617	−9,352	−12,365
Sources of Finance					
Net foreign borrowing	4,745	7,297	1,881	1,568	−1,389
Net domestic borrowing	4,260	5,350	4,182	5,961	8,684
Drawdown on assets	2,354	1,571	446	−1,823	−5,070

Source: Ministry of Finance, 1987: xxxii, Table 4-1.
Notes: [1]Estimated actual.
       [2]Latest estimate.

cut-backs in development expenditure. The budgetary constraints mean that development spending, without a foreseeable boost in revenues, can only increase by further domestic and foreign debt, both already at dangerously high levels.

As economic realities began to go against the economic and political agenda, the leadership became divided as to what to do next. In late 1983, Datuk Musa Hitam, then Deputy Prime Minister, sounded the voice of realism by saying that the government had become burdened with a massive budget deficit and could not hope to reach the 30 per cent ownership target of the NEP by 1990 (*The Star*, 19 December 1983). Tengku Razaleigh, on the other hand, took the politically popular route by saying that the NEP would be achieved by 1990, holding to this view even as late as the end of 1985 (see *ST* (S), 27 September 1984; James, 1986: 208, 222). Only in 1986, when it was obvious that the economy was in a major predicament, did the Prime Minister make the government's position explicit: 'The government will slow the redistribution of wealth whether we like it or not, now that there is no growth at all' (*AWSJ*, 22 September 1986).

All that the statement really meant was that the government was postponing its deadline for realizing its targets. The politics of ethnicity make policy adjustments very difficult. As we shall see in the next chapter, the state élite has had a strong desire to control Chinese business. Interestingly, most of the improvements in the incentive system to regenerate growth have been directed at the foreign manufacturing sector.

As for the role of the state, the politicians and bureaucrats appear to be playing a 'wait and see' game, restraining spending, especially in expensive capital-intensive projects, which have a small political pay-off per dollar spent, while waiting for commodity prices to increase. However, the economic difficulties have had an impact on politics. The Prime Minister has had to face new challenges to his position in UMNO from some of his former cabinet members.[46] UMNO is not as united as it was before—diminished state resources make it difficult for the top leadership to reward all the party's supporters, thus giving rivals the chance to court the disgruntled. The political system has also become more authoritarian in response to criticisms of and challenges to the regime from within and outside UMNO. In October 1987, opposition leaders from the DAP and PAS parties, unionists, and social activists were arrested, ostensibly for stirring up racial tension. In spite of these new tensions in the political system, however, the reserve of political legitimacy that the Prime Minister and his party have accumulated from fifteen years of boosting Malay economic capacity and group worth might see them through the economic crisis; at least for another five years or so.

Conclusion

Our analysis of the Malaysian state since 1970 cautions against simple generalizations about the economic role of the state. Its active involvement in the economy was not induced by the need to protect peripheral development from the global rationality of multinationals (Evans, 1979) or extract society's resources solely for the sake of expanding state power. In Malaysia, the state's economic role, reflecting its complex political, cultural, and economic setting, was a product of the Malay leaders' twin goals of consolidating their political power and realizing the deep cultural aspirations of elevating the relative economic power of their ethnic group in society. Economic development was subsumed under this politico-cultural goal. The government's vigorous policies to promote state enterprises and the Malay bourgeoisie resulted in few national economic benefits in spite of spending enormous resources. There were high economic costs in both. Even at its best, the state's effort was an enormous exchange of assets (that is, buying assets for cash) rather than finding avenues to increase the competitiveness of the economy and to develop new niches for future growth.

The vital compensation for the Malay political leaders and bureaucrats, which gave them a high tolerance for the society's inefficiencies, was the significant support they received from the Malay community for their policies. By bolstering the relative economic capacity of the Malays, the government was able to provide both material and psychological benefits to them. Although the élites benefited the most, the flow of benefits was essentially positive sum within the Malay community.

The burgeoning problems in the economy were camouflaged by the favourable external conditions in the 1970s and early 1980s, causing the political élite not to worry about the real costs of its programmes. When the international environment turned for the worse in the mid-1980s, the economy was in deep trouble and the state, which had started out fiscally strong in the early 1970s, was also in a weak position. Yet, because of political legitimacy gained from its vanguard ethnic role, UMNO continued to enjoy the support of its Malay base even at the height of the economic crisis.

In short, the enlarged and later, over-burdened state, was a product of a long history of inter-ethnic comparison of power and status. In the quest for group economic parity, the leaders were prepared to pay a high national economic cost. Their policies led to some important changes in the politico-economic system. In the 1960s, the state was fiscally solvent but had problems of political legitimacy. In the 1970s and up to the mid-1980s, the state was able to enjoy strong support from its Malay base, but ended up with deep fiscal problems. Further economic difficulties are bound to result in a significant loss of support for the regime. The golden mean between economic growth and political legitimacy had yet to be found.

1. For the changing racial pattern of intake into the nation's tertiary institutions, refer to Table 4.9.

2. PAS broke away in 1977 when a radical religious fringe captured party power and pushed the party's platform toward setting up a theocratic Islamic state in Malaysia. PAS's former strategy of championing Malay rights lost its force as UMNO embarked on its strong pro-Malay policies. The only party that stayed completely out was the DAP, the aggressive Chinese-based opposition party, which hoped to get the support of Chinese voters disaffected with the MCA and other opposition parties which had joined the government, like the Gerakan party.

3. Information provided by an EPU officer, January 1985.

4. Information on both these bodies was obtained from interviews conducted in February 1985 with a senior official in the EPU and a high-ranking official in the Ministry of Finance.

5. As we shall see in the last section of the chapter, the increasing centralization of decision-making ended up in the 1980s with the Prime Minister and his own narrow group of advisers initiating large, expensive projects, with little EPU input.

6. Price setting has been a particularly sore point with Chinese businessmen, whose companies are quoted exclusively on the local stock market, while foreign companies, who are often quoted abroad, have been able to get market prices. Some examples are provided later in this chapter.

7. Information obtained from an interview with a senior executive in a 'foreign' (now restructured) plantation company.

8. It is important to point out that there have been important factions in the UMNO party for power and influence. In the 1970s and early 1980s, the main rivalry was between Datuk Musa Hitam, the former Deputy Prime Minister, and Tengku Razaleigh (the former Finance Minister and Trade and Industry Minister) for the post of Deputy President of the party (and hence the Deputy Premiership). In the mid-1980s, a serious split occurred between Dr Mahathir Mohamad, the Prime Minister, and Datuk Musa Hitam (who was now allied with Tengku Razaleigh) over the leadership of the party. These splits have sometimes touched on the implementation of the NEP and its rate, especially in the adverse economic conditions of the mid-1980s, but there has never been disagreement over the desirability and legitimacy of the NEP among the Malay leaders and general population. See Chapter 6 for a discussion

of the relationship between internal UMNO struggles and economic growth at the time of writing.

9. The most controversial aspect of the bargaining between the oil majors and Malaysia was the government's stipulation that oil companies in downstream activities issue a special class of management shares which would carry the voting rights equal to 500 ordinary shares (*FEER*, 16 May 1975: 63). The oil companies regarded it as nationalization without compensation, and threatened to pull out. In the end, in 1976, the management share idea was dropped but Malaysia got the production sharing arrangement it wanted (see Chapter 6).

10. Tengku Razaleigh, the Petronas Chairman (1974–6) said in 1976:

We do not expect oil production to go beyond 250,000 barrels per day beyond 1980. We'd like to see the petroleum industry developed in a way that will help firstly to conserve whatever resources we have. We are not relying on oil for our revenue. We rely on things that we chop and grow again like rubber and palm oil, which are inexhaustible.

11. The Heavy Industry Corporation of Malaysia (or HICOM), which started operations in 1981 and enjoys the strong support of Dr Mahathir Mohamad, the present Prime Minister, will be considered briefly in the last section as part of its contribution to the national economic problems of the 1980s.

12. Tengku Razaleigh moved on to become the Chairman of Petronas, Minister of Finance (1976–84), and finally Minister of Trade and Industry (1984–7).

13. Many top Pernas executives were unhappy at the government's decision—it led to a marked dilution of Pernas's assets and profits. Nonetheless, they had to put aside their own organizational interests and comply with the political leaders' wider political goals.

14. The oil palm market was a free market and access to the rubber market, while intricate and involving a multi-layered dealer network, was outside the hands of the owners. Interview with a senior foreign executive of a major plantation company, February 1985.

15. Interview with a senior British executive of a tin-mining agency, January 1985.

16. Interview with a senior British executive of a tin-mining agency, January 1985.

17. Singapore clearly had reasons not to provide an easy precedent for state-backed Malaysian companies to take over its companies. Many of its companies made sizeable profits in Malaysia and were therefore vulnerable to Malaysian economic nationalism (Gale, (1981a: 119).

18. The deep problems of the tin market, which Malaysia partly contributed to, is discussed in the last section.

19. Tengku Razaleigh estimated in 1976 that Malaysia needed about ten to fifteen years to build up its expertise in mining (*NST*, 3 January 1976).

20. Malaysian leaders did not try very hard to ease some of these doubts. The Finance Minister, Tengku Razaleigh, said in 1975: 'We are not nationalizing. We could do that but we don't want to. We would do that if we are forced to. But first we want to try a partnership, do things in a commercial way' (*FEER*, 4 July 1975: 61).

21. OCBC had an extensive business in banking in Malaysia besides several large investments. It was quite likely that it did not want to risk the displeasure of the Malaysian government by undermining Pernas's objectives (Lim Mah Hui, 1981: 80).

22. The reaction of Ian Coates, the Managing Director was harsh:

I have been saying for years that self-regulation in the City didn't work. . . . I think it is disgraceful that [the majority of Guthrie's shareholders] wake up to find that their company is owned by the Malaysian government (*FEER*, 18 September 1981).

In reply the Minister of Finance, Tengku Razaleigh said:

[W]e are merely carrying out a business deal the way the British have taught us. The Guthrie takeover was nothing extraordinary and they [the British] should laud us for really believing in and practicing free enterprise (*NST*, 10 September 1981).

23. Interview with a senior British executive in a major plantation company, February 1985.

24. The pay-off has not been as high as expected. Pernas wanted a direct trading relationship with China, but the Chinese government has been unwilling to displace the role of middlemen merchants in Hong Kong and Singapore who supply Malaysian wholesalers.

Trade with Eastern European countries has been troubled by the fact that these countries have curtailed their purchases, especially of rubber, from Pernas as a bargaining chip for the government to buy more Eastern European products (see *SP*, 1982: 8(4)).

25. Bank Bumiputra was established in 1965 to increase the flow of capital to the Malay business community and, in the 1970s, because of oil-based deposits, became the largest bank in the country. Malayan Banking, another large bank, came under government control in 1966 after a run on the bank. It was previously owned by a syndicate led by Malaysian businessman Khoo Teck Puat. The government's ownership of the banks has been transferred to PNB.

26. Interviews with two expatriate executives in companies under PNB's wing.

27. Growing concerned about the SEDCs, the Ministry of Public Enterprises started only toward the end of the 1970s to collect information on all companies under its wing.

28. Further complications included the fact that the SEDCs submitted their reports to the Ministry of Public Enterprises and Auditor-General's Office three to four years after they were due. Furthermore, there usually had to be consensus between the Treasury, Ministry of Public Enterprises, and Prime Minister's Department before any drastic action was taken. Only the Johor SEDC took the step of closing down unprofitable companies on their own (*NST*, 4 January 1982).

29. In May 1981, amendments were made to the Constitution to make chief ministers of states step down as SEDC chairmen. New regulations also limited the number of members of a company board to twelve and gave greater powers to central authorities to intervene in the activities of the SEDCs (*NST*, 23 May 1981).

30. The high expectations of UMNO's Malay clients make it hard to impose sound policies because of the leadership's fear of losing its popularity and vote-getting ability. For example, MARA decided to freeze its loans in late 1982 because of the high rate of defaults among its borrowers. However, just four months later it lifted the freeze, although the problem had hardly been solved (*NST*, 6 April 1983).

31. Some examples were the issue of 50 million shares by Batu Kawan (a plantation company controlled by Lee Loy Seng) at $1.10 when the market price per share at the date of announcement was $1.68; 8.75 million shares offered by United Engineers at $1.00 each when the market price was $1.25; and Oriental Holdings' issue of 20 million shares (market value, $2.95) offered at $1.60 (Yong Poh Kon, 1980).

32. His family companies (Seri Iras, Pradaz, Baktimu, Dani and Daan) hold substantial holdings in public companies such as Raleigh Cycles Malaysia, General Lumber, Taiping Consolidated, United Estate Projects, Cold Storage, Roxy Electric Industries, and Development and Commercial Bank (*FEER*, 26 July 1984: 14).

33. An article by Raphael Pura in the *Asian Wall Street Journal* in September 1986 suggests that Daim has not been adverse to using his office for personal considerations (*AWSJ*, 26–27 September 1986). Rules limiting ownership of a bank to 20 per cent by a corporation and 10 per cent by an individual were established after Daim had bought his stake in UMBC. When Daim wanted to sell his share to Pernas, the same rules were changed to allow corporations to fully own banks, thus allowing Pernas to become the sole owner of UMBC. Daim's decision to sell UMBC was ostensibly made because the Prime Minister, long criticized for allowing his cabinet members to pursue their business interests while in government, decided that ministers should not have substantial stakes in companies. Another interpretation provided by the article says that Daim needed to raise money because of the heavy debt-service burden of his past borrowing from local and Singaporean banks.

34. These figures are highly controversial and are not accepted by many non-Malays, who think they are a gross underestimate. See Chapter 5.

35. Before 1970, Malaysia followed the pattern of former British colonies of giving an education to a minuscule percentage of the population. From pronounced under-investment in education, analysts believe Malaysia has over-invested in education, leading to the problem of absorbing graduates (see Mehmet, 1986: 121). The brighter Malay students were also sent abroad to acquire better skills, provide some spaces for non-Malay students, and to ensure that a sufficient number of Malays remained fluent in English (the language of instruction was switched to Malay from English in 1970).

36. In a 1983 sample of Malay scholarship holders, 14.2 per cent came from families with

a monthly salary of less that $300 (population share: 63.2 per cent); 32.5 per cent from the $301–500 group (population share: 19 per cent); 30.1 per cent from the $501–1,000 group (population share: 12.9 per cent); and 22.9 per cent from the above $1,000 group (population share: 4.9 per cent) (see Mehmet, 1986: 122, Table 5-12).

37. The ratio of mean to median income is used as a proxy for inequality because of the lack of proper official statistics.

38. Dividend payments have been as high as 18 per cent although with the recent recession, dividend payments have come down to around 16 per cent, still much higher than any other comparable investment. Out of $1.9 billion invested in the scheme as of 1985, $935.5 million had been paid out in dividends and bonus payments.

39. It should be mentioned that UMNO has also tried to win support against its Islamic rival, the PAS party, by elevating the status and symbolic importance of Islam in society. In other words, soulcraft has been an important accompaniment to economic statecraft. An Islamic Bank was established in 1982 (see AB, April 1983: 19–22) and an International Islamic University was established in the early 1980s. Thus far the essential capitalist economic framework has remained intact; for example, the rule against usury has been disguised in other forms, such as in profit-sharing schemes.

40. An example is the use of enormous resources for carrying out a large-scale exchange of assets strategy rather than for productive investment.

41. In the 1980s, the EPU had to defer to the Prime Minister on his selection of key projects. An economist there said that although many officials in the EPU had their reservations, they had no choice but to obey their political masters (interview with senior official in EPU: February 1985). The imposition of political criteria also extended to the Central Bank. The Bank was disinclined to see commercial banks lending for the purpose of purchasing shares. The Finance Minister, Daim Zainuddin, a close associate of the Prime Minister, thought otherwise, and removed its Chairman, Tan Sri Aziz Taha (see ST (S), 8 March 1985).

42. The date for exports has been brought forward because of the deep problems of the industry. The Malaysian car is to make its debut in the US market in 1988. Originally, the Japanese partners were unwilling to modify the car to meet the standards of foreign markets, saying the contract was only for the domestic market. The Malaysian side had to turn to Bricklin Industries of the US (which imports the Yugo and Hyundai models) for modification and distribution. Since the Bricklin link, the Japanese have decided to aid the export drive as well. The high appreciation of the yen was an important consideration, too.

43. The information on the tin scandal comes from an article, banned in Malaysia, by Raphael Pura entitled 'Malaysia Plan To Control Tin Led To Disaster' in the Asian Wall Street Journal, 22 September 1986.

44. Malaysia's primary commodities have suffered low prices because of substitution, sluggish demand from industrialized countries, and competition from other developing countries with cheaper costs. Thailand and Indonesia, especially, have intensified rubber and palm oil production to diversify their economies and take advantage of lower wage costs. Brazil, too, recently discovered the largest deposits of tin in the world and has overtaken Malaysia as the world's largest and cheapest producer of tin in the world. Oil, the new linchpin of the economy, also suffered from weakening prices in the 1980s, taking a plummet in 1986.

45. At the end of 1986, the national debt was $95 billion or 144 per cent of GNP (Ministry of Finance, 1986: 75–6). Public sector domestic debt was $47 billion and the foreign debt was $40 billion. Private sector foreign debt was $8 billion, making total foreign debt $48 billion or US $17.4 billion.

46. See the last section of Chapter 6 for a further discussion.

5 The State and Chinese Business

Introduction

THE Malay leaders' objective of elevating Malay economic status encroached on the relatively unfettered economic environment enjoyed by the Chinese business sector before 1970. Besides favouring state corporations and Malay individuals in business development, the government wanted Chinese businessmen to open up ownership and employment opportunities for Malays. This chapter looks at the limits and possibilities of Chinese resistance to state policies and examines how the Chinese eventually accommodated to them. The key factor is that while the Malay leaders were relatively successful in warding off Chinese protests against their policies, those policies had a cost. The Chinese business sector did not invest to its full potential. No effective state–Chinese capitalist alliance developed to enhance national economic capabilities. Although some of the larger Chinese firms were able to expand rapidly because of the high growth rates of the 1970s and early 1980s, they chose safe and easy areas of expansion, generally staying away from manufacturing.

The Emerging Economic Environment

Business élites usually want the state to provide generous subsidies, fiscal and monetary incentives, and various write-offs to increase their profits. If the state cannot or will not provide these benefits, the next best option for companies is simply for the state to leave them in peace. The most objectionable situation is when the state imposes a regime of controls and regulations that curtail business expansion or profits. Political élites, on the other hand, sometimes formulate policies which may not accord with the interests of the capitalist class but which allow them to expand their power and political support. In Malaysia, the Chinese did not want any changes to the relatively unfettered economic environment of the 1960s, but the state élites' priority of vigorously promoting Malay capitalist development went against this wish. What was the outcome?

To frame our analysis, it will be useful to consider two viewpoints about how the business class exercises influence over state policies. The 'instrumentalist' view maintains that the business class exerts influence over the state by fostering close and personal links with powerful political figures; in extreme cases its members personally occupy positions of political power directly (see Domhoff, 1970; Miliband, 1969). Campaign contributions, bribes, and common membership in the same social clubs reinforce the ability of business to get favourable state policies. The 'structuralist' view pays less attention to direct, personal links between officials and capitalists, arguing instead that state officials are obliged to treat the business class with circumspection because their political fortunes depend on a healthy economy (Block, 1977; Lindblom, 1977). When state officials implement unfavourable business policies, the business climate turns sour, causing capital flight or hesitancy in making new investments. If the economy is hurt badly enough, state officials are pressured to devise a more favourable policy.

This section looks at how the economic environment changed for the Chinese as their influence in government waned; the next section will examine whether the Chinese business class was able to exercise its 'structural' power to modify unfavourable state policies.

Although the Chinese were an ethnic minority, they played a very strong role in government in the 1960s. The leaders of the business-oriented Chinese party, the MCA, not only enjoyed close links with the top Malay leadership, but also held key economic portfolios in government. This arrangement worked to protect the Chinese business community from excessive bureaucratic interference.

However, the close ties between the Chinese business community and political leaders and the Malay leadership existed only at the apex of Malaysian society, making the Chinese position vulnerable to change in the Malay political leadership. Tun Tan Siew Sin, the MCA President from 1961 to 1974, sensed this vulnerability and occasionally exhorted Chinese businessmen to cultivate more links with the Malays, especially by way of joint ventures. In a speech given in 1966 (quoted in Morais, 1972), he said:

If, as time goes on, we can set up more and more of such joint ventures between Malays and non-Malays, particularly Chinese, the advantages will be more than merely economic. If past experience has proved anything, it has proved that mis-understanding breeds on lack of contact while understanding grows in proportion to the frequency of contact.

Except for some large Chinese businesses which gave board directorships to politically influential Malays, there was very little Chinese–Malay economic co-operation. The Chinese were more concerned with their immediate economic interests, and took for granted the congenial economic climate of the 1960s. Hence, they found little reason to cultivate stronger and closer links with the Malays which would have necessitated major changes in their business practices and assumptions. Ironically, it was the success of the MCA in defending Chinese business interests against adverse government policies that made them complacent, contributing to this short-term outlook.

When the Chinese business community did decide to help the Malays, it was too late. Just after the May 1969 racial riots, Chinese business leaders took a sudden interest in Malay economic development. In July 1969, the

President of the Associated Chinese Chambers of Commerce (ACCC), the umbrella organization of the numerous Chinese trade associations and regional chambers, sent a directive to the various local chambers asking them to help Malays sell their farm produce and fruits (*ST*, 5 July 1969). Later, in December 1969, the ACCC proposed setting up a unit trust in which the Chinese would contribute funds to be used for Sino-Malay joint ventures (*ST*, 23 December 1969). In effect, the proposal was a loan finance scheme. The President, T. H. Tan, was careful to point out that the profits would be given back to the depositors since no one should expect the Chinese to give away hard-earned money without any reward. Tan pointed out: 'We believe this fund should be participated in by all Chinese, rich and non-rich. They can contribute a dollar or a million dollars to the fund. After all, to help our Malay brothers is a matter which concerns every Chinese' (*ST*, 23 December 1969).

The government was surprisingly indifferent to the proposals of the ACCC. It turned down the unit trust scheme on the grounds that there were already too many credit and loan establishments in the country and there was no need for one more (*ST*, 26 February 1970). The government officials and politicians might have seen the ACCC's gesture as a ploy to get a licence for a finance firm, or as an ineffectual offer. However, it was also evident that the government was formulating its own economic plans for revitalizing its damaged Malay base. By not acting earlier, the Chinese had failed to remove Malay perceptions that Chinese and Malay economic development was essentially zero sum in outcome, and therefore had lost the initiative in shaping economic policies favourable to them.

The Chinese business community next hoped that the basic rules of the free market would remain intact, that the NEP meant a greater state effort to help Malays and not the restriction of Chinese business. Its spokesmen, therefore, did not protest very much over higher state spending or the establishment of state enterprises, although the President of the ACCC, Koh Pen Ting, cautioned the government in 1975 not to take the nationalist road of Britain and Burma: '. . . the adoption of nationalisation or quasi-nationalisation policies, and controls or restrictions on private enterprise in order to help bumiputras (Malays) in economic development would produce questionable effects' (*NST*, 26 May 1975).

The government leaders gave assurances that their policies would be moderate and pragmatic. In 1972, the Prime Minister, Tun Abdul Razak, stated that the government believed in free enterprise, but had to take the short-term measure of intervening in the economy to make incomes more equal (*ST*, 16 January 1972.) To give weight to these assurances, the Mid-Term Review of the Second Malaysia Plan promised that 'no particular group [would experience] any loss or [feel] any sense of deprivation in the process' (*MTR SMP*, 1973: 1).

The Chinese business community, however, was not assured for long because, by the mid-1970s, new controls and regulations had been introduced into the economy. In 1974, the government formulated the controversial Petroleum Development Act, which attempted to give the government extensive management control over companies in the petroleum and petro-chemical sectors. Although it was essentially directed at foreign companies, it was a sign of increasing government control. In 1975, the government alarmed the Chinese by introducing the Industrial Coordination Act. This act imposed a licensing system on manufacturing firms and gave the Minister of Trade and Industry enormous powers to impose conditions serving the 'national interest'. It was an important shift in policy because the NEP targets, originally defined in global terms, were now to be applied at the level of the firm.[1]

The next strategy of the the Chinese business leaders was to play up to the emerging nationalistic sentiments of the Malay leaders by targeting the foreign sector as the source of Malaysia's problems. In mid-1975, the President of the Associated Chambers said that '[t]o help the bumiputras develop their economy, we have to take back gradually what is at present in the hands of the foreigners' (*NST*, 26 May 1975). He gave full backing to Tengku Razaleigh's call for Malaysians to control their own resources, and suggested that the government gradually take back the existing 60 per cent foreign share of limited companies; at a later point, a certain portion could be redistributed to the non-Malays (*NST*, 15 July 1975). This appeal to economic nationalism by the Chinese against the foreign sector was unusual. The Chinese had always found that giving a strong role to the foreigners indirectly protected them against the state. But now, under threat, the Chinese business leaders wanted the foreigners to bear the whole burden of the NEP.

Unfortunately for the Chinese, this strategy did not succeed. One reason was that the Chinese business community had lost effective input into key economic decisions in government. The MCA party had by 1974 lost control of the Ministry of Finance as well as the Ministry of Trade and Industry. Chinese leaders were thus not in a position to determine the menu of policy options and methods for the realization of the NEP. Even if the idea of the state and the Chinese working together was a feasible one, there was no strong intellectual or political backing for it. The Malay leaders had good reasons for keeping a moderate, albeit reduced, foreign presence in the economy. While prepared to do away with the foreign role in the traditional primary export sectors, they looked to the foreigners to play a strong role in manufacturing, the anticipated leading sector of the economy.

The state élites were also not about to make the Chinese business class into a full-fledged domestic bourgeoisie. The Malays and their leaders, especially after 1969, saw Chinese economic power as a threat to Malay political status and cultural aspirations. Many Malays regarded Chinese demands, such as opposition Chinese parties calling for the abrogation of Malay special rights and Chinese educationists lobbying for a Chinese language university, as emanating from Chinese economic power. The nationalist leaders, therefore, wanted to control and dilute this power.

As state economic power and controls increased, Chinese consternation over their future grew. From the mid-1970s, Chinese businessmen acted like a besieged group. In a 1978 memorandum submitted by the Selangor

Chinese Chamber of Commerce (SCCC) to the Associated Chinese Chambers of Commerce and Industry Malaysia (ACCCIM), one business analyst described the Chinese business community as 'terribly "sick", like a patient suffering from "economic diabetes", which if not diagnosed timely and cured speedily would culminate in disastrous consequences endangering substantially national economic development' (Chin, Poky, 1978: 72). The rest of the memorandum spoke grimly of Chinese political weakness and a rigid family business system unable to cope with state-backed businesses (SCCC, 1978).

The reasons for this anxiety and pessimism were culturally rooted as well as founded on the many new constraints experienced by Chinese businesses. Chinese businesses now had to face new competition from Malay firms in their 'traditional sectors', such as construction, trade, and transport. For example, in the retail trade, the number of Malay establishments increased from 3,311 to 32,800 between 1971 and 1981; the rate of increase was much smaller for Chinese establishments, increasing from 18,957 to 55,417 in the same period (*Fifth MP*, 1986: 114). Entry was relatively easy in these sectors because of low start-up costs and the minimal expertise needed. The government, where it had direct control over entry and business opportunities, strongly favoured Malays. Licences in logging, sawmilling, timber export, vehicle import, mining, and rubber dealing were either solely or predominantly issued to Malays. In government contracts and purchases, business was heavily slanted to Malay individuals and companies. In construction, government departments in the late 1970s were reserving 30 per cent of all contracts to Malays, while in the open bids, a price preference of 2–10 per cent was given to Malay companies and state enterprises (SCCC, 1978: 15).[2] In supplies contracts, the government increasingly appointed Malay firms, especially state companies like Pernas Trading, to supply its requirements in items such as building materials, computers, elevators, and office equipment.

Even in private markets, Chinese businessmen had to face constraints, although they were not as severe. Public enterprises enjoyed special privileges from state authorities and competed with Chinese businesses to provide residential property and commercial complexes to buyers. An early source of consternation was Pernas Trading's attempt to take away some of the traditional trade conducted between overseas Chinese traders and the People's Republic of China (see Gale, 1981b: Chap. 3).

Real as these problems were, the Chinese businessmen's dire assessment of their situation was also a product of having to adjust to a new status in society. To the Chinese, their past economic strength was testimony to their acumen, diligence, adaptability, and even superiority as a race. The Selangor Chamber (1978: 12) echoed this self-image:

Their [Chinese] economic position today represents the path of painstaking and bitter efforts in the long strive to build up their share of the economic cake. In a nutshell, they started from scratch through hard work: from 'coolie' to become sundry shop operators distributing Western goods, from mine workers and rubber tappers to owners of small mines and rubber small-holdings; from intermediary merchants to shareholders of the nation's wealth.

Chinese businessmen found it difficult to accept that, in one generation Malays would achieve the stake that the Chinese had taken many generations to build up (SCCC, 1978: 15). They viewed with disquiet the emergence of a new crop of Malay senior managers running big organizations and companies and, in contrast, feared that their outmoded family system would result in Chinese businesses being stuck in the low profit sectors of the economy (ACCCIM, 1978: 103).

In politics, the Chinese business class had lost effective influence in government. The MCA and Gerakan parties were essentially reduced to placating their constituencies and reassuring them of the government's good intentions, but they could not initiate or veto any policy. The ACCCIM filled the vacuum by becoming more vociferous and active in representing Chinese business interests but its influence was limited. The Chamber was outside the government, and could not take part in the agenda-setting and deliberative processes. Chinese business interests could only react and object to policies once made. However, government ministers and officials were not predisposed to back down from their policies, and the more the Chinese protested, the more they risked being labelled as unnecessarily confrontational. In short, Malay economic and political ascendancy was inflicting a blow to the status and identity of the Chinese business community. Just like the Malays before them, the Chinese were fearing for their future in society. If, in the past, Chinese economic preponderance compensated somewhat for their subordinate political position, now it appeared that they were losing everything.

Not surprisingly, the Chinese business leaders began to show a distinct change of heart towards the NEP around 1978, questioning the basic provisions of the policy and coming close to contravening the Sensitive Issues Act, which forbade criticism of Malay special rights. The Selangor Chamber, very late in the day, quarrelled with the attempt to increase Malay ownership from 2.4 per cent to 30.0 per cent, saying it was an extremely lopsided effort to help Malays (SCCC, 1978: 15–17). During the conference of the Associated Chinese Chambers of Commerce in 1978, government bureaucrats were accused of being arrogant, inflexible, and unco-operative; state enterprises were attacked for their poor performance and for wasting public funds; and the NEP was assailed for bringing only transitory gains for some Malays (ACCCIM, 1978: 90–2). While the Chinese leaders agreed their family business system was a handicap, they saw it as one which would remedy itself over time (SCCC, 1978: 22).

For the time being, the major obstacles affecting Chinese economic status, at the grassroots level, are caused by legislation and regulations, as well as the inconsistent manner, whether it is deliberately manipulated as such or inadvertently so, by which Government socio-economic policies are being implemented. The Chinese community should strive to effect modifications of Government policies, and seek redress of whatever inconsistencies at grassroots level, as they arise. Under the present day circumstances, it is imperative that the Chinese business community strive for greater unity and co-ordination among themselves, spearhead essential transformations, and embark on a more dynamic and positive course of action in protecting and promoting their legitimate interests.

The key question was whether the Chinese business community could block or change state policies which it did not like. Over a large range of policy decisions, such as the issue of licences, the level of state spending, and the direction of state enterprise growth, Malay officials and state enterprise managers were firmly in control and bent on attaining the targets that had been set by the NEP. As long as Malay individuals and enterprises were benefiting from particular policies, it did not matter very much to the state élite if Chinese interests were being hurt. The criticisms the Chinese directed at state enterprise performance might at best lead to state officials supervising these enterprises better, but not to reducing their role.

The strongest argument for the Chinese was to demonstrate that the well-being of the Malays and the UMNO party would suffer if the Chinese economic position was badly weakened. In other words, under the circumstances, the strongest leverage of the Chinese was the exercise of their 'structural power'.

The Limits and Possibilities of Economic Protest

This section examines the limits and possibilities of Chinese protest against a policy they particularly disliked, the Industrial Coordination Act of 1975. Through this policy the government sought to impose strong administrative controls on the manufacturing sector. It is an apt policy to study because the government bureaucrats had designated manufacturing to be a leading sector in the post-1970 period; if the Chinese had any leverage over the government, it would have been demonstrated here.

The objectives for the manufacturing sector were drafted in the 'Outline Perspective Plan 1970–1990', published with the *Mid-Term Review of the Second Malaysia Plan 1971–1975* (1973). The manufacturing sector's share of GDP was projected to increase from 13.6 per cent to 35.2 per cent between 1970 and 1990, while its share of the work-force was expected to increase from 9.6 per cent to 21.7 per cent (*MTR SMP*, 1973: 68–70). Due recognition was given to the role of non-Malay entrepreneurs in the transformation. In the 'Outline', the non-Malay percentage of share capital in limited manufacturing companies was to increase from 37.9 per cent in 1970 to 40.0 per cent in 1990, while the Malay share was to increase from 2.5 per cent to 30 per cent, and the foreign share, to decline from 59.6 per cent to 30 per cent (*MTR SMP*, 1973: 86–7, Table 4-9). Of more importance was the planned increases for all groups in absolute dollar terms: from $34 million to $9.7 million for the Malays; from $804 million to $9.7 billion for the foreigners; and from $510 million to $12.9 billion (the largest) for the non-Malays. To give substance to these figures, the Mid-Term Review assured manufacturers that 'continuing efforts will be made by the government to maintain the excellent investment climate of the country, to provide fiscal incentives as may be required and to expand the supply of skilled manpower' (*MTR SMP*, 1973: 146).

For a short time, the government officials were careful not to harm the investment climate. While pursuing the NEP, they preferred to encourage the growth of state enterprises rather than impose severe controls on the private sector. The only requirement was that *new* manufacturing companies approved by the government had to make plans for reserving at least 30 per cent of their equity for Malay-based interests. At that point, such a requirement could not be said to be onerous. As many as 90 per cent of Chinese firms were outside the supervision of the various ministries. There was no legal requirement for manufacturing firms to get approvals before setting up their firms, and so many Chinese firms chose not to inform the government.[3] Only a small minority who wanted government incentives did so.

In 1975, there was a major reorientation in the Ministry of Trade and Industry's approach. The immediate rationale was that very few firms had submitted their blueprints to the government for restructuring their equity and ownership structure (*ST*, 5 March 1974). Wider political and economic forces were also at work. The Minister of Trade and Industry, Datuk Hamzah Abu Samah, was a candidate for one of the three vice-presidency posts in UMNO in June 1975. The winners could count themselves among the five most powerful men in the country. From past experience, ministers and state officials who had shown a tough-handed approach concerning the NEP were invariably rewarded with a fast track to top UMNO positions. Among Hamzah's chief competitors were some of the foremost architects of the NEP, such as Tengku Razaleigh Hamzah, Dr Mahathir Mohamad, and Ghafar Baba (see Milne, 1976: 255). There was thus a powerful motive for Datuk Hamzah to take a hard line in his Ministry and project himself as an equally avid custodian of the NEP.

The economic conditions were also very favourable. The Trade and Industry Minister and his officials could easily convince themselves that little harm could possibly result from greater state control and regulation. In 1974, the balance of payments registered a surplus of $452 million, the seventh consecutive year of surplus. The GNP grew by 12.1 per cent and 7.5 per cent in constant prices in 1973 and 1974 respectively (*AF*, September 1975: 53). In addition, new oil discoveries promised to augment national income, export earnings, and government revenues even more. In manufacturing *per se*, Malaysia received a record number of applications in 1973, around 660, compared to 300 and 400 applications in 1971 and 1972 respectively. The 1974 figure was almost as high, around 630 (see MIDA, *Annual Report*, 1977: 167). The high level of investment applications was due to large numbers of foreign textiles and electronics firms entering Malaysia to produce for export, and new state firms going into the manufacturing sector. In 1973 and 1974, the Malaysian authorities were in the unusual position of being able to pick and choose the investment projects they wanted, approving only 473 projects in 1973 and 525 projects in 1974.

In this state of mind, the Ministry of Trade formulated the Industrial Coordination Act. The Act was passed in parliament very suddenly in May 1975, with very little prior consultation with the private sector, and was to come into operation in May 1976.

When the ICA was passed, the detailed regulations governing the Act and the conditions for engaging in manufacturing had not been drafted by the Ministry. The Act only stated that '[n]o person shall engage in any manufacturing activity unless he is issued a license in respect of such manufacturing activity' (see Laws of Malaysia, Act 156, 1983: Clause 3). The Ministry exempted firms with less than $100,000 in shareholders' funds and fewer than twenty-five workers, but all other manufacturers were required to apply for a licence within one year of the Act coming into effect.

The Act's aims were stated innocuously as providing for the 'coordination and orderly development of manufacturing activities in Malaysia' (Laws of Malaysia, Act 156, 1983: 5). It was to facilitate the collection of better and more complete information on manufacturing, aid policy-making, and benefit existing manufacturers by preventing uncontrolled entry of unlicensed firms.

The private sector's response to the new controls was varied (see *AF*, December 1976/January 1977: 50). Except for the ACCCIM, none of the other chambers showed much alarm. The Malaysian International Chamber of Commerce and Industry (MICCI),[4] representing all foreign enterprises in the country, thought the Act had no particular significance for them, seeing the ICA as primarily directed at the large unlicensed Chinese sector (MICCI, *Yearbook*, 1975/6: 55). The Malay Chamber of Commerce and Industry showed little dismay, since further government regulations only promised to favour their interests. The ACCCIM, on the other hand, was hostile to the ICA from the very beginning. It felt that the Act was targeted primarily at the Chinese community and questioned the government's reasons for introducing it. The Chinese representatives argued that there were enough information-gathering bodies in existence, so that the ICA was superfluous.

The Chinese never enjoyed good relations with the bureaucracy, and feared further rules. Besides making life more difficult, regulations only increased their business costs because of the need to make under-the-counter payments to overcome bureaucratic intransigence. However, in 1975 and early 1976, the Chinese 'found themselves somewhat helpless and isolated because the other communities were not much worried by it [the ICA] at that time' (*AF*, December 76/January 77: 50).

In mid-1976, when the detailed regulations pertaining to the Act were drafted, the true meaning and scope of the ICA became clear. The provisions gave the Minister, armed with the prerogative to revoke or not issue the licence, extensive powers to control detailed aspects of a company's activities. Clause 4 stated: 'The Minister shall, in deciding whether an application for a license should be approved or refused, consider whether the issue of a license is expedient in the national interest and would promote the orderly development of manufacturing activities in Malaysia' (*MB*, June 1977: 12).

The Act itself did not spell out what comprised the 'national interest', which was left to the Trade and Industry officials to determine. Among the more important conditions the Ministry imposed were:[5]

1. Malaysian firms had to put aside at least 30 per cent of their equity for Malay interests. Foreign firms producing for the domestic market or using depleting resources had to provide 70 per cent ownership for Malaysians, out of which a minimum of 30 per cent was to go to Malay interests. For the export-oriented firms, foreigners could hold anywhere from 100 per cent to minority equity positions, depending on how much they exported and how much they depended on local materials.

2. All companies (that is, non-Malay) had to employ and train Malaysian citizens as far as possible, and at the earliest opportunity, to reflect the multiracial composition of the country's population in all grades of appointment up to the managerial level.

3. All companies had to adopt concrete measures over a reasonable period of time to use Malay distributors to the maximum extent possible, the minimum being 30 per cent of turnover.

4. The ex-factory price of products sold in Malaysia could not exceed the prevailing cost, insurance, and freight (cif) prices of equivalent imported products. Companies could not increase their prices unless the Ministry approved such a move.

5. Companies had to use local materials, components, and parts at least to the level indicated in their approved licences.

6. All agreements for starting-up operations, employment of expatriate personnel, technical know-how and assistance, trademarks and service, royalties, and marketing had to receive prior approval from the Ministry in writing before becoming effective.

Besides these new, more onerous conditions imposed on manufacturing companies, the ICA gave the Minister of Trade and Industry enormous discretionary power. An existing licence could not be transferred without his permission, and whatever conditions imposed on a licence could be varied 'either on the application of the manufacturer or on the Minister's own motion' (Clause 4, Section 4). Firms were also given very little room for manoeuvre when meeting the Minister's regulations. They could not vary the type of products and production volumes specified in their licences—increasing the capacity for a product line or substituting an existing product needed the Minister's permission. Even the deletion of an existing product needed prior approval, effectively giving the Minister the power to make a firm go on producing even when it was unprofitable to do so.

The ICA was a major departure in the country's industrial policy, not only in making the NEP the foremost objective, but also in expanding government power over firms. Not surprisingly, a wider segment of the private sector found the Act to be prejudicial to their interests. By the end of 1976, the International Chamber, MICCI, joined the ACCCIM to ask for changes to the ICA. Both agreed that the ICA brought enormous uncertainty to business planning, was a disincentive to investment, and put firms at the mercy of arbitrary decisions made by the Minister and his staff. The central complaint was the power of the Minister to change the rules and conditions of the ICA in mid-stream, once the decision to invest had been made. Such changes would violate the initial business plans and financial premises of the investment decision, which was not only unfair, but would also seriously damage the investment climate. The business representatives were also very much against those aspects of the ICA which threatened to substitute administrative fiat for basic managerial decisions. Only the firm's boardroom should decide, in response to market conditions, the price of a product, production cut-backs, and the product mix of a manufacturing operation. Finally, both Chambers resented the lack of an appeals mechanism in the Act to counter inflexible bureaucrats who, in spite of promises of fair play by their political masters, were apt to follow the letter rather than the spirit of the law.

Despite agreeing on many common points, the ACCCIM and the MICCI diverged on how much the ICA had to be altered. The ACCCIM insisted on the total repeal of the Act while the MICCI, acquiescing to the idea of linking the ICA with NEP objectives, only wanted sufficient modifications so that its existing members could live with it. The source of this divergence was in the different business organizations of the two groups and their sense of what was fair treatment.

Foreign firms were corporate bureaucracies with wide geographical interests. For most, their operations in Malaysia were only a small part of their parent's overall activities. Their 'bottom line' was to get a rate of return commensurate with the riskiness of the investment. The whole question of equity shares was not as critical to the firm as arbitrary changes in the conditions governing their operations. It was mid-stream changes in equity, sudden limitations on foreign managerial personnel, and bureaucratic controls on prices which threatened a firm's original investment assumptions. In these areas, the MICCI wanted changes. As for the question of equity, the MICCI regarded it as the prerogative of the host country to set. An incoming firm would have to decide for itself whether it was worth investing or not.[6] Many firms, from their experiences elsewhere, had become used to the idea of joint ownership.[7] Furthermore, there were other ways of making profits. In a survey of joint ventures between foreign and public corporations in Malaysia, Abdul Razak Abdul (1984: 272–89) found that foreign partners were able to exercise strong control through the use of loans, supply of technology, and by arranging special veto powers over important managerial decisions. In many cases, profits came not from having high equity stakes but from the exercise of managerial control, transfer pricing, management fees, interest on inter-company debts, and payments for various kinds of special services.

The MICCI was therefore not interested in defending abstract principles of free enterprise. The Chamber wanted fair consideration for firms which had been set up before the ICA, a mutually agreeable price for foreign firms divesting, and the assurance that no new conditions and restrictions would be imposed once a firm had complied with government policies.

In contrast, the Chinese business sector was against any form of government control in the manufacturing sector. Although the equity levels imposed on Chinese firms for Malay interests were sometimes lower than for the foreigners (particularly in domestic-oriented production), they viewed the ICA as an attack on the whole Chinese business system, particularly family-based enterprises. In a 1971 survey of manufacturing establishments, 65 per cent of the firms surveyed were either sole proprietorships and partnerships, all essentially family businesses. Many of the remaining 35 per cent or so private limited companies were also family-based organizations (Department of Statistics, 1971). These family businesses, unlike corporate bureaucracies, did not operate just to maximize profits, but were in important ways founded on non-economic lines. The 'old man', as the owner is often called, saw the organization as providing security for his family, as a way of linking the generations together, and ensuring independence by being one's own boss.

The ICA threatened this tightly knit structure, especially in its equity and employment rules. A high official of the Selangor Chinese Chamber, in an interview in January 1985, described the problem as follows:

Chinese businesses are mainly small-to-medium scaled. They are not recent companies or new entrants, but have been established for a long time. There is resentment, especially among the older generation, to a newcomer coming in and getting 30 per cent of the firm. This is difficult to accept after so many years of risk-taking, hard work, and sacrificing consumption for the well-being of the family. There is a great individualistic feeling of success, and sharing a business with anybody is very difficult. If there are partners, they are individually picked; workers too. A businessman won't even bring in partners and people from the same race or clan if they are not familiar. Malays belong to a different culture, race, and religion. Perhaps if the old man dies, the next generation will get Malay partners for the opportunities he brings.

The Chinese also used a different criterion of fairness than the foreigners in assessing the ICA. The Chinese claimed that they had no place to go, unlike the foreign multinationals, which came and went freely. They were citizens of the country and had a stake in national development. The government was already discriminating against them in civil service recruitment and educational enrolment. Only the Chinese could be counted on to employ their own in Malaysia, yet the ICA threatened the last sanctuary of Chinese employment (see ACCCIM, 1978: 99). Chinese businessmen also regarded it as unfair that Malays could pick and choose profitable companies for ownership, while ignoring the unprofitable and struggling ones, and thus incur no risks whatsoever. In addition, the Ministry also reserved the right to choose the Malay partners, appoint the distributors, and set the share price of the firm.

The Chinese business leaders resolved that the government had no business interfering with their existing establishments. The ACCCIM's strategy to fight the ICA was to get the whole private sector to adopt its own position against the government. It planned to use the National Chamber of Commerce and Industry as a platform.[8] The National Chamber comprised the various chambers of the ethnic groups, the International Chamber, and the Federation of Malaysian Manufacturers (FMM). The FMM comprised mostly Chinese manufacturers but also had foreign and Malay representation. When the National Chamber met in early 1977 to submit a joint memorandum to the government on the ICA, the

ACCCIM representatives insisted that the whole body vote to repeal the ICA. The ACCCIM threatened to block any other position, invoking the National Chamber's convention that decisions had to be taken unanimously (*AF*, 15 December 1976/14 January 1977). However, the ACCCIM failed in its bid and was forced by the other component chambers to state its demand for repeal as a minority and dissenting position. The majority recommendation of the National Chamber to the government was: (1) to set up an independent appeals mechanism for aggrieved manufacturers, and (2) to form a private sector industrial advisory committee which had the power to convene meetings with the Minister on industrial policy. The meetings of the existing Consultative Committee on Trade and Industry could be initiated only by the Minister.

The ACCCIM was again isolated. The Malay chambers were willing to see changes that would improve the investment climate without weakening the government's capacity to make firms comply with the NEP. This was a rational stand from the Malay point of view because their industrial expansion could not proceed without the capital, technology, and marketing support of the other private sector actors. The FMM, reflecting its membership composition, took an intermediate position; it did not press for a repeal but was the strongest advocate for the appeals mechanism and advisory committee. It also recommended that the cut-off point for exempting firms from the ICA be raised to $1 million in shareholders' funds (*AF*, 15 August 1978). The MICCI was the most moderate of all the non-Malay representatives. It accepted the NEP as a *fait accompli* and merely pressed for the removal of the excesses and inconsistencies in the ICA. The Chamber was not willing to unnecessarily alienate the government by asking for a repeal. The British Executive Director of the MICCI, in an interview in February 1985, expressed the position of the International Chamber as follows:

We try very hard to live with the socio-economic realities of a country. In Malaysia, we accept that there cannot be free enterprise. We show how government's policies affect investment and if the broad objectives of the government are consistent with implementation of policy. . . . The Chinese were adopting an explicitly political position by going against the government. We don't see our role that way.

It was ironic that men brought up in the home of Manchester liberalism were making allowances for strong state intervention while those with roots in the bureaucratic polities of East Asia were pressing for free enterprise. Had the MICCI taken the same position as the ACCCIM, the private sector challenge to the government would have been formidable.

It was unrealistic of the ACCCIM to expect solidarity from the Malay Chamber, but getting the MICCI's support was possible. As a provider of essential export markets and technological inputs for Malaysia's industrial development, the foreign sector could not easily be brushed aside. However, the foreign sector chose not to ally with the Chinese, which severely weakened the ACCCIM's position. The government was thus not compelled to pacify Chinese interests when it could first accommodate the foreign sector. State officials, for their part, could easily satisfy themselves that the Chinese were being negative for political reasons rather than advancing a genuine grievance since foreign companies, many of which had stricter equity conditions than Chinese manufacturers, were prepared to accommodate.

The initial response of the government to the private sector's complaints was to soft-pedal the import of the Act and accuse the manufacturers of over-reaction. The Deputy Prime Minister at the time, Dr Mahathir Mohamad, said to the Federation of Manufacturers (quoted in MICCI, *Yearbook*, 1976/7: 125):

I would like to re-iterate the Government's determination to implement the Act with pragmatism and the maximum of flexibility. You have my assurance that the Act will not be allowed to become a disincentive to private investment, for it is our fervent belief that the ICA will provide a healthy environment for industries to prosper for the mutual benefit of the nation as well as for investors, local and foreign.

Notwithstanding these assurances, the officials had to contend with the real investment picture. In 1975, there were only 471 applications for manufacturing projects (that is, new as well as expansion projects), a decrease of 157 from 1974 (FIDA, *Annual Report*, 1975: 108). Officials in both the Ministry of Finance and the Federal Industrial Development Authority blamed the general recessionary climate in the region for the shortfall, arguing that the decline in manufacturing investment was not unique to that sector (Ministry of Finance, 1975: 57). The argument weakened in 1976 as manufacturing investment worsened—a 16 per cent decline in applications compared to 1975 while overall private investment picked up (FIDA, 1976: 159; Ministry of Finance, 1976: 68). Whether they liked it or not, the government officials had to take cognizance of the ICA's effect on the investment climate, even as they dismissed the notion that the ICA, on its own terms, was a disincentive to investment.

On 30 April 1977, the government announced a number of amendments to the ICA (*FEER*, 6 May 1977: 38–42). The salient changes were: (1) the appointment of a licensing officer, who would be the issuing authority for ICA licences. This arrangement was an appeals mechanism of sorts because the Minister could now act as an appellate; (2) requiring the licensing officer to consult the manufacturer before varying the conditions of a manufacturing licence; (3) revoking the need for manufacturers to obtain prior approval before ceasing to manufacture a product; (4) making it easier to transfer licences under certain circumstances, such as death, incapacity, and bankruptcy of a holder; (5) allowing a revoked manufacturing licence to remain in force until an appeal had been heard; (6) excluding firms with less than $250,000 in shareholder funds and fewer than twenty-five workers from the Act, and (7) freeing firms with less than $500,000 in fixed investments from the equity condition. This last provision was undoubtedly aimed at placating the Chinese business sector.

The amendments removed the most objectionable aspects of the Act, but left intact the objective of enforcing the NEP through bureaucratic controls. The response from the foreign sector was far more positive than from the Chinese sector. The President of the MICCI, Mr Willey, in his presidential address to his Chamber regarded the amendments as a sincere move by the government to create a more favourable investment climate. He did point out that potential investors still harboured fears of living with the Act as presently constituted (MICCI, *Yearbook*, 1977/8). The Chamber's lingering concern was the absence of a consultative process which would help ensure that the ICA was applied consistently and would not undergo dramatic changes in the future. As for the ACCCIM, its members held an extraordinary meeting on 3 May 1977 and unanimously voted for the government to repeal the Act (*NST*, 4 May 1977). The ACCCIM considered the exemption of a wider segment of companies a minor concession, doing little to curtail the enormous powers of the Minister and to remove bureaucratic interference in the economy.

The government made another concession on the ICA in June 1979, when it added an amendment to allow for an Industrial Advisory Council to advise the Minister on all matters pertaining to the ICA. It was to comprise seventeen members; seven from the private sector, eight from the government, and two appointees of the Minister. Its bureaucratic representation was much stronger than the private sector had contemplated, but the MICCI welcomed the Council and, as expected, the ACCCIM, while not dismissing the latest government gesture, still considered repeal of the ICA as the only acceptable move. By the late 1970s, the ICA had ceased to become a critical issue with the foreign sector businessmen. They had acquired from the government roughly what they had asked for. The MICCI's position was to leave it to individual firms to decide on the merits of investing in Malaysia.

The Chinese were not successful at getting the government to substantially modify the ICA for the whole decade between 1975 and 1985. Even when Dr Mahathir Mohamad, who was regarded as being more open to business views, became Prime Minister in 1981, his message to the ACCCIM was blunt (*NST*, 7 August 1981):

It is not formed to oppose the government or government policies. Once this is realized, it will be seen that the objectives of the chamber can be achieved not by blind opposition but by carefully examining Government policies in order to take advantage of these policies.

Before we examine further why the government could ignore the fundamental demands of the Chinese business sector, let us first consider how Chinese investments in manufacturing have fared with the NEP and the ICA. Figure 5.1 demonstrates quite clearly that they have had a depressing effect on non-Bumiputra (that is, non-Malay) investments, which are essentially Chinese investments, and thus will be referred to as such. Chinese investments in 1971, before the full-scale implementation, comprised 66.9 per cent of all investments.[9] Since 1972 the percentage share of Chinese investments has fallen drastically. Before the ICA, Chinese investments were on the average just above 30 per cent, but since the ICA have fallen below 30 per cent, except for 1984. Certainly, Chinese investments have been below the 40 per cent target set for them in manufacturing

FIGURE 5.1
Non-Bumiputra Equity in Manufacturing Projects
Granted Approval, 1971–1985
(percentage share and nominal value)

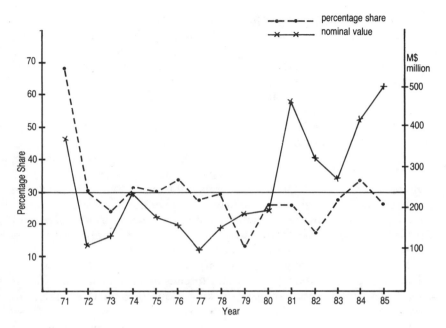

Source: MIDA, Annual Reports, 1971–85.
Note: Tourist and hotel complexes are not included in the years 1983–5.

in the NEP. The sluggishness of Chinese investments is also striking when the actual value of approved investments is considered. In 1971, Chinese investments totalled $377 million but the figure has been exceeded only on a few occasions—in 1981, 1984, and 1985.[10] If constant 1970 prices had been used, the figures in the 1980s would have been deflated by more than half, making the Chinese hesitancy in investing even more obvious.

Historically, Chinese businessmen in Malaysia, even under the best of circumstances, were wary of going into manufacturing. The opportunities for making good money in safe investments such as property development, plantations, tin-mining, and financial institutions were too alluring compared to the greater demands and risks of manufacturing. The new restrictions further exacerbated the lack of attraction of manufacturing. Prospective investors, who in normal circumstances would have initiated projects, found the pay-off simply not worth the effort. An official in MIDA described the Chinese manufacturers' dilemma as follows:[11]

Chinese businessmen do initiate projects because they can't wait for partners, whether foreign or Malay to come to them. But many Chinese firms need some kind of foreign technical or technological input because their sophistication isn't very high. This means that they have to give equity participation to foreigners and

Malays. For example, if it is an export-oriented project, they might have to give the foreign partner 49 per cent. The Malay partner takes another 30 per cent. The Chinese partner ends up with 20. This is so little considering that he does all the homework, and goes through all the initial trouble. It surely deters many and lessens their will to invest.

Government leaders frequently placed the blame for non-investment on the Chinese themselves. Sometimes they accused the Chinese of dwelling on irrational fears and, at other times, of lacking the necessary expertise to go beyond manufacturing the simplest products. In 1979, the Prime Minister, Datuk Hussein Onn, chided the private sector for being pre-occupied with negative rather than positive factors and warned them against living in an environment of perpetual doubt and fear (*BT* (S), 19 May 1979). The Finance Minister, Tengku Razaleigh, criticized the 'paucity of depth and vision in the private sector, compared to the intellectual leadership and influence exerted in other parts of the world' (*ST* (S), 29 May 1978). In late 1979, the Deputy Prime Minister also expressed disappointment in the modern generation of Chinese, whom he said were losing their traditional role as the driving force of the Malaysian economy. He argued that Chinese capital expanded only because of government policies requiring Malaysian participation in foreign companies. Otherwise, they would be worse off (*BT* (S), 29 August 1979).

Many of the views of government officials were self-fulfilling in nature. The correlation between Chinese and foreign manufacturing investment was negative rather than positive, making it questionable that foreign investments were the motor of Chinese manufacturing expansion. These were issues the politicians were not willing to thoroughly investigate. They had other options, in the form of state-based investments as well as foreign investments. The message to the Chinese was clear: either invest on the government's terms, or fall behind.

Figures 5.2 and 5.3 illustrate how foreign and Malay investments acted to offset the sluggishness in Chinese manufacturing investments. First, let us consider foreign manufacturing investments. When government officials realized that Chinese investments were not going to be strong, they set about attracting foreign investment. Their first task was to reverse the substantial decline in foreign investment in 1975 and 1976, resulting from global recession and uncertainty about the ICA. From 1977 onwards, top government officials, nearly always headed by Dr Mahathir, went on numerous investment missions abroad, selling Malaysia and exorcizing doubts and uncertainties about the Malaysian government's economic policies. The high-level delegation highlighted Malaysia's good labour relations, political stability, and leadership commitment to foreign investment, and visited business groups and prominent businessmen in Western Europe, the US, Eastern Europe, Japan, and Hong Kong. Stressing Malaysia's lower wage costs, the delegates sought to attract companies suffering from high wages and cost increases in their respective countries.

These missions apparently paid off. Foreign investment picked up after 1977, helped by the general improvement in world economic conditions.

FIGURE 5.2

Non-Bumiputra and Foreign Equity in Manufacturing Projects
Granted Approval, 1971–1985
(percentage share)

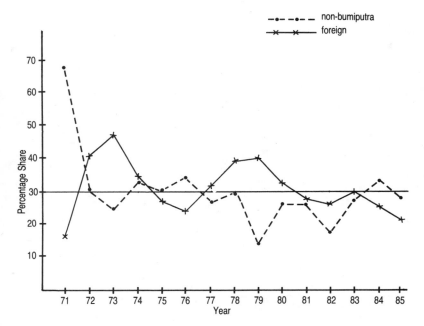

Source: MIDA, *Annual Reports*, 1971–85.
Note: Tourist and hotel complexes are not included in the years 1983–5.

The government managed to get new investments from labour-intensive,
export-oriented firms in the US and Japan. Investment also came from
new areas, such as Germany and Australia, in engineering products and
palm oil-based food products. Figure 5.2 shows that the percentage of
foreign investment, except for 1984 and 1985, has been higher than Chinese
investment since 1977. The highest levels recorded were in the late 1970s,
when Chinese investments were at their nadir. In the early 1980s, foreign
investment declined, but generally stayed around 30 per cent, the figure
the government set for foreign participation. The sharp decline in the
mid-1980s has prodded the government to come up with new incentives
for foreign investment, which will be discussed in Chapter 6.

Figure 5.3, on the relationship between approved Bumiputra equity and
approved Chinese equity from 1971 to 1985, shows the state was even
more important than the foreign sector in shoring up manufacturing investments. Since 1975, Malay-based investments,[12] except in 1978, have
been systematically above 40 per cent, reaching a peak of 56.3 per cent in
1982. The manufacturing projects were of all types, from the dispersed
manufacturing investments of the SEDCs and Pernas, to the heavy industrial projects undertaken by HICOM.

The state's ability to provide employment, especially to Malays, and

FIGURE 5.3

Non-Bumiputra and Bumiputra Equity in Manufacturing Projects
Granted Approval, 1971–1985
(percentage share)

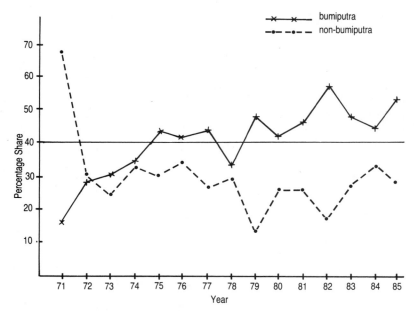

Source: MIDA, *Annual Reports*, 1971–85.
Note: Tourist and hotel complexes are not included in the years 1983–5.

engage in industrial projects on its own gave it a strong lever over Chinese
businessmen. This partly explains why the Chinese, despite vociferous
protests, only managed to get minor concessions from the state.

The same logic, in which the state and to a lesser extent, foreign capital,
acted to offset Chinese sluggishness in investing, applies at the general
macro-economic level. This fact can be demonstrated by examining the
original targets and actual outcomes of the Fourth Malaysia Plan (1981–5).

The drastic shortfall in planned private sector investment, a rough
proxy for Chinese investment, resulted in the state pumping in an enormous amount of its own resources, almost double what it planned, in the
Fourth Malaysia Plan (see Table 5.1). In addition, the government relied
on greater inflows of capital from abroad to buttress 'private' investment.

However, the recourse to state investment as a compensatory factor did
not mean that the state was able to achieve its targets for manufacturing.
For example, manufacturing's share of GDP stood at 19.1 per cent in 1985
and is projected to reach only 20.5 per cent in 1990, far short of the original
target of 35.2 per cent set in 1973 (*Fifth MP*, 1986: 62). Clearly, the
government's failure to provide a conducive climate for the full-scale
mobilization of domestic resources and talent was a factor. And, although
the government was able to maintain high growth rates between 1970 and

TABLE 5.1
Public and Private Investment/Expenditure,
Fourth Malaysia Plan, 1981–1985
(in M$ million)

Investment/Expenditure	Original Target	Actual Result
A. Public development expenditure	42,830	80,331
B. Private investment	74,111	62,198
1. Self-financing of private sector	52,585	39,027
2. Public sector financing of 'private investment'	12,121	10,060
3. Private long-term capital inflow	9,405	13,111

Source: FoMP, 1981: 255; Fifth MP, 1986: 209.

1984—through enormous public spending—the cost paid was very high since public debt has become a major problem.

This section has argued that as long as the state had plentiful resources and was able to get adequate amounts of foreign participation, the Chinese business sector was in a weak position to challenge unpalatable policies. Differences in interests between the foreign sector and the Chinese sector made it difficult for the Chinese to mobilize a common private sector stand against government policies.[13] Chinese businesses had to resign themselves to state policies, and seek ways of protecting their stake within the rules set by the government.

The NEP and Chinese Strategies of Accommodation

The NEP, which brought new regulations, unwanted competition, and constricted markets for the Chinese, made them think of ways of preserving their economic stake in the country. It was not only individual business-men who tried to find an economic niche for themselves, but also Chinese political and representative organizations, such as the MCA and the ACCCIM, who felt they needed to increase Chinese economic and political leverage by direct involvement in business.

A distinction needs to be made between the large Chinese businessmen and their smaller counterparts. Their enterprises not only face different environmental pressures but also diverge in the responses they are able to make. We will discuss each in turn.

Small- and medium-scale businesses are concentrated in the retail and wholesale trades, transport, and in the lower end of the construction and manufacturing sectors. Since they tend to have low profit margins, Malay businesses are usually not interested in becoming shareholders in them; thus the question of being forced to bring in outside partners does not arise (Tan Tat Wai, 1982: 303). Their problems are of a different order, such as increased competition and the loss of government contracts re-sulting from Malay entry in business. For example, in construction, the government gave out contracts to Malays generously, especially in small-scale jobs. In agricultural wholesaling activities, government agencies such as the Malaysian Rubber Corporation (Mardec) and the Padi and Rice Board (LPN) invested heavily in processing rubber and rice, getting involved not only in distribution and exports but also in appointing Malay dealers as produce collectors and wholesalers (see Gosling, 1983: 159).

As a result, Chinese small businesses suffered, especially in construction and wholesaling.[14] Nonetheless, they enjoyed a number of 'in-built' advantages which forestalled any serious deterioration in business activity. Their strength lay in the buyer–seller–retail nexus, linking customers, retail shops, and wholesalers into a tight network. Because buying decisions are influenced by ethnic ties and loyalties, Chinese retailers were able to depend on the large urban Chinese population for a secure business. Unless Malay retail and service establishments could offer better prices, credit terms, and the same range of products, they could not easily penetrate the Chinese consumer market.

The figures bear this out. The number of Malay retail establishments increased from 13 per cent to 34 per cent of total retail establishments between 1971 and 1981 while the Chinese share fell from 74.6 per cent to 57.7 per cent (*Fifth MP*, 1986: 114). In terms of turnover, however, the Malay share only increased from 3 per cent to 11.5 per cent while the Chinese fell only from 81.2 per cent to 74.6 per cent. Indeed, the average Chinese retailer increased his turnover from $70,000 to $180,000 in the ten-year period, while his Malay counterpart increased his from $15,000 to $46,700. These figures suggest that Malays were competing against each other for a limited market.

In businesses requiring some skill, as in certain services, the Chinese were able to expand even further. For example, the turnover of Chinese photographic studios as a percentage of total turnover increased from 93.1 per cent to 96.5 per cent, and in hair-dressing and beauty salons, from 63.2 per cent to 73.3 per cent. The already small Malay shares fell even further in both. Although no figures are available, the Chinese also seemed to dominate the sale of home computers and their accessories, having developed sufficient expertise to perform on-premise repairs and to give customer advice on software and hardware.

The Chinese retail strength also allowed Chinese wholesalers to maintain their dominant role in urban markets outside the government sector. The close connection between wholesalers and retailers played a critical role in warding off market encroachments from Malay companies and state corporations. This fact was amply demonstrated in early 1985 when Chinese wholesalers frustrated Pernas's attempt to displace them in the import of perishables and fruits for the Chinese New Year festivities.[15] In 1985, Pernas set up its own company, Satria Utara Sdn Bhd, in association with other Malay businessmen, to buy 410,000 crates of mandarin oranges. It then denied, for the first time, permits to the traditional Chinese wholesalers (*ST* (S), 24 January 1985). After strong protest from Chinese merchants, Pernas, at the last minute, issued thirty-three Approved Permits to Chinese wholesalers and cancelled 270,000 crates of its own order. Pernas had to pay a penalty of $1 million to the shippers in the process. While it was too late for the Chinese wholesalers to import, they refused to buy Satria's remaining shipments in spite of the great symbolic value of the oranges during the Chinese New Year. Instead, fruit sellers sold Colifornian Sunkist oranges and Chinese customers were content to celebrate their New Year with an 'imitation' product. Pernas did not make the same mistake in 1986. However, this economic action by the Chinese was a circumscribed form of economic power. It could help the Chinese keep away state intrusions in markets where Chinese were the dominant customers but it could not shape broad national priorities, such as the nature of state spending and the government's ethnic priorities.

Chinese small businesses have also survived by slipping through the state's regulatory net or reach. One common practice was Ali–Babaism, a local colloquialism describing the situation when a Malay front acts as a shield for a Chinese businessman. This practice was prevalent in construction, transport, and agricultural wholesaling, where the government zealously issued licences to Malays while limiting them to the Chinese. Nonini (1983: 195) describes how the relationship works in the truck transport business in a north Malaysian town. The Malays, in return for 'procuring the truck operating permits from the Ministry of Transport and by being available to hold shares of private limited companies . . . receive monthly or lump sum payments from their Chinese colleagues in each transport company'. Most Malays, according to Nonini, distrust their Chinese associates and prefer a known monthly payment to an uncertain dividend arrangement.

The inefficiency of the state bureaucratic apparatus has sometimes worked to the advantage of the Chinese. In construction, Malays, who might hold several government contracts, are nonetheless unable to proceed with their jobs because of cash flow problems. These are often brought about by having to wait as long as five months before finding out if their loan applications have been approved by the state financial institutions. Rather than risk losing their contracts, they enter into an Ali–Baba relationship, where the Chinese confederate puts up the cash and does all the work, providing the Malay with an assured return (NST, 1 December 1978).

Manufacturers have also been known to restrict the size of their businesses or split up an existing company into two or more units in order to remain inside the ICA threshold.[16] In the latter case, an offshoot company is given a completely new identity, and has, in name, a new owner, who usually is another member of the family or a trusted associate. Presumably this practice is undertaken by manufacturers who are adamant about restructuring their enterprises, because they do not want Malay partners or fear they will have to sell off their shares cheaply. However, they are obviously enjoying sufficiently good sales to be willing to go through the trouble of undertaking this complex arrangement.

These practices are the second best option, and not the preferred choice of the small-scale Chinese businessman. They are strategies for making the best of a constrained environment. Splitting up companies does not contribute toward rationalizing production or management, or saving on transportation costs. The profit margins are probably very thin as well, since the generous supply of permits to Malays adds to excessive competition.

Chinese big business comprises individuals who own some of the country's largest companies and conglomerates. Their accumulated wealth, knowledge, and ability to mobilize funds gives them many advantages not available to the small businessman. Many of the large Chinese businesses were able to grow rapidly during the NEP's expansionary period, made possible by the oil and commodity boom. This growth, however, cannot be attributed to a state–Chinese capitalist alliance.[17] The large businesses were able to take advantage of their historical strengths to benefit from high growth, despite the state's regulations. Many would have been happier if there had been no NEP.

In general, large Chinese companies are less concerned about being displaced than about how to expand further. The minimum requirement is the ability to offer at least 30 per cent ownership to Malay interests. Indeed, failure to do so can result in co-ordinated attempts by the various state regulatory agencies to hurt the company's business. Selangor Properties, a publicly listed property development company, was controlled and largely owned by Dato T. K. Wen and his family up to 1983. In the early 1980s, its associate company, Bungsar Hill, which was also mostly owned by the Wen family, planned to develop a 54-acre tract of land in Kuala Lumpur into a town centre. However, the government announced in 1982 that it was going to acquire most of the site (see KLSE, 1984: 832–3). Following protracted negotiations with government departments, the notice of acquisition was withdrawn, but not until Selangor Properties agreed to restructure the ownership of the company. Both Datuk Ibrahim Mohammed, one of the members of the new Malay 'bourgeoisie', and Koperasi Bersatu Bhd, an investment arm of the UMNO party, were given a 30 per cent share of Selangor Properties at a marked-down price (see *Insight*, April 1983: 45–6).

The example of Selangor Properties—besides showing how the state exercises its leverage—also demonstrates the willingness of large Chinese corporations to get rid of their former exclusivity and adopt a more multiracial complexion. Being large, they have the financial power and the incentive to absorb the costs of incorporating Malay partners. Indeed, the owner need not lose much money when giving new Malay shareholders substantial discounts[18] because he can first go public before restructuring, selling the company to Chinese middle-class investors, while retaining a sufficient stake for managerial control. In this way the new shareholders can be made to bear a portion of the cash discounts given to Malay interests.

Incorporating Malay partners, however, does not solve all the problems of big Chinese businesses. They are still considered 'non-Malay' by government departments[19] and must therefore line up behind state corporations and Malay businesses in the queue for getting land, government contracts, or buying into lucrative foreign companies. While restructured companies may not be as harassed by the government as non-restructured ones, they still operate in a constrained and uncertain environment.

The regulated environment has led many large Chinese businesses to take a short-term view of their economic activities. This mind-set results in finding the quickest way to realize profits. The following characteristics are common among large Chinese businesses: (1) a gravitation toward commercial projects, especially property development instead of manufacturing; (2) a heavy reliance on take-overs and mergers instead of starting fresh companies as a means of expansion, and (3) the spread of their assets and activities outside Malaysia.

A good example combining these three facets is Malayan United Industries (or MUI), one of the largest capitalized corporations in Malaysia. MUI was founded in 1960 by Khoo Kay Peng, a Malaysian-born Chinese who started off as a clerk in Singapore's Overseas Chinese Banking Corporation (OCBC) in the 1950s (*Insight*, March 1982: 50). Khoo, like many who passed through OCBC, was able to use his banking experience to propel himself into the world of big business. After his stint in the bank, Khoo went into the manufacture of enamel household utensils and, later, of tooth-brushes and paper products. In 1971, MUI went public and Khoo, by winning the stock market's confidence, expertly used his company's high-priced shares to acquire new companies by share swaps and raising cash from the public (*FEER*, 6 March 1981: 60). The most rapid expansion came between 1979 and 1984, when MUI's paid-up capital increased from $11.5 million to $823.5 million. The company became a large conglomerate with assets in property, finance, hotels, and manufacturing.

Since the 1960s, MUI has tended to refrain from establishing new projects in manufacturing. Its industrial involvement has primarily been the acquisition and selling of existing manufacturing companies. In the mid-1970s, MUI acquired Central Sugars, an ailing sugar-refining concern, which also owned other substantial assets, among them 50 per cent equity of a cash-rich cement company, Pan-Malayan Cement Works. In 1983, Central Sugars Refinery was sold for a large profit to Pernas and Grenfell Holdings. MUI has ventured into new manufacturing projects only when the risks involved are small, such as the manufacture of ready-mixed concrete and concrete beams for its property development projects (*BT* (S), 24 February 1984).

MUI's main domestic effort has been in commercial banking and acquiring properties. In finance, Khoo's strategy has been to acquire small companies and build them into national entities. In the mid-1970s, MUI bought Tong Bee Finance Bhd, a Chinese-owned financial and leasing company. At the time, it had only two branches, a deposit base of $2.8 million, and a loan portfolio of $3.3 million. By injecting MUI's resources and expertise, the company became by 1984 the third largest non-bank finance company in the country, with eleven branches, $861 million in deposits, and a loan portfolio of $626 million (*MB*, 16 May 1985: 89). In 1982, MUI went into commercial banking by taking over Kwong Lee Bank, one of the smaller commercial banks in the country, through a share swap. After just two years, the bank, renamed MUI Bank, tripled its loans syndication and vastly expanded its branch network. In property, MUI acquired a number of large hotels, and built office and commercial complexes in Kuala Lumpur's prime business area.

While MUI has seized business opportunities in Malaysia when possible, the company has also diversified internationally to escape the constraints of Malaysia's regulated environment. Most of its acquisitions have
been in the property area. In the mid-1980s, MUI, through its subsidiary,
Malayan United Manufacturing, bought properties in Canada, including a
first-class hotel in Vancouver, and developed an international hotel-cum-
office complex in downtown Perth, Australia (*BT* (S), 25 February 1984).
MUI's other international investments include a property investment
company in California, a food distributing chain in Western Australia,
hotel chains (under the 'Ming Court' banner) in Hong Kong, Singapore,
and Canada, and a host of miscellaneous companies in the US, Singapore,
and Hong Kong (see KLSE, 1984: 324–6). Its diverse geographical
spread earned it the title 'Malaysia's first home-grown multinational' from
the local stockbroking and journalistic communities.

Despite MUI's high public profile, Khoo Kay Peng is believed to retain
substantial ownership in the company. One of his private companies,
KKP Holdings, alone holds 18 per cent of the paid-up capital of the $832
million company (*MB*, 16 May 1985: 90).

Most of the large Chinese companies share MUI's strategy and pattern
of expansion, although on a smaller scale. Even companies which began as
manufacturers have avoided manufacturing in their later development,
going instead into property and finance. For instance, Lien Hoe Industries was started in 1969 by the Tee family to manufacture a wide range
of building materials, such as wooden doors and zinc ridges (KLSE,
1974: 435). It went public in 1970, but kept to manufacturing in the
early 1970s, producing sulphates used by palm oil and rubber factories (*MB*,
September 1983: 125). In the 1980s, Lien Hoe changed its strategy. It
sold off some of its interests in building materials and chemicals and
diversified into property and finance. In 1983, the company spent $125
million acquiring two finance companies and four property development
companies.

The Chinese were hesitant to go into manufacturing for a number of
reasons. First, government controls created many uncertainties. It was a
guessing game as to whether a firm might be allowed to expand with market demand. The bureaucrats, through the Industrial Coordination Act,
regulated the production capacity of firms. Secondly, opportunities in
manufacturing lessened as foreign manufacturers started forming partnerships more frequently with state corporations and Malay firms. Table 5.2,
on Japanese investment patterns, illustrates this trend. Since national
policy required foreign firms to have at least 70 per cent Malaysian ownership, of which at least 30 per cent had to be Malay, many foreign firms
formed partnerships solely with Malay firms. State and Malay companies
provided better access to the government market and to high-level
decision-makers.

Property development, in contrast, provided few of the hazards of
manufacturing and promised large profits and quick returns. Demand
for housing and commercial space was high because of the growth of the
middle class, brought about in no small part by the oil and commodity

TABLE 5.2
Japanese Investments and Ownership Structure, 1970–1980
(percentage in parentheses)

Period	100 Per Cent Japanese	Japanese–Chinese	Japanese–State/Malay	Total
1970–1975	17 (43)	16 (40)	7 (18)	40 (100)
1976–1980	4 (17)	7 (29)	13 (54)	24 (100)

Source: This table is constructed from the best publicly available data on Japanese overseas investments in Malaysia, reported in *The Oriental Economist*, 1981: 65–74. Firms were left out if the information was vague.

boom of the 1970s. The government also contributed to housing demand from its subsidized loan scheme for all government civil servants. Property development, and its spin-off, loan financing, were probably the most lucrative sectors to enter in the 1970s and early 1980s. Large Chinese companies had accumulated choice urban land in the past, and could benefit from housing demand.

Chinese manufacturing investments, though sluggish, were not entirely absent. Foreign firms sometimes had to seek Chinese partners because they controlled the urban distributive trade. Some examples, culled from Japanese manufacturing investments in the 1976–80 period, were Fumakilla partnering a Chinese trading firm, Texcham Trading, to manufacture insecticides; Toshiba Corporation partnering Kee Huat Radio, an electrical appliance distributor, to manufacture electrical appliances; and Yuasa Battery partnering with Boon Siew Sdn Bhd, a motor-cycle assembler and distributor, to manufacture storage batteries.

Chinese participation remained relatively strong in wood and wood products, plastic products, fabricated metal products, and food manufacturing (see MIDA, *Annual Report*, 1981). These were typically low technology-intensive industries. The comparative advantage of Chinese manufacturers was their link to the urban distributive network, which sold consumer products such as furniture, household utensils, and food preparations to the mass market. Products such as plastic materials, carrying bags, wooden boxes, and cardboard cartons were used by retail establishments for packaging and shipment. However, using the 1960s as a benchmark, it is hard to say that the Chinese progressed very far in their manufacturing capabilities.

The other common feature of Chinese big business, obvious from a quick perusal of company reports in the *Annual Companies Handbook* of the Kuala Lumpur Stock Exchange, was their reliance on acquisitions and mergers as the predominant means of expansion rather than on starting their own businesses. While this behaviour accorded with their desire to accumulate assets and realize profits easily and quickly, it was also a product of existing constraints. Prime urban land was a limited resource; the authorities were hesitant to give agricultural land to the Chinese for development; and there were strict controls on the number of banks, finance companies, and merchant banks that could operate in the country. Understandably, there was a scramble for existing lucrative businesses, thus encouraging the larger companies to buy or merge with smaller companies, almost all Chinese.

Finally, many large Chinese businessmen took, in Albert Hirschman's terms, the 'exit' option (or voting with one's feet) as an alternative to 'voice' (protest) and 'loyalty' (accommodation) (Hirschman, 1970). Business diversification abroad was a way of escaping domestic constraints and spreading economic and political risks more widely. Not all instances of internationalization resulted from the NEP; even without the NEP, some enterprises would have been induced to go abroad because of the small domestic market. But there were sufficient disincentives to make Chinese enterprises think of going abroad first before trying to intensify their activities further in Malaysia. For example, locals could have produced some of the relatively simple manufacturing products which were carried out by multinationals, but chose not to.

Only the largest Chinese companies, possessing strong foreign links, resources, and knowledge went abroad, most commonly to Singapore and Hong Kong, places where Malaysian businessmen had friendship and kinship links. Australia has also become a haven. Investment abroad has followed essentially the same pattern as domestic expansion: buying up trading and commercial companies, and promoting property development and speculative ventures.

The most prominent business group to expand abroad has been the Kuok family business group, who built up in the 1960s Malaysia's most dynamic conglomerate. Before 1970, the Kuoks had around eleven companies in Malaysia and only four in Hong Kong; by 1978, they had added fifteen more companies, mainly in properties, trading, and shipping to the Hong Kong list, but only five in Malaysia (*Insight*, August 1978: 55). In 1976, the leading Kuok figure, Robert Kuok, moved to Hong Kong where, according to Verchere (1978: 43), the wheeling and dealing of Hong Kong became attractive to him as government controls increased and a new generation of unfamiliar leaders took over the reins of power in Malaysia. Recently, the Kuoks built a luxurious hotel in Kuala Lumpur, but the aim appeared to be to expand their Shangri-La hotel network in the region, rather than to make a comeback in Malaysia (see *FEER*, 30 October 1986: 60).[20]

Large Chinese capital, through the use of the devices described, managed to maintain their profitability in the 1970s and early 1980s. Table 5.3 shows that there was no clear trend toward declining profits among a sample of Chinese public companies during the NEP. However, much of their expansion came from buying out smaller Chinese firms. Their activities, from a national viewpoint, were not conducive for building a strong economy; they were weak in capturing new domestic and foreign markets in industrial products, and large funds went abroad to seek alternative investment outlets.

We turn briefly to consider the Chinese group response to the NEP.

TABLE 5.3
Return on Shareholders' Funds in a Sample of Chinese Public Firms,
1974–1982

Name	Activity	Return on Shareholder Funds		
		1974	1978	1982
SEA Development	discount house	0.16	0.25	0.22
Selangor Properties	property	0.09	0.08	0.12
Batu Kawan	plantations	0.08	0.08	0.07
United Motor Works	manufacturing, trade	0.12	0.04	0.08
Oriental Holdings	manufacturing, property	0.22	0.20	0.25
Paramount	property, plantations	n.a.	0.04	0.06
Lien Hoe	property, manufacturing	0.16	0.11	0.03
MUI	property, finance	0.02	0.06	0.07
Khong Guan	manufacturing	0.12	0.15	0.06

Source: KLSE, 1974, 1978, 1980, and 1984.
n.a. = Not available.

The most innovative, controversial, and ultimately most disastrous response to the NEP was the MCA party's scheme to formulate a collective Chinese strategy. The MCA party leaders, while complying with the Malay leaders' policies, wanted an economic strategy that would bolster the party's support and also increase Chinese economic bargaining power with the state. The party was losing considerable support because of its weak position in government and needed a new political initiative. To this end, the party leaders established Multi-Purpose Holdings Bhd, commonly known as MPH, in 1975. Its role was to pool Chinese economic resources and compete, in the way small enterprises could not, with large Malay corporate organizations.[21] The precipitating factor for MPH's formation was the ICA, which threatened the interests of Chinese small businesses in manufacturing and exposed the MCA's political weakness (Gale, 1985: Chap. 2).

The political leaders of the MCA chose two prominent Chinese businessmen to lead the company—Lee Loy Seng, Malaysia's 'rubber king' and respected businessman was made the Chairman, and Tan Koon Swan, a shrewd corporate take-over artist, the Managing Director. Tan was to play a pivotal role in the direction and fate of the corporation, and his business role would later put him at the centre of MCA politics. Tan, starting out as an officer in the Income Tax Department in the 1960s, went on to work in several prominent companies and, from speculation in the stock market in the early 1970s, ended up with a controlling interest in Supreme Corporation, a diversified public company (see MB, September 1977: 85). Tan was also one of the first Malaysians to take the Harvard Business School's three-month management course, and received wide attention from the business community.[22]

Chinese support for MPH was enthusiastic in the late 1970s and early 1980s. Its maiden issue of $30 million shares in 1977 was over-subscribed and, subsequently, the company did not have problems in raising cash. The Chinese expected MPH to be the answer to state organizations and, at its height, MPH had more than 200,000 shareholders.

Although MPH was formed in response to the ICA, it avoided manufacturing and behaved very much like any large Chinese corporation. It went on the acquisition route, and among its initial purchases were Bandar Raya Developments, a property company, Plantation Holdings, a UK-based plantation company, and a large minority stake in Magnum Corporation, which operated a profitable lottery business. MPH rationalized its purchases in terms of serving the national good.[23] It was probably hoping to get legitimacy from the Malay leaders, many of whom were suspicious of MPH's intentions.

MPH, however, could not become just another large Chinese company like MUI. It sought visibility, and its political and communal agenda led to collisions with existing economic and political interests. Not just Malay politicians but, ironically, Chinese businessmen began to see the corporation as a threat. Rather than increasing Chinese economic bargaining power, these conflicts put constraints on how MPH could expand.

The rift with the traditional Chinese business community began in late 1977, when Huaren Holdings, the investment arm of the MCA and linked to MPH by common directorships, tried to wrest management control of Southern Banking, a small Penang-based bank (see Gale, 1985: 105–8). The Hokkien business community, to which the top executives of the bank belonged, were incensed at MPH, suspecting that the corporation was trying to usurp their traditional role as business leaders. To make matters worse, the Multi-Purpose group fielded twenty-two candidates in the 1979 annual elections of the Selangor Chinese Chamber of Commerce. It was an open challenge to the leadership of the existing business community, who had shown lukewarm support to MPH and were contemptuous of MCA's weakness in dealing with the ICA and advancing the cause of a Chinese-medium university (*New Nation*, 10 March 1979). All of MPH's candidates, including Tan Koon Swan, lost and the message to MPH was clear: respect the preserve of traditional businesses or expect opposition.

Since the company had to be cautious of taking over Chinese businesses, the alternative was to either buy Malaysian assets owned presently by foreign companies or start its own businesses. It chose the former but soon ran afoul of Malay interests. In June 1981, MPH purchased for $204 million a 56 per cent share of United Malayan Banking Corporation (UMBC), the nation's third largest bank, from Chang Ming Thien, a Singaporean businessman who was shifting his base to Hong Kong. The state corporation Pernas had earlier acquired a 30 per cent share of the bank. The purchase was approved by the CIC and FIC, as well as the Minister of Finance (*ST* (S), 10 March 1981). However, the leaders of UMNO Youth, who were the party's ambitious second echelon leadership, created an uproar, insisting that Pernas should have majority control. Its leader, who was standing for re-election, put the matter in grave terms: 'These acts [take-overs] will not only affect the economic situation of the Malays and other bumiputras but also threaten national solidarity and security' (*NST*, 22 March 1981). The political pressure was strong enough to produce a top-level compromise in which Pernas and MPH would have an equal 40 per cent share in UMBC.[24]

Only a few months later, MPH was involved in another brush with UMNO Youth, this time involving a 51 per cent share in Dunlop Estates Bhd (DEB), a giant plantation company which owned 58,000 acres of rubber and palm oil land. The $252 million purchase was a result of a complex arrangement worked out between Dunlop Holdings of UK (DEB's parent company), Pegi Malaysia, which had 17 per cent equity in Dunlop Holdings, and MPH. Dunlop would sell DEB to MPH, which in turn would form a joint company with Pegi to share their assets in Dunlop Holdings and DEB. In return, Pegi would agree not to buy further into Dunlop (see Gale, 1985: 165). Suhaimi Kamaruddin, the UMNO Youth leader, criticized the deal, arguing that it undermined the NEP because Dunlop should have given PNB, the National Equity Corporation, the 'first option' to buy. He calculated that DEB would be only 40 per cent owned by Malays from this transaction when their minimum stake should be 51 per cent (*BT*, 13 October 1981). The controversy resulted in MPH calling off its alliance with Pegi, and promising the authorities that it would raise Malay participation to 50 per cent in the near future.

MPH's move to acquire foreign-owned Malaysian assets in natural resources, while seemingly in agreement with national policy, ran into trouble because Malay organizations were also interested in the same assets. The company finally embarked on a less controversial, but more risky and costly route—the buying of foreign assets abroad—which was to result in deep financial problems.

Before MPH's problems became severe, however, the corporation was an important asset politically to the MCA party. Its rapid growth and collisions with Malay politicians made the MCA appear as though it had an economic answer to the NEP. Strongly supported by the Chinese middle class and co-operatives, MPH's paid-up capital escalated from $87.2 million in 1980 to $450 million in 1982 (KLSE, 1984: 392; *MB*, 16 August 1984: 76). The party's political popularity also increased. In the 1978 general elections, the MCA won only seventeen of the twenty-seven parliamentary seats it contested, and polled only 70 per cent of the votes received by its major rival, the DAP.[25] In the 1982 elections, it won twenty-four of the twenty-eight seats contested, and increased its share of votes to 90 per cent of what the DAP polled. This increased Chinese support could not be attributed to better economic benefits since MPH had not paid out dividends since 1977 and its role in creating employment was limited because its expansion came from take-overs of existing companies (*MB*, 16 August 1984). The simplest explanation was its role in reinforcing Chinese ethnic identity and giving it concrete expression in an economic enterprise. Its supporters and shareholders were prepared to overlook some of the more troublesome aspects of its finances, such as the company's debt, which stood at $573 million or 80 per cent of paid-up capital in 1984 (*BT* (S), 13 June 1984).

MPH's political success led its executives to push it further along the expansion path, in spite of its high debt and politically circumscribed opportunities for expansion. In 1983, MPH bought into a Hong Kong shipping company, Promptshipping, which had a bulk carrier, thirty-five vessels, and a monthly China–West Africa line operation (*FEER*, 19 January 1984: 92). The company had large debts but had been averaging US$5 million in profits since 1978. By 1984, MPH had paid out US$48 million for a 75 per cent stake in Promptshipping.

The prolonged recession in commodities and general trading made its impact. MPH's financial structure was such that it could not afford sudden losses in its subsidiaries. In 1983, it was paying out $45.2 million in interest payments alone, nearly equal to its profits for the year. In 1984, MPH's shipping business reported a loss of $30 million because of low charter rentals and high financing costs (*BT* (S), 24 May 1985). Pretax profits stood at $41 million out of a paid-up capital of nearly $750 million. In 1985, MPH reported a loss of $200 million. Its trading firm in Singapore, Mulpha, reported a loss of $15.5 million, while Promptshipping made a loss of $40 million. The shipping company also had to write down $150 million of the value of its assets since the value of its vessels had declined. The only respectable showing was the corporation's plantation interests. The financial crisis of MPH was reflected in its share price which fell, in 1986, to about half its par value.

As MPH's financial problems mounted, its executives began to use the company for their own ends. In November 1985, Tan and some fellow directors transferred MPH's funds amounting to $23.2 million for their personal use in stock market machinations in Singapore (*ST* (S), 19 January 1988). Tan's manoeuvres eventually resulted in Singaporean authorities sentencing him to two years' imprisonment in 1986 for criminal breach of trust and stock market manipulation.[26] The charges were related to the collapse of Pan-Electric Company, a Singaporean public company in which Tan had substantial personal shareholdings (see *ST* (S), 5 August 1986). Later, Tan and a few former MPH directors were also sentenced to jail in Malaysia.

Just as MPH was a boon to the MCA in the 1982 elections, it was a liability in the 1986 elections. Far from spearheading the Chinese economy, the MPH had become a financial embarrassment. It was also responsible, indirectly, for the debilitating leadership struggle that started in 1983. When Lee San Choon, the MCA President, resigned in 1983, Tan Koon Swan and his associates, who had become politically prominent via MPH, made a bid to oust the Acting President, Neo Yee Pan. Neo had risen through normal party channels and not through business. In 1984, Neo, under threat, expelled Tan and seven other supporters from the Central Committee, accusing them of engaging in 'money politics'. For more than a year and a half all attempts to resolve the internal strife by the National Front leaders failed. Only in November 1985, under the pressure of looming general elections, did both factions agree to settle the dispute. Tan emerged the victor but his party only won seventeen seats in the August 1986 general elections compared to twenty-four in 1982. The DAP won in nearly all constituencies with a Chinese majority while MCA's victories came in 'marginal constituencies where substantial Malay voters helped to offset the Chinese votes which went to the DAP in droves' (*ST* (S), 4 August 1986).

In retrospect, the MPH's group approach to the NEP, while seemingly an innovative attempt to mobilize idle funds in the Chinese community for investment, failed because it contained conflicting economic and political objectives. Frantic expansion was preferred over caution in the build-up of assets, and economic soundness was sacrificed for high corporate visibility in order to build loyalty and patronage for the MCA and some of its leaders. MPH's ties to the party, rather than facilitating bargaining with the top Malay leadership, hurt its opportunities for domestic expansion because it brought negative reaction from Malay politicians, who were also looking for popularity from their constituencies.[27] Finally, as the company's original agenda frittered away, its executives and directors merely used the company for their personal economic interests.

The NEP thus elicited interesting responses from the Chinese business community, ranging from Ali–Baba arrangements to the collective pooling of resources. Small- and medium-scale businesses suffered the most from economic displacement and lower profit margins as a result of Malay entry and state favouritism. However, Chinese businesses which were linked closely to the urban consumer market, such as retail and service shops, urban wholesaling operations, and manufacturing for the mass consumer market, enjoyed built-in advantages and managed to remain entrenched. Large Chinese businesses, on the other hand, did not appear to have been hurt very much by the NEP. Their superior financial resources allowed them to buy over existing businesses, especially smaller Chinese finance and property companies, and take advantage of high demand for housing and credit in the 1970s and early 1980s. However, their thinking became short term as shown by their preference for take-overs instead of building up their own enterprises, and over-commitment in ventures bringing quick profits such as in finance and property.

The Failure of a State–Capitalist Alliance

What stands out, from examining available figures, is that the chief characteristic of the Chinese sector is *not* any pronounced reduction of its stake in the economy but the failure of a state–Chinese capitalist alliance to congeal in order to upgrade and diversify the national economy. Government data, while disputed by many people, show that Chinese ownership of limited companies increased from 23 per cent in 1970 to 33 per cent in 1982 (*MTR SMP*, 1973: 12; *Fifth MP*, 1986: 109). When the shareholdings of ethnically unidentifiable owners are added to the Chinese share (which government statisticians often do), then the Chinese share increased from 35 per cent to 47 per cent between 1970 and 1982.[28] (The foreign share, on the other hand, fell from 61 per cent to 34.7 per cent, with the Malay share increasing from 2 per cent to 16 per cent.) Thus, the Chinese share has not only exceeded the allocation of 30 per cent but also the 40 per cent NEP allocation for non-Malays as a whole. Many Chinese business spokesmen have not been impressed by the figures, arguing that they are a mere artefact of statistical definition.[29] First, they claim that many Chinese businesses have corporatized themselves from their previous status as sole proprietorships and partnerships (for tax and financial reasons), so there is really no actual net gain in tangible assets. Secondly, many enormous state organizations and enterprises which serve primarily Malay interests, such as Felda and Petronas, are not included in the calculations, and hence make the figures meaningless (*The Star*, 29 June 1981). It suffices to say that Chinese businesses do not appear to have lost out markedly, certainly not as much as they initially feared.

The critical point is that the Malay state élite and Chinese business have viewed each other in zero sum terms and have gone on divergent paths in their economic activities. In a study completed in 1985 of the country's industrial sector by UNIDO experts (IMP, 1985: 13–14, 16–17), this key aspect of Malaysia's shortcoming was highlighted:

The modern industries in Malaysia which demand high technology are either foreign-owned or joint-ventures involving foreign equity or foreign technical collaboration, and therefore have direct access to foreign technology from their principals. This complacency, probably derived from easy access to the foreign partners, has hindered the formation of any coherent and comprehensive policy designed to develop indigenous industrial technology in Malaysia (apart from the technology in the areas of primary products). . . . In addition, little attention is paid to the generation of a minimum level of indigenous technology which is necessary to absorb technology from foreign sources and adapt them to gain comparative advantage in the market. . . . [T]here is no synergistic effect of interactions between government policies and the activities of the private sector.

The lack of effective co-operation between the state and Chinese capital is clearly demonstrated in the behaviour of state enterprises. In the previous chapter, we noted that nearly all of Pernas's partnerships were with foreign enterprises. Where there has been joint ownership with the Chinese, this has come about only because of Pernas buying into Chinese interests to meet the 30 per cent ownership requirement. The only instance of a Chinese firm involved in a Pernas project was in the manufacture of refrigeration equipment in 1978. The partners were Hall Thermotank Ltd of Britain (30 per cent), Pernas Trading (60 per cent) and Wong Brothers Electrical and Refrigeration Sdn Bhd (10 per cent). Wong Brothers Sdn Bhd was a previous distributor of Hall Thermotank products, and came in as a minority partner, presumably for its distributing and marketing role. Being the only case of Chinese participation in a Pernas project, it was often used by Pernas executives to defend their company against charges that Pernas only formed partnerships with foreign enterprises (*SP*, 1978: v.5(2)).

The Heavy Industry Corporation of Malaysia or HICOM also put its own desire to expand rapidly at the expense of Chinese enterprises. When the government of Dr Mahathir decided to build a 'national car', there were already eleven automobile assembly manufacturers in the country, mostly joint ventures between Chinese car distributors and foreign principals. There were good reasons for these companies to form the nucleus of the national car project. There was over-capacity in the industry, and these companies had accumulated considerable expertise and experience in basic car assembly (*IMP*, Transport, 1985: 41–2). However, these existing companies were completely bypassed, and instead HICOM, which had been set up only in 1980, entered as a majority partner in a joint venture with Mitsubishi Motor Corporation of Japan.

Government officials often rationalize their policies by saying the state, in entering capital-intensive industries, is only doing what the Chinese will not do. In fact, Chinese businessmen do agree that if the state must get involved in commerce and industry, it is better for it go into heavy industry, where there is little Chinese participation, instead of competing with them in the other sectors. Nonetheless, Chinese business spokesmen reject the idea that the Chinese are simply not interested in large-scale manufacturing projects. According to the Executive Secretary of the Federation of Malaysian Manufacturers:[30]

The private sector will not go on its own into large-scale projects. But the government does not tell us what tariffs, subsidies, and prices it will allow for in any project. If they do that, we will make our own calculations and see if it's profitable. Many car assemblers would have been interested in the car project had the government announced the concessions it was willing to give. If the government keeps coming up with its own projects and doesn't tell us anything, how are we to get involved?

One important conclusion from studies of 'late' developers such as Japan, South Korea, and Taiwan is that close collaboration between the societies' corps of public administrators and entrepreneurs has been critical for their tremendous economic and entrepreneurial success (for example, Lim Hyun-Chin, 1982; Gold, 1981; Vogel, 1979). Malaysia's national leaders have not been unaware of the East Asian success and have even come up with their own slogans, such as 'Look East' and 'Malaysia Incorporated'. Interestingly, however (since it is always easier to point one's finger at others), officials and politicians have appealed to those aspects of the model which stress the necessity for a strong work ethic rather than bringing up what the appropriate role of the state should be in facilitating development. Some of the steps taken to further control the weak labour movement have found their justification in the 'East Asian' company union structure.

In Malaysia, the lack of co-operation between the state and Chinese capital has compromised the nation's ability to enhance its technological capabilities and develop a strong manufacturing sector. However, for many years, there was little incentive on the part of the Malay state élite to change the status quo because of the high political pay-off to the government's programme, good growth rates, and the ability to rely on multinationals.

Since the mid-1980s, it has become increasingly difficult to generate economic growth. In 1985 and 1986, the economy entered into a deep recession. Future improvements in commodity prices are unlikely to result in the high growth rates of the 1970s and early 1980s. There does not appear to be an economic catapult on the horizon that could replace the role of the oil boom of the 1970s. There are also new strains on investible funds because of the large public and foreign debts. The past formula, of high state spending and reliance on multinationals to provide jobs and generate economic growth, cannot work as well as before. The critical question is whether the government will now enter into a new accord with the Chinese sector, relaxing its unpopular regulations and providing new incentives for the Chinese to play a more dynamic role in the economy. Will the need for economic rationality override the politics of ethnicity?

Indeed, a few minor adjustments have taken place. The Fifth Malaysia Plan (1986–90), which was released in early 1986, announced that the exemption level for companies having to meet the ICA's provisions had been raised from $250,000 to $1 million in shareholders' funds and, in addition, conditions regarding capacity expansion were relaxed, especially in export-oriented projects (*Fifth MP*, 1986: 215). These changes were much less than what the FMM and the ACCCIM wanted; both organizations, since the early 1980s, had been asking for the exemption level to be raised to $5 million in paid-up capital (to encourage small and medium enterprises as well as to take into account inflation). So far, these changes have not impressed Chinese businessmen, coming at a time when investment opportunities are limited to begin with because of the economic recession.

There are a number of reasons why a major reorientation of policy toward a renewed pro-growth coalition might be very slow. First, the bureaucracy has operated so much on controls, regulations, and ethnic zeal that only a major intellectual and political shift will make them think of their roles as promoters and not controllers of business development. For nearly two decades, Malay bureaucrats and politicians have measured success in their policies in terms of achieving ethnic targets and quotas.[31] To provide a new, powerful impetus for Chinese business development would be going back to the beginning, and an open admission of years of misguided policies. It is both politically and psychologically difficult for the present leaders, who were the force behind the NEP, to embark on a major change of direction. Secondly, it is always easier to hope that events and conditions will change for the better, and permit the old *modus operandi* to work again. Hence, only minor policy adjustments will be made, while the bureaucrats hope commodity prices will improve in the near future. Thirdly, the government has the option of turning to the foreign sector to provide the new impetus for growth. The most important policy changes have actually been directed at increasing the flow of foreign investment. When the Minister of Trade and Industry, Datin Paduka Rafidah Aziz, was asked in 1988 why special incentives were offered to foreign companies only, she replied: 'The only difference is the equity. As locals, they should subscribe to their own national policy' (*ST* (S), 7 January 1988). Only when it is plain that foreign capital will not come at adequate levels can we perhaps expect a more accommodating policy toward local Chinese capital. Fourthly, politics always threatens to work against more nationally beneficial economic policies, not just from the Malay quarter but from the Chinese as well. After the 1986 elections, the leaders of the MCA and Gerakan parties, the two Chinese parties in government, attacked the NEP for their poor showing, saying that the discriminatory policies made it difficult for them to maintain Chinese support. Naturally, the UMNO leaders became very defensive and exchanged verbal blows with the Chinese leaders. Such mutual attacks only make it harder to think about an effective national economic strategy.

Conclusion

This chapter, on Chinese business since the NEP, has shown how mutual ethnic distrust between the Chinese and the Malays has resulted in their working at cross purposes in national economic development. Because of Malay group resentment and envy of Chinese economic success, both aggravated by past Chinese exclusivity in their businesses, the Malay leaders strove to control Chinese business development. New terms were set for Chinese participation, while entry was curtailed in some sectors of the economy. The Chinese did not like the state's new policies, but they were unable to have them revoked against a determined Malay government. Their failure was not just a matter of their ethnicity. The Chinese business sector was disadvantaged by its failure to get the foreign sector on its side. In addition, the state was able, in the face of Chinese investment shortfalls, to pump in its own resources and rely on multinationals to sustain economic growth and employment.

The impact of state policies on Chinese businesses varied according to the type and scale of the business, but in general, the small firms came under greater competitive pressures and suffered from lower profits than the larger ones. However, some establishments were protected from state and Malay encroachments because they belonged to the tight nexus between Chinese customers, retailers, and wholesalers. Surprisingly, the large firms were relatively unhurt by the NEP because their superior financial and organizational resources allowed them to profit from the high demand for commercial property and residential housing. However, in the restricted and uncertain economic environment, they pursued easy and safe areas of expansion, investing heavily in property development and finance, and avoiding sectors like manufacturing which entailed larger risks and longer periods to recuperate investment outlays. In conformity with this mentality, Chinese big businessmen opted for take-overs and acquisitions rather than starting new businesses, and transferred assets abroad to diversify their economic and political risks. From a national point of view, it is difficult to say that their activities have led to enhancing the nation's productive base or technological level. The saliency of ethnic group differences has failed to weld an effective state–Chinese alliance, so critical in accounting for the success of contemporary capitalist development. Despite the current deep economic slump, where all groups stand to lose, the Malay state élites, who have made inter-ethnic economic differences their prime *raison d'etre*, have been slow in forging a new economic consensus. Not only are there obvious political constraints, but also, the state appears to be looking to the multinational sector to re-crank the economy. To this third leg of the Malaysian economy, we now turn.

1. This Act, which pitted the Chinese business community in a protracted fight against the government, will be studied in the next section.

2. The quotas have increased since. In 1985, for example, Felda and Telecoms gave out only 0.1 per cent and 22.6 per cent of their total contracts to non-Malay companies, including foreign firms (*Fifth MP*, 1986: 116).

3. This was revealed by the Minister of Trade and Industry, Datuk Hamzah Abu Samah, to the Malaysian International Chamber of Commerce and Industry in 1975 (see MICCI, *Yearbook*, 1974/5: 217).

4. The MICCI now has about 400 members from twenty-five different countries. Nearly every type of business is represented in the Chamber although the majority of its members are manufacturers. Companies with significant foreign equity are eligible for membership. Its members account for 80 per cent of the total foreign investment in the non-primary sector in Malaysia (MICCI, brochure, undated, around 1984).

5. Information about the conditions imposed were obtained from MICCI, *Yearbook*, 1974/5; Wu and Wu, 1980: 185.

6. This point was made by the Executive Secretary of the MICCI, in an interview in January 1985.

7. This topic is treated in more detail in Chapter 6.

8. The National Chamber was formed in 1974 at the request of Tun Abdul Razak. He wanted only one business body for the government to deal with when seeking feedback from and assessing the reaction of the private sector.

9. Comparable data on the breakdown of manufacturing investments by Bumiputra, non-Bumiputra, and foreign investors are not available before 1971 from public sources.

10. In 1981, the Chinese made large investments in tourist and hotel complexes ($124 million or 27.4 per cent of Chinese investments), a sector which MIDA classified under manufacturing activities up to 1982.

11. Interview with a MIDA official, February 1985.

12. The public enterprise share of Bumiputra equity, as opposed to private entrepreneurs, was the predominant component. For example, it was 72 per cent and 85 per cent in 1981 and 1982 respectively (MIDA, *Annual Report*, 1982: 56, Table XVII).

13. The recent crisis in government finances promises to increase Chinese economic leverage. However, while the state has made a few concessions to Chinese manufacturers, the main thrust of the policy revisions has been directed at resuscitating foreign investment (see Chapter 6).

14. While Chinese wholesale establishments increased from 78.5 per cent to 81.8 per cent of total establishments between 1971 and 1981, their share of turnover fell from 66.2 per cent to 55.5 per cent, and in terms of turnover per establishment seem to have, in real prices, suffered from a marked decline (*Fifth MP*, 1986: 114, Table 3-11).

15. Pernas previously played a regulatory role in the Malaysia–China trade by issuing permits to wholesalers for importing made-in-China products. In 1972, the company had tried to bypass the role of overseas Chinese merchants in Singapore and Hong Kong in Malaysia's trade relations with China. The Chinese government did not oblige because it wanted to preserve its links with these merchants. Pernas, instead, began to regulate import permits given to Malaysian Chinese wholesalers, and charged them a 0.5 per cent service commission (effectively a tax) on the value of the import shipments (Gale, 1981b, Chap. 3).

16. Interview with a Chinese businessman in Penang, March 1985.

17. To use the word 'alliance' fruitfully, one should demonstrate, at a minimum, that the state carried out specific policies for the benefit of a particular group. Just because a group does well economically does not mean it enjoyed special benefits. The creation of good economic conditions cannot be seen as a special benefit. Many groups might benefit under these circumstances, in spite of some experiencing discrimination. Can we still therefore say that the state has entered into an alliance with all these groups?

18. Chapter 4 gives examples of price discounts Chinese companies make when they issue special shares to Malays.

19. The criteria for being 'Malay' varies from department to department as well as from time to time, but the minimum is 50 per cent Malay shareholding in a company.

20. The *FEER* article contains a detailed chart of the enormous stable of companies

belonging to the Kuok empire in Malaysia, Singapore, and Hong Kong.

21. Bruce Gale (1985) also deals with this topic.

22. It has been speculated that Tan's sojourn at Harvard Business School inculcated the idea of rapid expansion through borrowing and acquisitions (see Rowley, *FEER*, 10 May 1984: 88).

23. Tan, for instance, claimed that his objectives in acquiring Bandar Raya were: 'The first was social in nature—to help accelerate . . . housing development; the second was economic as it is an industry which stimulates growth. It supports 104 other industries and brings in good profits' (*Insight*, February 1983: 10).

24. Lacking effective control, MPH sold off its UMBC stake in 1984 to Daim Zainuddin, the present Finance Minister, in exchange for a controlling interest in a small bank, Malaysian French Bank (*AF*, 15 August 1984).

25. Beating the DAP was difficult because the MCA never enjoyed strong support from the Chinese working class and, by the logistics of seat allocations amongst the component government parties, could not contest in as many seats as the DAP.

26. Stock market manipulation and business fraud were common practices in Malaysia but no one, until the precedent set by Singapore in sentencing Tan, had been caught or punished for them. Singapore, always very sensitive about international business confidence, took a very serious view.

27. Partly as a response to MPH, the ACCCIM started its own company, Unico Holdings Bhd, in 1981 with the aim of providing a non-political alternative to MPH. By 1986, it had $50 million in paid-up capital and an oil palm mill in Sabah. The shareholders of Unico, mainly rich Chinese businessmen, appear to have learnt from the mistakes of MPH. When its executives contemplated buying Tan's Supreme Corporation, shareholders argued against it, pointing out that it was a bad idea to buy into ailing companies and raise cash through high debts (*ST*, 26 February 1986). Unico's recent plans also suggest that it is more willing to enter manufacturing projects and start businesses from scratch (*BT* (S), 10 January 1986).

28. Strictly speaking, it is classified as the non-Malay share, but the Indian share is negligible (less than 2 per cent). In the Fifth Malaysia Plan (1986–90), the non-Malay share was put at 56.6 per cent in 1985 (1986: 107), but on closer reading of the text, the figure was merely a statistical estimate (see p. 106). We report this figure but do not use it. One suspects that officials have been trying to overstate the Chinese but understate the foreign figures. No reason was given for the rise of the Chinese share from 44.6 per cent to 56.7 per cent, and the accompanying decline of the foreign share from 42.9 per cent to 25.5 per cent between 1980 and 1985. Such large changes did not take place previously over the much longer period from 1970 to 1980.

29. To illustrate just how indeterminate the NEP's achievements have been to date, the former Prime Minister, Tun Hussein Onn, said in 1987: 'There should be a White Paper to show whether the 30 per cent has been achieved. We don't know the actual achievements. Maybe there are Malays who are unhappy and non-Malays who are more unhappy' (*ST* (S), 1 July 1987).

30. Interview with the Executive Secretary of the FMM, February 1985.

31. Interestingly, the leaders have, instead, asked the private sector to change their behaviour and become less racial. In December 1986, the Prime Minister suggested that there should be only one Chamber of Commerce and not the present four, split up into ethnic segments. With one chamber, the question of race would be less salient. However, business leaders, especially from the Malay Chambers, said the move was premature because the political reality was based on communal lines (*ST* (S), 17 December 1986).

6 The Role of Multinationals

Introduction

ALTHOUGH the New Economic Policy strove to reduce the role of the foreigners in many sectors of the economy, the Malay leaders, nonetheless, turned to multinationals to play a strong role in manufacturing. This chapter argues that the leaders were more interested in using multinationals to help realize their political goals than to intensify industrial development. As the state carried out its restructuring goals, multinationals helped to keep the economy afloat by absorbing labour and providing ownership opportunities for Malay interests in manufacturing. However, they failed both to generate many linkages in the economy and to wean the economy from its high dependence on the commodity sector. Given tapering multinational investments in the 1980s and a weak economy, we end by asking how foreign investment levels in the future might affect political and economic outcomes in the country.

State Interests and the Business Climate

Theorists from the dependency school have had much to say about the effects of multinational participation in the Third World. Their analyses commonly portray governments as relatively weak *vis-à-vis* the interests of multinationals. A typical example, which is worth quoting at length, is an article by Bornschier and Ballmer-Cao in the *American Sociological Review* (1979: 487–506) on the effects of MNC penetration on national income distribution:

The hypothesis can be put forward that, driven by self-interest, MNCs try to influence the pattern of purposes as well as the pattern of priorities of state expenditures. . . . More precisely, the argument is that MNCs use direct and indirect political pressure (legal as well as illegal, e.g., bribery) to bring about a pattern of purposes and a pattern of priorities of government expenditures which favors them. Indeed, their demand for infrastructure, which is necessary for their type of capital intensive production, cuts down on the resources which would be potentially available for redistribution of income to poorer regions and to poorer segments of the population. But MNCs probably do not only block possible redistributions indirectly by cutting down what is available for such purposes. They also are vitally opposed to any redistributive policy that withdraws money from those who are actually or potentially their customers; in other words any policy which transfers money to poorer segments of the population. . . .

After these 'hypotheses' are made, the usual strategy in the analyses of this genre is to employ a regression model of carefully selected variables using cross-national data. When the tests show significance (usually most do), the original assumptions are casually accepted as confirmed. How these behavioural assumptions might play themselves out in a single concrete case is never demonstrated.

While governments undoubtedly make many concessions to attract multinationals, the dependency view is simply too one-sided in seeing governments as basically instruments of multinationals. Only in extreme circumstances, such as when a government is hopelessly fragmented or externally dominated, might this characterization have some plausibility. Otherwise, it is vital to consider how governments use multinationals for their own economic and political purposes. In addition, many of the social structural consequences usually attributed to multinationals might, upon closer investigation, be found to stem from the state's own interests and policies.

The state élites in Malaysia found multinationals useful in several ways. First, they provided an alternative investment source to the Chinese business sector. Although many multinationals carried out activities that locals could not have done, there were also other foreign companies that were only marginally ahead of the Chinese sector in technological sophistication.

Moreover, multinationals had a number of attributes which the Malay leaders and policy-makers favoured. Foreign companies were removed from struggles over the internal distribution of power and the appropriate cultural forms of the society. There was less fear that the economic power of multinationals would translate directly into strong influence over the political process.

Secondly, many foreign companies found it easier to provide Malays with ownership opportunities and executive positions than the family-oriented business organizations of the Chinese. The nature of their business organizations allowed them to better comply with government policies even though some of the equity conditions for domestic production appeared more onerous than for Chinese companies.

Thus, while state corporations embarked on replacing the role of foreigners in technologically simple sectors such as banking, plantations, and tin-mining, the state made multinationals an important ally in the more demanding ones, such as manufacturing. Not surprisingly, state policies were consistently more responsive to the opinions of the foreign sector than the Chinese business sector. In the Industrial Coordination Act, the state made concessions up to a point which allayed the foreign sector but not the Chinese sector. And recently, faced with sagging foreign investment commitments and diminished economic growth, the government targeted most of its concessions to the foreigners to intensify their investments.

Thirdly, the state also wanted multinationals to provide high levels of employment. The leaders and policy-makers in Malaysia have been sensitive to the undesirable consequences of high unemployment levels in society. As an electoral regime, the pressure of mass demands could not be so easily dismissed politically as in more authoritarian societies. The second prong of the NEP promised to eradicate poverty irrespective of race. The main strategy to appease the poorer sectors of the population was to increase the rate of employment creation, particularly in the envisaged growth sector, manufacturing. Redistributionist measures and welfarism were eschewed as solutions. Although the idea of 'anti-poverty' was a constricted one, it was not mere political rhetoric, since the government had equated unemployment with political instability after the May 1969 riots.

Both the state and Chinese business sectors, however, were inadequate for generating high levels of employment. The state's principle objective was the restructuring of ethnic wealth ownership. Many of its economic activities, such as the buying over of existing companies, did not create much employment outside the bureaucratic sector. There were also many failures and a lot of waste in the state enterprise sector. As for Chinese businesses, state policies were not helpful in encouraging them to play a strong developmental role. A number of large Chinese companies engaged in take-overs and mergers while some others channelled their funds abroad. Many medium-sized businesses preferred not to invest at all. The multinational sector was hence relied upon to counteract these deficits in the NEP as the state concentrated on building a Malay bourgeoisie and managerial class.

For the most part, the leaders and bureaucrats were able to provide a climate attractive to multinationals. In a survey of 'country risks' conducted by the Japanese magazine *Nikkei Business* in the mid-1970s, Malaysia was put in the same category as Singapore, Portugal, Brazil, and Mexico in terms of investment risk. These countries ranked lower than the industrialized countries but were above South Korea, Thailand, Chile, Kenya, and India (see *FEER*, 18 March 1977: 88).

In a 1984 survey of foreign companies in Malaysia commissioned by MIDA for a special supplement in *Business Week*, Malaysia was ranked just below Singapore and Taiwan, but ahead of South Korea, China, the Philippines, Sri Lanka, Indonesia, Thailand, India, and Brazil as a desirable investment location (*BW*, 9 July 1984).

However, Malaysia did not score uniformly high on all facets of the business climate. Its main weakness was the mixed signals the bureaucracy gave to foreign executives regarding its commitment to foreign investment. Two policies which particularly tainted the investment climate for a period of time were the Industrial Coordination Act (ICA) of 1975 and the Petroleum Development Act (PDA) of 1974 and its amendments. We have already considered the ICA in Chapter 5. The PDA, which covered the petroleum sector, unilaterally cancelled the previous oil production arrangements with multinational oil companies. What was worse was a 1975 amendment which sought to gain control cheaply of companies in the distribution, marketing, and refining of petroleum products. It empowered the government to make these companies issue a special class of management share to the national oil company, Petronas. These shares were to be sold at the cost of an ordinary share, but would carry the voting power of 500 ordinary shares (see *NST*, 18 April 1975). Malaysia had simply gone too far, and Esso Malaysia pulled out of its oil exploration efforts pending a more favourable policy. This policy also gave the country bad international press coverage. After protracted negotiations, the management share idea was dropped and its strongest advocate, Tengku Razaleigh Hamzah, was transferred from his job as Chairman of Petronas and made the Minister of Finance in 1976. According to Gale (1981a: 1137–8):

. . . Tengku Razaleigh's cabinet colleagues felt they could no longer support policies that were being increasingly interpreted by foreign investors as the first moves towards nationalization of the oil industry. Malaysian development plans laid heavy stress on the need for foreign capital and powerful ministers such as Dr Mahathir and Ghazali Shafie, the Home Affairs Minister, were known to be particularly concerned about the dangers of excessive government regulation of the economy.

The élites, as they embarked on economic nationalism, were trying to test how much they could squeeze the foreign sector, and rather clumsily overstepped the acceptable bounds of commercial logic. Most of the leaders, however, were sufficiently flexible and pragmatic to correct excessive controls and over-nationalistic ambitions.

However, whatever lingering uncertainties foreigners had about whether the government possessed an adequate understanding of their vital interests were largely counterbalanced by the high marks foreigners gave to Malaysia for its political stability, good labour relations, and generous package of financial incentives.

In the 1984 *Business Week* survey, 95.9 per cent of the foreign respondents rated Malaysia as politically stable. Only 14.4 per cent indicated that ethnic tensions in the country caused them concern. In Malaysia, unlike countries such as Sri Lanka and Lebanon, ethnic conflict was kept within bounds by long periods of good growth which helped to lubricate the relations amongst the ethnic groups. The strong position of UMNO in the polity also gave predictability to the political system. Any open challenge to the Malay position by the non-Malays would not only be costly but would probably fail since the army and the military were firmly in Malay hands. Polarization was also contained by some Chinese parties (that is, the MCA and Gerakan) opting to co-operate, often uneasily, with the UMNO government rather than be in the opposition. The Chinese community, therefore, did not act as a unified bloc against the government. The opposition Chinese party, the DAP, which relied on a working-class Chinese base, had little choice but to work within the political system. The Islamic Malay party, PAS, was also kept at bay by UMNO's ability to distribute benefits (fertilizers, loans, and social amenities) to poorer Malays, on whom PAS relied for support.

The union movement also provided very little consternation for foreign firms in Malaysia. In the 1984 survey, 88.7 per cent of foreign firms approved of the labour relations in the country and 72.2 per cent rated labour productivity positively. Their chief complaint was the difficulty of getting

TABLE 6.1
Number of Strikes and Man-days Lost, 1978–1986

Year	Number of Strikes	Man-days Lost	Year	Number of Strikes	Man-days Lost
1978	36	35,032	1983	24	7,900
1979	28	24,868	1984	17	9,800
1980	28	19,600	1985	22	34,700
1981	24	11,800	1986 (January		
1982	26	9,600	–July)	15	10,400

Source: MIDA, *Modern Malaysia* (brochure), 1984: 6; Ministry of Finance, 1986: l–li, Table 6.1.

skilled labour (56.7 per cent). Malaysia's labour problem did not reside in the militancy of the workers but in the failure of the educational system to generate a technical corps of skilled craftsmen and machinists. Malaysia's main 'asset' was the provision of an unskilled, relatively docile work-force. In the government's investment promotion exercises abroad, its frequent boast was the low incidence of strikes in Malaysia (see Table 6.1).

The historical cause of labour's weakness was the suppression of communist-linked unions in the late 1940s by the colonial authorities, and ongoing government policies ensured that the unions remained weak. In the early 1970s, union membership was only 10 per cent of all employment in West Malaysia; in 1985 it had increased to only 11 per cent (Edwards, C. B., 1975: Appendix 4/1; Ministry of Finance, 1986: Appendix 6.1). The unions were also small and fragmented—of the 287 unions in West Malaysia in 1982, nearly half of them had fewer than 500 workers and only six unions had more than 10,000 workers (Ministry of Labour, 1984: 172).

Government controls on the union movement tended to be imposed in times of national 'emergency', such as the period of 'confrontation' with Indonesia in the mid-1960s and the period of emergency rule following the 1969 racial riots. At present, stringent regulations govern the use of the strike weapon, the recognition and formation of unions, and the political involvement of unions. Some of these include: (1) the prerogative of the Minister of Labour to refer any dispute for compulsory arbitration; his power to recognize or not to recognize a union, and his right to suspend any union up to six months, for acting in a manner prejudicial to the 'national interest'; (2) the curtailing of the role of union leaders by requiring union members to conduct secret ballots over decisions to strike, amalgamate with other unions, and join a federation of unions; (3) the barring of union leaders from holding office in any political party and disallowing the use of trade union funds for political purposes, and (4) the disqualification of any person, union, or group not directly involved in a trade dispute to carry out sympathy strikes, wildcat strikes, and secondary picketing.

The main government parties have had little incentive to cultivate the union movement because of their reliance on ethnic mobilization for political power. The UMNO party has consciously encouraged vertically structured patronage relations between Malay leaders and workers through

TABLE 6.2
Monthly Wages in Selected Industries, 1974 and 1980 (in M$)

Industry	1974	1980	Wage Increase, 1974–1980 (Per Cent)	Annual* Real Wage Increase, 1974–1980 (Per Cent)
Rubber latex processing	155	216	39.3	2.0
Rubber products	227	343	51.1	3.9
Tobacco products	329	327	−0.01	−4.5
Textile products	100	155	55.0	4.6
Saw-milling	172	513	198.2	28.5
Plywood	113	193	70.7	7.3
Chemical products	255	352	38.0	1.8
Industrial machinery	175	277	58.2	5.2
Electronics	164	241	47.0	3.3

Source: Ministry of Labour, 1984: 142–3.
Notes: *Fourth column figures calculated from Wage Increase–Inflation (1975–1981)/6.
   CPI index obtained from FoMP, 1981: 29.

various communal and welfare organizations. In addition, many of the government party leaders and bureaucrats are involved in business, either in their own capacity or as managers of state enterprises. Their economic and managerial interests go against the establishment of strong working-class organizations.

Government policies have endeavoured not so much to suppress wage increases as to ensure that unions do not have the power to push up wages much higher than the market rate. Between 1975 and 1980, for example, during the period of high growth, wage increases kept up with the government's Consumer Price Index but fell short of productivity increases. Table 6.2 provides data on wages in selected industries for 1974 and 1980.

Between 1975 and 1980, the gross domestic product per capita grew by about 6.2 per cent. Only in saw-milling and the plywood industry did real wage increases exceed this figure. In most of the other sectors, real wages increased but failed to keep up with general economic growth. The base wages in electronics and textiles, both strongly export-oriented and essentially non-unionized sectors, were quite low, although these sectors also experienced real wage increases. An important reason for the real increases in nearly all the sectors was the falling unemployment rate in Malaysia between 1975 and 1980—from 7 per cent to 5.3 per cent (TMP, 1975: 68; FoMP, 1981: 226).[1] In short, the chief determinant of wage levels has been the market rather than the institutional role of the unions. This fact created a vicious circle. There was little incentive for workers to join unions because they provided few benefits and this weakness made it politically easy for the government to control the labour movement.

Foreign companies also appreciated Malaysia's financial and fiscal policies. Foreign investors were free to repatriate capital and remit profits, dividends, royalties, fees, and commissions in any foreign currency other than those of Israel and South Africa. The government also provided a large package of tax incentives for investing firms. Some 82 per cent of foreign companies in the 1984 survey liked the government's investment tax incentives. The incentives have varied from time to time, but as of 1986, they included:

(1) Pioneer Status: This incentive gave full tax relief for a period of five years for a company manufacturing a 'promoted' product. Pioneer firms could also get tax relief at the expiration of their pioneer status for capital expenditure incurred during the pioneer period.

(2) Investment Tax Credit: This incentive was the most common. Profits were exempted from tax up to 100 per cent of capital expenditure over a five-year period.

(3) Abatement of Adjusted Income: This incentive adjusted income according to a company's level of exports, use of local materials in export-ed products, and location in designated industrial areas (see MIDA, *Annual Report*, 1985: 14, for further details).

(4) Other incentives included Accelerated Depreciation Allowance, Re-investment Allowance, Incentives for Research and Development, Capital Allowance for Plant and Machinery, and Export Credit Refinancing Scheme (see Ministry of Finance, 1986: 144–5).

Overall, up to 1983 the leaders were able to get foreign investment at levels they considered adequate for their goals. How did the strategies of foreign companies fit in with Malaysian policies? What were the benefits and shortcomings of foreign companies in Malaysia?

Capitalizing on International Diversity

If we were to go by the assumptions of the dependency theorists, the Malaysian state élites would have found it difficult to get strong multinational participation. Multinationals were portrayed as large capital-intensive firms interested only in large markets and rather unwilling (unless huge profits could be made) to enter into joint ventures as minority partners. In contrast, Malaysia's market was small and the state élites wanted multinationals to provide both high employment and significant ownership to locals, particularly Malay interests.

The international economy, however, should be seen as offering greater diversity than suggested by the dependency theorists. Multinationals exhibit a greater range of firm types than just the large capital-intensive multinational. The dependency image of multinationals had its origins in the experience of Latin American countries with US multinationals. However, the types of foreign investment available to a country depend on its particular policies and characteristics as well as its regional environment. Malaysian officials were able to enjoy some degree of choice in picking multinationals from East Asia, Europe, and the US.

To generate employment, the leaders promoted labour-intensive, export-oriented multinationals, primarily from Japan and the US. And to increase local ownership, the officials turned to all those multinationals which were willing to take minority positions, seeking them out from diverse national origins.

Labour-intensive, Export-oriented Production

In the late 1960s, the planners realized that Malaysia's easy phase of import-substitution manufacturing was running against the country's small market size. Already in 1968, new incentives, under the 1968 Investment Incentives Act, were introduced to encourage export-production in order to increase manufacturing output. The major impetus for export-production, however, came after the 1969 racial riots when employment creation became a major goal.

The key to the export strategy was the establishment of special Free Trade Zones (FTZs) in 1971 outside the Principal Customs Territory of Malaysia. Raw materials, component parts, and semi-finished and finished products could be shipped into and out of the FTZs without being subject to any customs and excise duties. Many special benefits were given to firms entering these zones to produce for export. Very few of the bureaucratic controls of the NEP and the ICA applied to them. Companies could be wholly foreign owned if they exported their entire output. They were also given pioneer status, which exempted them from income tax for a period up to ten years. Many restrictions were put on union formation in these zones as well.

As a result of the special provisions, the textiles and electronics sectors grew rapidly. In the electrical machinery sector, comprising mainly semiconductor component assembly, the percentage of total manufacturing value-added increased from 2.4 per cent to 17.1 per cent between 1968 and 1982 while the share of manufacturing employment grew from 1.7 per cent to 17.1 per cent (Osman-Rani, Anuwar Ali and Toh Kin Woon, 1986: 2, Table 1). Textiles' share of manufacturing value-added increased from 3.1 per cent to 7.1 per cent while the employment share grew from 6.6 per cent to 12.4 per cent in the same period. In 1985, the electronics sector contributed 54.1 per cent of manufacturing exports while the textile sector contributed 11.8 per cent (*Fifth MP*, 1986: 338).

The Electronics Industry. The electronics industry in general can be divided into three sub-sectors: industrial electronics (large computers, robots, and telecommunications equipment), consumer electronics (for example, radios, televisions, personal computers, and VCRs), and components (for example, passive devices and semi-conductors).[2] The overwhelming portion of Malaysia's electronics industry has been in the assembly of semi-conductors using cheap labour.

Prior to 1971, there were only two Japanese companies, Matsushita and Toshiba, in the electronics sector. Both companies assembled black-and-white television receivers for the domestic market. The great change in the electronics industry came with the active wooing of US companies to locate their labour-intensive assembly operations in Malaysia's FTZs. The US companies were under constant pressure to reduce their costs because of the need to quickly capture market share, given the short product life of electronic components (Chang, 1971: 11–13). Most of them went initially to Singapore, Mexico, and Taiwan. However, by the mid-1970s Malaysia had become the favoured investment location because of its cheaper wage costs. Japanese electronics companies later followed suit in order to compete with the US companies.

In 1982, there were more than 100 electronic companies in Malaysia; among them were nearly all the world's major companies. The US companies included Hewlett–Packard, Intel, National Semiconductor, RCA, Mostek, ITT, and Motorola. From Japan came Hitachi, Omron, NEC, Toshiba; and from Western Europe, Siemens of West Germany.[3] Their assembled products were exported to the US, Japan, and Western Europe. The largest exporters were the US firms, which collectively exported 70 per cent of the industry's total exports, mainly to the US (NST, 20 June 1984).

By 1978, Malaysia had become the largest producer of semi-conductor devices in the world, overtaking the more established industries in Hong Kong, Singapore, and Taiwan (BT, 30 August 1978).[4] From a gross output of $24 million in 1970, the figure had reached nearly $6 billion in 1984 (IMP, Electronics Industry, 1985: 8, Table II-1).

In spite of these impressive statistics, the most important contribution of the electronics industry was only in the provision of high levels of employment. From a mere 577 full-time workers in 1970, employment increased to 41,000 in 1976 and to an estimated 83,000 in 1984 (IMP, Electronics Industry, 1985: 8, Table II-1). The electronics industry became the most important absorber of low-skilled labour in the manufacturing sector, and directly contributed to the lowering of the country's unemployment rate in the 1970s and early 1980s.

However, there were several weaknesses in the electronics industry, resulting from the enclave nature of its production. Most of the intermediate products, such as the IC brain, lead-frames, gold wires, and ceramic packaging, were imported from abroad. In 1983, the semiconductor industry exported $3.85 billion worth of semi-conductors but imported components and machinery amounting to $3.54 billion, earning only $310 million in foreign exchange (BT, 6 October 1984). Very few linkages were established with local firms, which merely supplied items such as plastic packaging materials and cardboard boxes, and fitted the factories with furniture, electrical wiring, and carpets.

The industry was also heavily concentrated in the component sub-sector. In comparison to other countries, there was a noticeable absence of forward linkages extending from components to the manufacture of consumer and industrial products (see Table 6.3).

There was no improvement from 1976 to 1984. In 1976, the distribution of the component, consumer, and industrial sub-sectors was 82.3 per cent, 11.6 per cent, and 6.0 per cent; in 1984 it was 84.2 per cent, 11.8 per cent, and 4.0 per cent (IMP, Electronics Industry, 1985: 14). The consequences of over-concentration in the components sector were (1) low wages for workers because of the concentration in lower value-added activities, and

TABLE 6.3
Comparison of Electronics Sector with Selected Countries, 1982
(sub-sector percentage)

Sub-sector	Malaysia	Singapore	South Korea	Japan
Industrial	5.7	14.8	16.0	35.9
Consumer	8.7	33.3	38.6	32.2
Components	85.6	51.9	45.4	31.9
Total	100.0	100.0	100.0	100.0

Source: IMP, Electronics Industry, 1985: 15, Figure II-6.

(2) the volatile nature of the industry in Malaysia because of rapid product obsolescence, leading to severe retrenchments during recessions.

There was very little incentive to manufacture intermediate inputs such as aluminium and gold wires, lead-frames, ceramic packages, and wafers because these could be flown in cheaply from abroad. Equally serious was the government's lack of leadership in building up the electronics industry. It merely looked to the electronics sector to absorb labour since its priorities were elsewhere. According to a high-level local executive in a major US electronics firm:[5]

There is much more the Malaysian government could have done in electronics to increase value-added. The person who was in charge of electronics in the Ministry of Trade and Industry did not know much about electronics. I do not think he visited a single factory before, yet he made policies for the electronics industry. There is six to seven hundred million dollars worth of components that can be potentially import-substituted. The government should have given incentives for joint ventures between locals and foreigners to fabricate these products. Our company makes some intermediate products in Singapore but not in Malaysia. It is not a question of avoiding putting all the eggs in one basket. Malaysia has done a poor job of selling itself and pushing for the further development of electronics.

From time to time, state officials expressed interest in silicon wafer production in Malaysia, an extremely delicate operation that superimposed integrated circuit patterns on silicon wafers. This industrial process depended on large amounts of electricity, but more importantly on an extremely constant voltage supply. The government, however, was slow in providing the necessary infrastructure—Malaysia's electricity charges were very high and its electricity supply suffered from high voltage fluctuations.

The critical shortcoming in establishing extensive forward linkages in electronics, such as disk drives, keyboards, and television receivers, was the absence of a strong supporting local sector. Multinationals producing these items in Singapore, Taiwan, and South Korea usually relied on ancillary firms to supply disk drive parts, and plastic and metal shells for various equipment. In Taiwan, for example, small- and medium-scale local enterprises with fewer than 100 workers engaged in various precision engineering activities, such as the machining of metal parts, die casting, and plastic moulding. The small business sector in Malaysia did not get much support from the government and failed to enjoy the same tax incentives as the large multinationals. Part of the problem was the bias of bureaucrats for large-scale projects, since they had very little understanding of how small enterprises functioned or fitted into the activities of the larger companies. A further problem was that the more capable entrepreneurs in the small- and medium-scale sector were the Chinese. The government did not show much interest in their vigorous development.

Toward the end of 1985, the government began to make a more concerted effort to develop the micro-electronics sector. The weakening commodity sector and the emerging economic crisis were undermining all previous assumptions. The electronics industry was also generating less employment because of rapid strides in the automation of many assembly activities. The government's hope of taxing electronic companies when their pioneer status expired did not materialize as companies threatened to go to more lucrative tax havens like Thailand. The next best alternative was to intensify the development of the electronics industry. The Prime Minister's Department established the Malaysian Institute of Micro-Electronic Systems to carry out basic and applied research in micro-electronics and new incentives were granted to foreign companies to develop more backward and forward linkages in the electronics sector. Whether the new effort will bear fruit remains to be seen. Malaysia will have much catching up to do since countries such as Taiwan, South Korea, and Singapore had early on in the 1970s moved strongly into the manufacture of disk drives, computer clones, and other consumer electronics products.

Textiles. For many countries, the textile industry constituted the first stage of their industrialization process. This was true not only in the Western industrialized countries but also in the industrially more advanced Third World societies. Local demand, cheap labour, and protected markets supported the industrial efforts of indigenous entrepreneurs in textiles. In Malaysia, cheap imports during the colonial era forestalled the development of a strong textile industry. In the 1960s, when the government encouraged local industrialization, the initiative for textile development came from East Asian investors, particularly from Hong Kong. Hong Kong textile firms, sometimes in partnership with local Chinese or with Japanese interests, entered Malaysia to take advantage of quota allocations under the Generalized System of Preferences given by the US and European countries. The most important activities were the manufacture of spun cotton, cotton fabrics, and cotton garments.

In 1970, there were only fifteen textile establishments in pioneer industries (FIDA, *Annual Report*, 1971: 77). The most prominent firms were Textile Alliance Limited, a partnership of Hong Kong and Japanese interests based in Hong Kong, and Yangtze-Kiang, a Hong Kong company started by Shanghai industrialists. At the end of the 1960s, the textile industry was only weakly developed, accounting for 3.1 per cent of the value-added of the manufacturing sector and 6.6 per cent of employment. The distribution of paid-up capital was 41.5 per cent foreign and 58.5

per cent local (FIDA, *Annual Report*, 1971: 77).

As with the electronics sector, the textile industry began to pick up with the setting up of free trade zones in Malaysia. The main investors in the 1970s were from Japan, although companies from Hong Kong and, to a lesser extent, from Singapore, also made sizeable investments. The strong pull factors were the tax holidays and the duty-free import and export of goods in the zones. However, there were other important considerations, particularly the lower costs of production in Malaysia and its quota allocations under the Multi-Fibre Agreement.

Japanese firms were suffering from high wage and land costs, and were under pressure to go offshore to remain competitive. Companies from Hong Kong were not so much relocating their textile activities in Malaysia as using the country as a convenient platform for further expansion. With Malaysia's lower wages costs, these firms could use their obsolete machinery in Malaysia and still produce competitively.[6] In the mid-1970s, land values in Malaysia were one-fifth the cost in Hong Kong, while labour costs were 30 per cent lower (*BT*, 17 November 1978).[7]

In addition, as the US and the EEC became more protectionist in textiles, the East Asian firms, particularly from Hong Kong, were under great pressure to capitalize on whatever quota allocations they could amass. Although quota allocations to Malaysia were very small (being an international latecomer to the textile and garment industry), the foreign firms still considered it worthwhile to produce and export from Malaysia.[8] Malaysia also had a favourable policy of not discriminating against foreign companies in its quota allocations, which were given out on the basis of a company's track record.

A major difference between some of the new companies and past investors was the highly integrated nature of textile production and the movement into synthetic fabric manufacture. Japanese companies were primarily responsible for this change. The Pen-Group was set up in the early 1970s by Toray Industries Inc of Japan in partnership with Textile Alliance of Hong Kong. Six companies formed an integrated complex, involved all the way from synthetic fibre-making to spinning and weaving, and the manufacture of garments. Figure 6.1 shows the group's structure.

Penfibre was the only synthetic fibre-making plant in Malaysia. Toray's main reasons for investing were to utilize inexpensive labour, reduce costs, expand into third country markets, and benefit from the government's tax incentives. In 1982, the company had invested a total of $600 million in the project and was employing 7,000 workers (*MB*, December 1982: 13).

Two other examples of Japanese investment in textiles were Kanetso Malaysia and Kanematsu–Gosho. Kanematsu came to Malaysia to manufacture wool tops, which were used for making yarn for woollen suiting. Wool imported from Australia was sorted out and washed in Malaysia, and then exported to Japan, Singapore, Hong Kong, West Germany, and the UK. Malaysia was chosen primarily for its cheap labour. The company considered setting up its plant in Australia, the raw material source, but found the labour unions to be too powerful and disruptive (*MB*, April 1974). Its executives also found Malaysia to have a more favourable

FIGURE 6.1
Structure of the Pen-Group

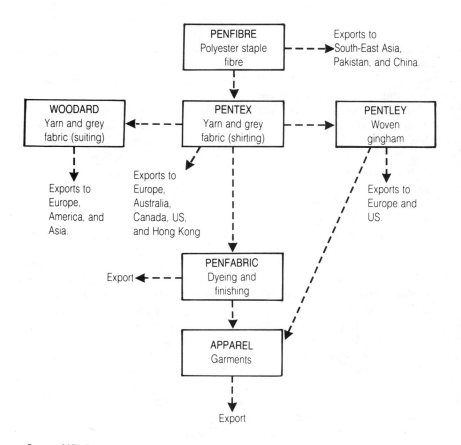

Source: *MB*, December 1982: 16.

location and wage structure than Korea and Taiwan, while its bureaucratic machinery was more efficient than Indonesia's.

Kanetso Malaysia was a joint venture between Kanebo and the trading company Mitsui. It began production in Malaysia in 1975 (*BT*, 6 May 1983). The company made yarn from a fibre developed and manufactured by the parent company. Kanetso became the largest producer of acrylic yarn in Malaysia, and its products were exported to Europe, Australia, the US, and the Middle East. It started to go into fabric production in the early 1980s.

Investors from Hong Kong, unlike those from Japan, concentrated on cotton rather than synthetic products. Some of the larger firms that came were Dragon and Phoenix, Kamunting, and Imperial. They came to benefit from Malaysia's quota allowance in the highly regulated world market for cotton garments, and produced name brands such as Levis and Texwood under contract from their principals in the West.

TABLE 6.4
Main Foreign Investors in Textiles, 1983

Country	Paid-up Capital (M$ million)	Share (Per Cent)
Japan	168.1	44.3
Hong Kong	102.4	27.2
Singapore	61.5	16.2
West Germany	21.2	5.6
Others	25.7	6.7
Total	378.9	100.0

Source: IMP, Textiles/Apparel, 1985: 23, Table II-6.

With the FTZs, the output of textiles increased rapidly from $0.4 billion to $1.97 billion in 1981. Table 6.4 shows the main foreign investors in textiles in 1983 by paid-up capital. Overall, foreign firms had 41.3 per cent of total paid-up capital while local firms had 58.7 per cent. Local firms were typically small- and medium-scale establishments in garment-making, knitting, and batik printing, producing principally for the protected domestic market (see IMP, Textiles, 1985: 24).

The main contribution of the textiles industry, as in electronics, was in the provision of high employment. There were 33,552 workers in the industry in 1973, and this figure increased to 51,363 in 1979 and 72,925 in 1981. In 1983, textiles employed 18 per cent of the manufacturing labour force (BT, 3 November 1983). As an extremely competitive and low-profit sector, the textile industry paid amongst the lowest wages in the country.

The enclave nature of production in the Free Trade Zones resulted in poor spin-off effects for the economy. The industry was divided into the foreign-dominated export sector located in the FTZs and the local sector, which produced for a protected local market. There was no benefit for local firms to purchase their inputs from the FTZ companies, since these would be taxed as imports. The foreign firms bought nearly all their intermediate products such as fabrics, fibres, and chemicals abroad, particularly from their parent companies. In 1982, for example, only 6.5 per cent of total raw material procurement worth $486.5 million was purchased from the principal customs area (IMP, Textiles, 1985: 38). The segmentation of the industry was not conducive to the development of the local sector, which was further handicapped by the fact that non-FTZ firms did not enjoy duty exemptions and generous tax privileges.

In short, labour-intensive, export-oriented multinationals generated high levels of employment but failed to create many linkages in the economy. The government was relatively passive in formulating policies to lay the basis of a more dynamic electronics and textile sector; its main interest in that sector was the quick provision of employment while it concentrated on the creation of a Malay capitalist and managerial class under the NEP. The jobs in the textiles and electronics sectors were hardly sufficient for a decent livelihood for the worker. The main benefit of these jobs, it appears, was to help augment family income by providing new employment opportunities for unemployed and underemployed family members in poor rural and urban poor households. McGee (1986: 663), for instance, has pointed out the role of these urban sector jobs for augmenting the income of poor households, particularly in the rural areas:

For instance, why is it that so many households in Kedah with incomes falling below the 'poverty line' have television sets, as shown from village surveys conducted in the 'Labour Force Formation in Penang Study'? There are many explanations, but our data strongly suggest that remittances from urban-based workers are a major factor contributing to rural income and ownership of material possessions. The fact that one solution to the problem of rural poverty is the growth of the Malay urban working class and middle-class is not seriously considered. . . .

Casting the Multinational Net Widely

The other principal concern of the state élites was to get multinationals to provide ownership opportunities for local interests, particularly state enterprises and Malay businessmen. The general rule was that foreign companies that relied significantly on the local market or on local raw materials were required to have 70 per cent Malaysian ownership, of which at least 30 per cent had to be allocated to Malay interests. Even though the equity conditions the country imposed were rather stringent considering the small domestic market, the leaders nonetheless counted on multinationals for large capital inflows and technological know-how.

However, one of the problems of foreign investment in the 1970s and 1980s was that traditionally strong investors from the UK and the US were not making broad-based investments in the country. There were very few investment projects from the UK.[9] Although Table 6.5 shows that the accumulated fixed assets of UK companies as of 1983 were high, most of

TABLE 6.5

Top Ten Foreign Investors (Fixed Assets) in Malaysia
as of 31 December 1983

Country	Fixed Assets (M$ million)	Percentage of Total Foreign Investments
1. Singapore	1,069.8	25.0
2. Japan	766.6	17.8
3. UK	755.2	17.6
4. US	473.0	11.0
5. Hong Kong	305.0	7.1
6. Australia	131.5	3.1
7. West Germany	114.9	2.7
8. Holland	88.1	2.1
9. India	57.9	1.3
10. Switzerland	50.9	1.2
Others	483.5	11.2
Total	4,296.4	100.0

Source: MIDA, Investment Promotion Division.

TABLE 6.6
Sectoral Distribution of Fixed Assets
by Nationality (Selected), 1983 (percentage)

Sector	Japan	USA	UK	Germany	Singapore	Hong Kong
Food manufacturing	7.0	1.9	17.7	2.6	21.2	16.3
Beverages/tobacco	—	6.1	21.3	—	14.3	—
Textiles	22.0	0.8	—	16.6	3.5	29.2
Wood products	3.3	2.1	—	—	2.9	3.2
Chemical products	2.7	9.7	12.0	8.7	3.1	18.4
Petroleum	—	n.a.	21.9	—	1.3	—
Rubber products	2.0	7.6	5.2	5.2	2.6	3.9
Non-metallic mineral products	8.9	0.6	10.7	—	13.2	0.3
Basic metal products	4.8	—	—	4.3	7.2	—
Fabricated metal products	2.7	0.1	—	0.8	5.7	0.3
Electrical/ electronic	29.9	58.9	6.2	26.3	9.1	12.4
Transport equipment	6.2	3.8	0.9	3.2	2.2	2.6
Scientific equipment	—	0.4	—	16.6	—	—
Others	10.5	8.0	4.1	15.7	13.7	13.4
Total	100.0	100.0	100.0	100.0	100.0	100.0

Source: Calculated from data provided by MIDA, Investment Promotion Division.

the increase came from the expansion of British companies established in the 1960s. Large investments were made by one company in particular, the Anglo-Dutch Shell Company, which was expanding its petroleum refining and petro-chemical facilities to meet greater domestic demand (see Table 6.6).

A major reason for the sluggishness of new British investments was the change in the country's political and economic orientation when it joined the European Economic Community in 1971. British manufacturers, lured by the potentially larger market of the EEC, preferred to strengthen and build commercial relations with Europe rather than with the Commonwealth.[10] British equipment manufacturers of electricity meters and boilers, for example, took the Malaysian market for granted and preferred to simply export from Britain. But gradually they lost their market in Malaysia because they failed to cultivate strong ties with local salesmen and to keep up with changing market trends and tastes.[11] Only the manufacturers which entered to produce locally in the 1960s, such as ICI and Lever Brothers, managed to remain entrenched in the market against new competitors for East Asia.

New investments from the US were heavily concentrated in the electronics sector. There were very few new projects in the other sectors. As with the British case, most of the investments went to expand existing capacity, especially in the chemical and petro-chemical sectors.

New US firms were reluctant to enter Malaysia because of their distaste for holding minority positions in joint ventures. According to an official in MIDA:[12]

The US firms seem to be living in a world of their own. They are the least sensitive to the national aspirations of Third World countries. Companies from other countries have learned to share ownership, although they are still able to have management control by holding key posts in the project. You can have management control without ownership control. Some US companies were given approval for certain projects, but as soon as they learned that they could only have minority positions, they opted out of the projects.

The preference for majority-controlled and wholly owned subsidiaries stemmed from a corporate culture that gave a strong role to the board of directors. US companies, therefore, exercised control through ownership rather than management. Unlike Japanese companies, US companies in electronics, for example, were quite prepared to have a fully Malaysianized management structure but made sure that the boards exercised ultimate control. Existing US companies producing for the domestic market had little choice but to adjust to minority positions, since firms from other nations were prepared to take minority positions. But Malaysia's regulated environment kept potential US investors away, and encouraged them go to places such as Singapore, where minimal controls existed.

The lower than anticipated participation of British and US companies was, however, compensated by investments from other countries. Table 6.5 shows some interesting features about the top ten investing countries in 1983: (1) Three countries from among the less developed nations—Singapore, Hong Kong, and India—were among the top ten investors. Indeed, Singapore was the largest investor in Malaysia; (2) No country had more than 25 per cent of total investments in Malaysia, showing that there was no major reliance or dependence on a single investment source; (3) Compared to the 1960s, many new investors, particularly from Western Europe and Australia, became prominent in Malaysia. Japan, too, moved up several notches to become the second largest investor in Malaysia.[13]

The diversification of investment sources was part of a broader strategy to give Malaysia greater manoeuvrability in pursuing its economic policies. In 1980, the Finance Minister, Tengku Razaleigh Hamzah, highlighted Malaysia's approach in a seminar on 'Negotiating With and Regulating Transnational Corporations' (cited in *MB*, June 1980: 37):

Multinationals are no longer exclusively identified with one major industrial country only. In recent years multinationals have sprung up in many industrial countries and in some developing countries as well. One further way therefore of dealing with multinationals more effectively is to encourage as much competition as possible amongst multinationals of different origins and orientations. We have done this in Malaysia and perhaps could do more.

The strategy of increasing national bargaining power by getting wide multinational participation was aimed less at making foreign firms carry out greater R and D activities, transfer technology, or maximize local content but merely at increasing local ownership opportunities.

Third World multinationals were attractive because they did not consider the retention of high equity and control as paramount criteria for investment. Singaporean, Indian, and Hong Kong firms were not global entities with large capital bases, and often sought local partners for capital and equity. They were slightly ahead of local entrepreneurs in technological sophistication, while their competitive edge over the advanced multinationals resided in their ability to produce goods for the lower end of the market cheaply and in relatively small volumes (see Wells, 1981: 27; Lecraw, 1981: 41). We have already noted the strong role of Hong Kong firms in the export-oriented sector; here we will only consider Singaporean and Indian investments.

In 1984, there were 776 Singaporean firms in Malaysia (MIDA, unpublished). Most were small- and medium-sized establishments, although a minority were foreign firms entering Malaysia from Singapore (for example, Matsushita) or were large public companies listed in the stock exchanges of both countries. In 1982, the largest number of Singaporean companies were in food manufacturing, followed by wood products, chemical products, fabricated metal products, and textiles. The primary motivations for investing were to cut down on the high costs of production in Singapore, get access to raw materials (especially in wood products and non-metallic mineral products), and to expand into the Malaysian market.

As the Singaporean population became increasingly wealthy, they turned to more sophisticated, imported, name-brand goods. Many Singaporean firms were, therefore, forced to seek new markets for 'low-income' products, such as kerosene stoves, simple cooking utensils, and garments, in Malaysia. Increasing wage and land costs in Singapore, too, forced large numbers of Singaporean firms in low value-added, labour-intensive industries, such as textiles, to shift to Malaysia to remain competitive.

Typically, the Singaporean companies had Malaysian Chinese friends and relatives as partners. When it was necessary to have Malay co-owners, it was usual to choose Malay individuals rather than state firms as partners. The former were probably considered more pliable and profit oriented.

India was the third largest source of foreign investment among the less developed countries. In 1982, there were 228 Indian joint ventures abroad. Malaysia had the largest share (29), followed by Indonesia (10), and Kenya (10) (BT, 9 November 1982). Indian investments were a relatively late phenomenon in Malaysia. The pressure to go abroad came from the Indian government, who wanted Indian firms to earn their own foreign exchange because of foreign exchange shortages in India. In its investment guidelines, the government also stipulated that Indian joint ventures could only have minority Indian equity, which should be financed by the export of plant, machinery, and technology (BT, 10 September 1982).

The Indian joint ventures were owned by the large industrial houses of India, such as Birla, Tata, Godrej, Kirloskar, and Gajras. Most of the investments were in food production, especially in the refining of palm oil and manufacture of derivatives. India was the world's largest buyer of refined palm oil, so entering Malaysia allowed the Indians to capture value-added operations in palm oil products and save on foreign exchange. The other important investments of Indian joint ventures were in the making of non-metallic mineral products (glass containers), transport equipment (bicycle and scooter chains, pistons, cylinder liners, and the assembly of trucks), and textiles (cotton of blended yarn and synthetic and blended fabrics) (*Economic Times*, Bombay, 18 July 1984).

The Indian joint ventures eagerly formed partnerships with state corporations, particularly the Negeri Sembilan SEDC, since these state organizations had liquid funds and access to banks, which the Indians needed. But Indian joint ventures tended to perform poorly. Some went bankrupt—there were thirty-seven joint ventures in the late 1970s but the number fell to twenty-nine in 1982—while others were barely breaking even. Except for the import of palm oil products, the Indians had not established a market for their products in Malaysia. Enjoying a sellers market at home, they were poor at marketing their products in Malaysia. They also got little help from the Chinese-dominated retail market, which showed 'an almost xenophobic antagonism . . . to goods manufactured by these companies' (Kumar, 1975: 14).

Part of the problem was that the Indians bore little risks in their investments. They relied on their partners for capital and only supplied their surplus machinery. In spite of losses, they could collect managerial and technical fees. In the case of NS Gula, for example, the Indian partner was willing to go on with a sugar-refining venture in spite of enormous losses since the Negeri Sembilan state corporation bore all the costs. For the local partners, Indian joint ventures promised easy ownership opportunities but entailed very high risks.

Among the investors from the more advanced countries, the Japanese played an important role in compensating for the weakness of British investments and the reluctance of US companies to be minority joint venture partners. Japanese investments were most prominent in the export-oriented electronics and textile sectors (see Table 6.6), but they were also high in domestically oriented sectors, such as transport equipment, fabricated metals, basic metal products, and non-metallic mineral products. In the 1970s, Japan had become Malaysia's predominant supplier of manufactured goods and the major source of machinery and transport equipment.[14] Japanese companies, therefore, had a stake in keeping costs down and maintaining their market share by investing in Malaysia.

Some major Japanese joint venture projects were actually initiated by the Malaysian government. The state-owned Heavy Industry Corporation of Malaysia (HICOM) was the majority partner in a number of joint ventures with Japanese interests. These included the establishment of Malaysia's largest steel-billets mill with a group of eight Japanese companies led by Nippon Steel Corporation, three joint ventures with Yamaha, Suzuki, and Honda for the manufacture of small motor-cycle engines, the manufacture of a national car with Mitsubishi Motor Company, and a cement plant (*FEER*, 14 February 1985: 90–1). Although these projects were questionable in view of the limited domestic market, the Japanese firms were probably enticed by the prospect of selling machinery to these large projects. Moreover, as minority partners, the Japanese did not have to bear the major risks of the projects. Whatever profits resulting from strong market protection would be a bonus. The chance to capture a large market share was critical for Mitsubishi's entry into car manufacturing. Prior to the car project, Mitsubishi had only a small share of the automobile market but now the venture promised a near monopoly position for Mitsubishi.

One of the favourable features of Japanese investors from the Malaysian government's point of view was their willingness to enter as minority partners. In contrast to US multinationals, prominent Japanese companies such as Lion Corporation, Seikisui Chemical Company, NGK Spark Plug, Dainippon Ink and Chemicals, and Nippon Electric easily took up local partners. However, by taking the key financial and technical positions in the joint ventures and maintaining constant channels of communication with the parent company, Japanese executives essentially controlled the company's operations. The main complaint of Japanese executives and investors was not the government's equity conditions but the stringent limitations it placed on the number of expatriate personnel in Malaysian companies.[15]

Except for powerful state corporations like HICOM, where some accommodation of interests was necessary, Japanese executives made most of the important managerial decisions in their joint ventures with the smaller state enterprises. In a study of joint ventures between state enterprises and foreign companies, where Japanese constituted the largest group in the sample, Abdul Razak Abdul (1984: 279–90) found that local managers were relatively weak in advancing Malaysian interests. This situation was not surprising given the government's priority of nominal Malay ownership.

Western European investments from Germany, Switzerland, and Holland entered Malaysia in the 1970s. Malaysian officials made frequent trips to these countries to familiarize businessmen there with Malaysia and its economic conditions. The industrial structures of these countries were dominated by specialized, medium-scale enterprises, which did not have the informational base of the large multinationals. Information, therefore, had to be brought to them. These enterprises were suitable for Malaysia because they were adept at producing in moderate volumes and were willing to give majority stakes to locals when required.

In the first phase, Western European firms, particularly from West Germany, came to Malaysia to assemble electronic components and scientific equipment such as optics and surgical tools for export. Wage costs and tax incentives were the primary considerations in investing. In the second phase, German, Swiss, and Dutch companies entered Malaysia to utilize Malaysian raw materials, including wood and rubber, for manufacturing products such as shuttering boards, catheters, and condoms for the home markets. Coming to Malaysia gave these firms a competitive edge over rival firms and importers in their countries by saving on wage and transportation costs. In the most recent phase, Western European firms have come to produce for the local and regional markets. Some examples are Swiss companies manufacturing plastic collapsible tubes and earth leakage circuit breakers, and German companies manufacturing welding machines and solid rubber tyres.

In conclusion, the government's ability to draw on diverse multinationals helped Malay businessmen and state enterprises to enter the manufacturing sector. It also generated high rates of employment and some industrial diversification. However, there were several weaknesses in the government's promotion of multinationals. The projects had an *ad hoc* pattern, since the primary criterion for entry was conforming to the government's equity rules. In both sectors—export-oriented and domestic market-oriented multinationals—the government failed to strategically link up multinational and local capabilities toward the development of a more innovative manufacturing sector. The joint ventures that were formed took advantage of good demand conditions during Malaysia's years of high growth but were weak at coming up with innovations that could generate new markets within and outside the country. For example, while Third World multinationals readily granted ownership opportunities to locals, they hardly added much sophistication to the nation's industrial capacities. Some merely came to take advantage of export quotas while others came to accumulate foreign exchange for industrial expansion at home. In other Third World countries of comparable national income, locals would probably have undertaken the activities of these companies. However, in Malaysia they replaced the role of the local Chinese businessman, since political factors hampered and weakened the latter's economic role. The government's promotion of multinationals was not aimed at an elaborate division of labour for 'national accumulation' but at meeting its immediate political objectives. When the commodity sector weakened, the nature of the manufacturing sector was such that it could not re-invigorate economic growth and development on its own.

Foreign Investment and Economic Crisis

A central policy goal of the state authorities was to ensure that foreign investment in manufacturing was about 30 per cent of total investment. However, starting from 1981, the foreign percentage of paid-up capital started to fall below this level (see Chapter 5: Figure 5.2). The fall was quite precipitous in 1984 and 1985 when it was 22.7 per cent and 17.8 per cent respectively.

Several factors were responsible for the decrease in foreign investment. All the major electronics component manufacturers had already established themselves in Malaysia. Thus, while this sector had been a major area of investment in the past, it was gradually becoming saturated. Furthermore, Malaysia was becoming less attractive as a place for further investment. Many electronics companies, particularly from Japan, had begun to automate assembly operations in component manufacture using sophisticated robots. It was thus becoming cost-effective to produce in the advanced home countries. As for companies that were still looking for cheap or non-unionized labour, neighbouring countries like Thailand had even lower wage costs and were giving the same tax incentives. Although the multinational subsidiaries in Malaysia decided not to relocate elsewhere—they still found Malaysia a good place to do business—the new expansion projects were coming less and less to Malaysia.

Malaysia was also being bypassed in the higher value-added operations of the electronics sector. Many Japanese and US companies in consumer electronics went to Singapore to manufacture disk drives, name-brand micro-computers, precision parts for audio, video, and automation products, as well as to establish their regional research headquarters. The Malaysians, although offering lower wage costs, could not offer the same infrastructural facilities, ancillary industries, and skilled and technical work-force as Singapore. In particular, the educational system suffered from major weaknesses, especially at the tertiary level. It was preoccupied with questions of ethnic representation in the student body and faculty, as well as the use of the Malay language. Academic excellence and the development of a skilled technical cadre enjoyed low priority.

Finally, the possibilities for manufacturing for the domestic market were becoming increasingly limited. Import-substitution was nearly complete in most mass consumer goods and some intermediate goods. Malaysia did not offer the economies of scale for further import-substitution in machinery and heavy industry. Only the large state enterprises dared to enter into such ventures. They were willing to put aside questions of profitability and, in other instances, were able to enjoy high protection or engage in various oligopolistic arrangements with other domestic producers.

Around 1985, the government leaders and bureaucrats started to worry seriously about the decline of foreign investment. During this time the government's finances had begun to weaken dramatically from low commodity prices, falling oil prices, and increasing domestic and foreign debt payments. Although Chinese manufacturing investments had been sluggish for a long time, the government could overlook this fact by relying on its own resources and foreign capital for manufacturing growth. With state revenue in a perilous condition, the government's role in providing employment for Malays in the bureaucracy and state enterprise sector was in jeopardy. Graduate unemployment became a serious matter, and sagging foreign investments exacerbated the employment situation.

The government's response was to relax some of its equity rules for foreign participation and to remove some of the capacity controls imposed on firms. Most of the liberalization was aimed at export-oriented firms. Some controls were removed for the small Chinese business sector but it was clear that the main thrust of the policies was to count upon foreign investment to resuscitate the economy. The favourable treatment of the foreign sector was based on pragmatic and political considerations. The top leadership was desperate for quick economic growth and employment generation to forestall a serious weakening of its political position. The fastest way was to get foreigners with available technology and markets to set up production. This route was also less controversial. Giving a liberal hand to the Chinese would have signified a fundamental change in the existing political practice. Neither the leaders nor the Malay middle class and business groups who had a stake in the NEP wanted this option.

New guidelines on foreign equity were announced in July 1985 (see

Ministry of Finance, 1985: 154). They were:

(1) For projects exporting 80 per cent or more of production, foreign equity ownership of up to 80 per cent would be allowed. A higher percentage, up to 100 per cent, would be allowed depending on the level of technology, size of investment, spin-off effects, value-added, location, and local content.

(2) Projects exporting between 51 per cent and 79 per cent could have foreign equity of at least 51 per cent, and up to 80 per cent depending on the merits of each case.

(3) Projects exporting between 20 per cent and 50 per cent could have foreign ownership of up to 51 per cent while projects exporting less than 20 per cent would have a maximum of 30 per cent.

(4) In high technology and priority projects, notwithstanding the above, foreign ownership of 51 per cent would be considered.

In the past, only companies exporting 100 per cent of their production could have complete ownership; otherwise even substantial exporters could hope for only 51 per cent. The rest of the companies were usually allowed only 30 per cent foreign equity.

Amendments were also made to the Industrial Coordination Act in December 1985 (see MIDA, *Annual Report*, 1985: 21). In the past, a company that wanted to increase its export capacity needed the government's approval first, while a company that wanted to export a new product could not be assured of getting government approval. Now, provided a company was exporting at least 80 per cent of its production, permission was not required for increasing capacity. Approval would also be given automatically if a company wanted to export a new product. Previously, a company that wanted to increase production for the domestic market was also not assured of approval; the new amendment gave a company automatic approval if its shareholders' funds were below $2.5 million and 30 per cent of its equity had been reserved for Malay interests. The old rules remained for companies making a new product for the domestic market. An important concession, which reduced uncertainty, was the assurance that the original equity conditions would not be changed for a company undertaking expansion or diversification. The most important concession for small businesses, provided they did not already enjoy tax concessions, was the waiving of the 30 per cent Malay equity condition in companies where shareholders' funds were less than $1.5 million. In the past, the threshold had been $0.5 million.

In September 1986, the Prime Minister announced a further round of concessions to foreign investors when he addressed a group of American businessmen and bankers in New York (*ST* (S), 1 October 1986). It came at a time when oil prices had plunged drastically and unemployment was continuing to rise. Foreign companies were now allowed 100 per cent equity if they exported 50 per cent or more of their production or sold at least 50 per cent or more of their product to the Free Trade Zones and Licensed Manufacturing Warehouses. Companies producing for the domestic market could also qualify for 100 per cent foreign ownership if they employed at least 350 full-time workers. The only condition was that employment in all work categories had to reflect the racial composition of the population. In addition, a company with more than $2 million would be automatically allowed five expatriate personnel. These concessions appeared to be directed at both US investors, who preferred full ownership control, and Japanese investors, who liked a strong Japanese managerial presence.

The new relaxations in foreign investment policy were greeted enthusiastically by the foreign business community. In 1987, the Secretary-General of the Japanese Chamber of Trade and Industry in Malaysia (JACTIM) said: 'The third wave [of Japanese participation] is already here. Prime Minister Datuk Seri Dr Mahathir Mohamad got it started with his announcement in New York of a large scale easing of policy over foreign investment' (quoted in MIDA, *Malaysia Industrial Digest*, March–April 1987). The 'third wave' was a reference to the renewed interest of Japanese companies, following the significant appreciation of the yen, to relocate part of their manufacturing base in South-East Asia.[16] At the moment, the most promising sources of investment are from Japan and the other capital surplus nations of East Asia, such as Taiwan and South Korea.[17]

Recent data show that the percentage of foreign paid-up capital in total paid-up capital in Malaysia's manufacturing sector has increased. In 1986 it was 28 per cent or $524.5 million in value, but in the first six months of 1987 it had increased to 47.2 per cent, amounting to $309.1 (MIDA, *Malaysia Industrial Digest*, January 1987; May–June 1987). The increase in the absolute value of investments has not been spectacular; so far foreign investments have only compensated for shortfalls by domestic actors. It is too early to predict how high foreign investments will go, but it is certain to have important consequences for Malaysian politics and the economy. Here we speculate on some possible scenarios.

If foreign investment does not enter in adequate amounts (such as less than $500 million annually), long-term economic stagnation might result. Commodity prices, even if high, are unlikely to lead to the strong growth rates that occurred with the oil boom in the 1970s. Also, even if the Malay leaders were to go against their ingrained attitudes and the sentiments of the Malay middle and business classes by relaxing state regulations on Chinese businesses, the benefits of deregulation would not be immediate. The Chinese business sector has not had the right environment in which to develop its industrial skills; it would take many years to upgrade its capabilities. Without high foreign investment, unemployment could reach 15 per cent. Unemployment has become a major problem, not just among the poorer groups but also among college and university graduates, where the number of unemployed is estimated to be anywhere from 30,000 to 50,000.

In a weak economy several problems are likely to develop. As the means to provide for a positive sum distribution of resources diminish, new divisions will occur in the Malay community. The leaders of the UMNO party, whose support is based on a vast patronage system incorporating disparate socio-economic groups, will face much greater internal dissent. It is unlikely that UMNO can remain strong with the Malays experiencing unmet expectations, despite the legitimacy the party has accumulated from past policies. The Chinese will probably withdraw the little support they give to UMNO's non-Malay allies and turn completely to the non-Malay opposition. With the weakening of the political centre held by UMNO and its allies, the population is likely to become extremely racially polarized. The experience of other ethnic societies shows that it is rarely the case that inter-ethnic majorities form to challenge unpopular regimes. The pattern has been either racial strife, as in Sri Lanka, or an authoritarian regime, as in Guyana, where political leaders from the majority group use coercion to maintain power in the midst of serious disaffection of all the ethnic groups; the inability of the ethnic groups to unite makes it hard to challenge the authoritarian regime.

Malaysians have already witnessed the move away from the controlled pluralism of the past toward greater authoritarianism and personal rule. Dr Mahathir Mohamad, the Prime Minister, facing internal challenges to his rule in UMNO and the upsurge of communal politics, has been the main engineer of this shift. In April 1987, Tengku Razaleigh Hamzah, the former Finance and Trade and Industry Minister, backed by the former Deputy Prime Minister, Datuk Musa Hitam, challenged the Prime Minister for the UMNO presidency. After his narrow victory, Dr Mahathir purged cabinet ministers allied to the Razaleigh–Musa faction. He has since centralized his powers as the President of UMNO, changed the party's rules to favour incumbents, and filled cabinet and party positions with loyalists.[18]

The Prime Minister's most drastic action has been the arrest of 119 people under the Internal Security Act. The justification for the detentions, which began in October 1987, was to quell the build-up of racial tension. Much of the racial provocation was actually initiated by politicians in the government. The Ministry of Education, for example, started to promote non-Chinese educated teachers to administer Chinese primary schools, provoking Chinese educationists and politicians from different parties to come together to oppose the postings (*ST* (S): 1 January 1988). The arrests, however, seemed to be aimed at the administration's critics rather than the racial instigators. Many opposition leaders and parliamentarians from the DAP and PAS parties were roped in, as well as environmentalists, social activists, and trade unionists. Since quashing his critics and potential opponents, Dr Mahathir has gone on to increase the powers of the executive over the judiciary. He has been annoyed by a number of court rulings against his administration. In one case brought by the DAP leader, the judge issued a restraining order blocking a $1.2 billion government contract awarded to a firm owned by the UMNO party.

Thus far no attempt has been made to dismantle the electoral system or bring in the military. However, if there is prolonged economic malaise, it is unlikely that the Prime Minister, or any other Malay leader, can rule with a majority coalition. The political system could then become much more authoritarian. Under these conditions, Islamic fundamentalism might be the only effective channel for political expression. Even if PAS were to lead the movement initially, one can conceive the UMNO leaders trying to follow suit to stay in power. With the economic route to individual and group well-being in obvious jeopardy, cultural chauvinism might prove irresistible in the assertion of Malay group power. For sometime, at least, UMNO might be able to mobilize both lower class and middle class support. Recently, for example, the Johor state government tried to impose the Islamic law on promiscuity (*khalwat*) on non-Muslims. Such actions are bound to have unpleasant effects on racial relations.

If foreign investment inflow is high, such as around $1 billion annually, it will help to stabilize the economic and political situation in Malaysia. Economic recovery might prevent a drift toward greater authoritarianism by allowing the leadership to regain the loyalty of disillusioned former supporters via improvements in their material circumstances. High foreign investment, for example, will help generate sufficient employment opportunities to permit limited mobility for members of poorer Malay households, and ease the potentially explosive situation of graduate unemployment. Giving educational credentials to Malays, especially to those from poor rural families, was a cornerstone of UMNO's claim of being able to provide mobility to Malays. Employment creation will also help to contain disaffection against the political system among the non-Malay poor and middle class. With foreign investments propping up the economy, scarce state resources can then be used for subsidy schemes for the depressed rural sector, whose condition has been worsened by many years of poor commodity prices, and for ongoing programmes to support the new Malay business class, also deeply hurt by the economic crisis.

By regenerating a positive sum economy, high foreign investments might make political competition less of a threat to the present administration. The old game of providing selective benefits to each section of the Malay community can then continue, and will help undercut support for Dr Mahathir's opponents within and outside UMNO. Moreover, the population is less likely to be responsive to government and opposition politicians engaging in extreme racial and religious politics. Such a climate might reassure the present leaders that electoral processes at the party and national levels can work to their advantage.

However, it is unlikely that the recent policies to centralize the powers of the UMNO presidency and weaken the judiciary will be reversed. Future leaders, too, will find these provisions helpful in protecting their power, especially in view of the fact that UMNO may not be as hegemonic in the political system as in the past. Even with economic recovery, the government's foreign and domestic debt burden will act as a crimp on state resources, and will make it difficult to meet all the expectations of UMNO's diverse political base. Although the basic features of the political system might remain, we can expect more voters to turn to opposition Malay and Chinese parties, as well as continued internal struggles within UMNO.

1. The rising unemployment rate at the present time, estimated to hit 10.1 per cent in 1990, will certainly have a deleterious effect on the wage gains of the past (*Fifth MP*, 1986: 141).

2. Semi-conductor devices are divided into discrete circuits (for example, diodes and transistors), integrated circuits such as semi-conductor integrated circuits (MOS, Bipolar), and hybrid integrated circuits (thick and thin films).

3. MIDA: list of electronics companies in production 1982, mimeo.

4. The primary reason was Malaysia's lower wage costs compared to its competitors. It compensated for the country's lower value-added per employee. In the early 1980s, the annual remuneration per employee in the semi-conductor industry was $4,688 in Malaysia, $6,600 in South Korea, $11,164 in Singapore, $24,680 in Japan, and $40,001 in the US. The ratio of value-added to remuneration per employee was highest in Malaysia (3.25), followed by South Korea (2.48), Japan (2.57), the US (2.09), and Singapore (2.08) (*IMP*, Electronics and Electrical Industry, 1985: 17, Table II-2).

5. Interview, March 1985.

6. Interview with a MIDA textile official, February 1985.

7. In the early 1980s, country wage costs comparisons (including social charges) in the textile sector were as follows: US—100, Germany—88, Japan—83, South Korea—22, Hong Kong—19, Taiwan—19, Singapore—18, Malaysia—11, India—8, Thailand—7, China—3, Indonesia—3, and Sri Lanka—3 (Werner, Spring 1984 quoted in *IMP*, Textiles/Apparel Industry, 1985: 42).

8. In the early 1980s, Malaysia had only 0.34 per cent of the world's textile trade and 0.5 per cent of the world's apparel exports.

9. Interview with a MIDA textile official, February 1985.

10. The irony was that as British manufacturers focused on Europe, many Western European manufacturers were getting interested in investing in Malaysia.

11. Interview with a MIDA textile official, February 1985.

12. Interview with a MIDA official, February 1985.

13. See Chapter 3, Table 3.2.

14. In 1985, Japan supplied 33.0 per cent of Malaysia's manufactured imports, followed by 7.8 per cent from the US and 7.5 per cent from Singapore. In machinery and transport equipment imports, Japan's share was 32.9 per cent, the US's 23.9 per cent, and West Germany's 5.7 per cent (Ministry of Finance, 1986: xxix, Table 3.4).

15. Interview with a Jetro official, March 1985.

16. The first wave was the rush of Japanese manufacturing investments in 1973 and 1974 in the export-oriented sectors. The second wave was the flood of general construction companies in 1982–3 to compete for government contracts in dams, roads, power generation facilities, and buildings.

17. Interestingly, Taiwanese companies manufacturing for export have also started to become prominent in Malaysia; they appear to be diffusing possible US protectionism against them by using other offshore export bases.

18. In Chapter 4, we mentioned that one interpretation of Razaleigh's near victory was the support he received from small- and medium-scale Malay businessmen who saw Dr Mahathir as closely tied to and favouring a narrow clique of Malay businessmen and state capitalists. This view is consistent with the author's argument that the long economic drought has produced new divisions in the Malay community, but more research is necessary to determine whether a clear-cut class basis underpins the conflict.

7 Conclusion

WE began by advancing two rational models of economic development. One was the market approach of the neo-classical development economists and the other the 'state activist' model of the new dependency theorists. The market approach insisted on a minimal role for the state in economic development. Among its many stipulations, a primary one was that the general social welfare was best served by leaving the market to judge who the most capable entrepreneurs were. The state activist approach, on the other hand, argued for a prominent role for the state. Leaving economic development to the market in Third World countries would result in short-term profit maximization and in multinationals dominating the economy. Successful economic development needed a strong state that was free from the narrow interests of the dominant economic classes. This autonomy was necessary to control multinationals, while enlisting their participation, and to forge an effective entrepreneurial alliance among state enterprises, local capital, and multinationals for successful national development.

Both approaches failed to take root in Malaysia. Underlying these models was the premise that the interests of the state élites and the capitalist classes were ultimately congruent. We argued that such a view was inapplicable in Malaysia where the politically dominant group was also economically weak. Malay insecurity and sense of weakness, and the dynamics of Malay élite competition for political power precluded any long-term convergence of interests between the state élites and the non-Malay capitalist classes.

The closest Malaysia came to the *laissez-faire* model was in the 1960s. In this period, the moderate Malay leader of the UMNO party, Tunku Abdul Rahman, concentrated on laying the basis for multiracial accommodation in society, and made important compromises with the Malayan Chinese Association, a party controlled by Chinese economic élites. There was little interference in the activities of the foreign and Chinese business groups, who were looked upon to diversify and build up the economy. The principal avenue for sponsoring Malay mobility was through bureaucratic recruitment and expansion, and only limited measures were undertaken by the state to promote their business development. The economy grew at a moderately high rate. It had a healthy balance-of-payments situation, and the government's fiscal debt was kept under control.

These economic arrangements were, however, contingent on the

UMNO and MCA parties getting substantial support from their respective ethnic bases. But it was increasingly difficult to do so. The Chinese
lower classes did not get many economic benefits from the MCA and
resented the party for not challenging Malay political predominance. More
damaging was the fact that Malay support for the UMNO began to erode.
Malays across all classes saw their economic weakness as a general debility,
and feared that Chinese economic superiority would eventually result in an
attack on their political status. Poor Malays turned to the communal PAS
party. The Malay middle class of bureaucrats, professionals, and aspiring
businessmen compared themselves unfavourably to the Chinese rich and
agitated for a more vigorous state programme for Malay business. After
1969, following the weakening of UMNO and the eruption of racial riots,
a new group of Malay nationalists took over the party. Under the banner
of the NEP, they sought to expand their political base by devoting more of
society's resources for the creation of a broader Malay capitalist and
middle class. The liberal economic approach had failed because market
outcomes were at variance with the bases of political rule and the interests
of a politically powerful, though economically underdeveloped, middle-
class group.

In the state interventionist phase, the government imposed various controls on the activities of the foreign and Chinese business sectors to allow
for state enterprise and Malay capitalist development. The state was able
to enjoy a high degree of autonomy from the existing dominant economic
groups. It had strong political support and was blessed with enormous
financial resources due to the discovery of oil in the early 1970s and good
commodity prices throughout the decade.

Indeed, the economy grew at relatively high rates up to the early 1980s.
However, it was deceptive in suggesting that the state's new role was
having beneficial consequences for the economy. The state's large resources allowed the political élites to carry out high levels of spending for
their economic restructuring goals, which ricocheted throughout the
economy and created high demand. Amidst recessionary signs in the early
1980s, the state contracted high levels of domestic and foreign debt to
sustain its programme, which propped up growth.

However, beneath the surface, the state's economic policies were weak
in advancing the nation's productive base and technological and managerial capabilities. None of the economic actors—the state, Malay individuals, local Chinese capital, and multinationals—played strong roles
in diversifying the economy away from its heavy reliance on primary
commodities. Because of the easy dependence on commodities, the leaders
and bureaucrats were more interested in controlling the dominant entrepreneurial groups for ethnic and political goals rather than in maximizing
national accumulation. Below we summarize their activities:

The State: One of the main activities of the large state enterprises was the
buying over, with payments amounting to billions of dollars, of foreign
companies in plantations and tin-mining. This route provided a quick
means for state ownership, the creation of a Malay managerial class, and

access to profits for distribution to Malay interests for political support building. However, this route committed resources in slow growth sectors and was weak in creating employment. The state also pumped large resources into new commercial and manufacturing activities, but numerous companies failed. The hurry to expand resulted in little attention being given to questions of viability and managerial competence. The central authorities were often confused about whether to use profit or 'social' criteria, allowing for abuse and corruption among state enterprise managers. A few large capital-intensive and prestigious manufacturing projects, such as making the 'national car', were also undertaken in the 1980s, ostensibly to diversify the economy. In spite of high protection, they ran into severe problems as they faced the realities of the country's limited domestic market.

The government, anxious to extend state patronage and see the development of Malay tycoons, also provided generous financial and policy support to aspiring Malay businessmen. Unfortunately, the failure rate was very high among small Malay businessmen since many entered the same saturated markets. Aiming for quick status, many Malay businessmen put their businesses in jeopardy by using their loans and profits for luxury consumption and by over-stretching themselves. A small group of well-connected Malay tycoons (some present government ministers included) emerged by means of buying corporate shares cheaply through large borrowing from state-controlled banks. Very few of them started their own enterprises and they made marginal contributions to employment and national diversification.

Chinese Business: With the NEP, Chinese businesses came under a regimen of controls aimed at either restricting their participation in sectors where small Malay businesses were concentrated, or making them share ownership with Malay interests at discount prices. Many Chinese businessmen, especially in manufacturing, found the benefits not worth the costs, and refrained from investing. Large Chinese companies were able to cope with the state's requirements, but tended to develop a short-term outlook and to invest in projects with quick returns, such as property development. They also engaged in paper entrepreneurialism, that is to say, they preferred to buy up smaller Chinese companies as a way to grow and make profits, rather than start new ones. Another common strategy was to invest in and buy companies abroad, particularly in Singapore, Hong Kong, Australia, and North America, in order to escape from shrinking opportunities and domestic constraints.

It is hard to say if Chinese industrial capabilities advanced much after the 1960s. The Chinese were historically weak in manufacturing, but now government regulations like the Industrial Coordination Act further inhibited manufacturing involvement. The progress they were making in the 1960s did not carry forward strongly in the 1970s and 1980s.

The Multinationals: While some multinationals carried out activities which locals could not have undertaken, the state did not, in general, strategically link multinationals with local capabilities toward the development of a strong domestic manufacturing sector. The multinationals' role tended to be a 'mopping up' operation to remedy some of the problems of the state's economic policies. Multinationals counteracted the weakness of national actors in providing employment, particularly outside the bureaucracy, and invested in manufacturing when the Chinese hesitated. The labour-intensive, export-oriented electronics and textiles industries provided high employment but failed to generate strong linkages with the rest of the economy. Many Third World multinationals came to Malaysia to take advantage of export quotas given to the country, to earn foreign exchange, and to sell surplus machinery. They were willing to provide ownership opportunities for locals, including Malay interests, but their technological capabilities could not be said to be much higher than those of the Chinese sector.

As long as commodity prices were good, and multinational inflow adequate, national income and employment growth were high. However, when the international economy turned for the worse, especially with the collapse of oil prices in 1986, the underlying problems in the economy were exposed. The economy entered a deep recession and state finances were in dire straits. The domestic economy was not in a position to pull itself up on its own. The Malay leaders looked desperately toward improvements in commodity prices and provided new incentives to increase foreign capital inflow. The zealous pursuit of ethnic priorities had transformed a well-functioning economy in the 1960s into an economy suffering its worst crisis since independence. In a regional context, Malaysia, which had a higher per capita income than Taiwan and South Korea in the 1960s, had by 1980 fallen behind them.[1]

What were the forces at work which resulted in the failure to recognize and check the underlying problems of the economy? Here we offer three main factors:

Competing rationalities: The economic programme of the state gave new support to the UMNO leaders. The party was able to reverse its weakened political position in the late 1960s and ward off the intrusion by its main rival, PAS. Many poor Malay supporters switched their loyalty to UMNO from PAS to benefit from state patronage. Although the middle class benefited the most, the plentiful resources of the state provided a sufficiently positive sum situation to gain the support of poorer rural supporters. By sponsoring Malay entry into commerce, an area where Malays had played a marginal role historically, the party also gained legitimacy by increasing the sense of Malay efficacy and worth. Here, UMNO provided an important psychological benefit. Even in the midst of the economic crisis of 1986, UMNO managed to do well in the elections. The leaders could therefore easily convince themselves that their policies were working. There were few incentives to examine the long-term economic consequences of their policies since these had more immediate political pay-offs.

The Malays who were likely to sense the underlying problems of the economy, and were in a position to influence the government, were the bureaucrats, professionals, and businessmen. But it was precisely this group which benefited most from the government's economic and educational policies.If they had any concern about national economic well-being, it was truncated by short-term self-interest. For many in this group, it was obvious that a weakened economy and financially strapped state would hurt their long-term interests. Loans would be cut, educational and job opportunities for their children would shrink, and demands for their goods and services would weaken. However, after many decades of feeling economically marginal, the sudden bonanza provided by the state was too good to miss. During the whole period of the NEP, the voices in the Malay community speaking out for greater caution in economic management were rare indeed.

Weakness of the private sector in disciplining the state: In many capitalist societies, the private sector plays an important role in checking excessive state encroachment in the functioning of the market. The means used vary from exercising political influence, political mobilization, and withdrawal of capital from the market. In Malaysia, the private sector failed to act as a check on unfavourable state policies. The political power of Chinese business was limited against a state with a strong political base and by the sector's weakness in getting strong working class Chinese support. The Chinese business sector also had weak economic leverage. When it hesitated to invest in the manufacturing sector, the state was able to pump in its own resources and enlist the participation of multinationals. The Chinese sector was further weakened by its inability to forge a common private sector alliance with the foreign sector against the state. There were important differences in their business organizations and attitudes toward state policy-making prerogatives. Only in late 1985, when economic problems were severe, did the state make minor concessions to Chinese businesses.

The foreign sector chose not to vociferously protest the government's economic policies. The foreign business chamber regarded the fundamental objectives of the government as a domestic political matter, and as such not subject to external challenge. Instead, the chamber took the more limited route of advising the government on the inconsistencies between its broad policy objectives and the specific regulations that were imposed. It was left to the individual firm to decide on the merits of investing or expanding its operations in Malaysia. In short, the foreign business sector did not feel obliged to fight for what it considered an ideal economic environment.

The illusion of a constraint-free economy: The state élites in Malaysia operated on the illusion that there was little they could do that would seriously jeopardize the economy. This unbridled optimism was based on the fact that Malaysia had not suffered from severe economic crises or recessions in the past. There was hence no memory of an economy that could go awry. The discovery of oil further buoyed spirits, and gave a false sense of an economy with unlimited possibilities. State élites, therefore, interpreted their policies only in the most favourable light and blocked out any consideration of potential negative consequences. In other words, they became risk-takers instead of being risk-adverse. While such behaviour might be commendable in individuals, it was dangerous for the government, as the custodian of the nation, to act in such a fashion. An outstanding instance of such risk-taking was the government's recourse to massive foreign borrowing after 1981 amidst growing signs of a recession. It worked on the premise that the recession would not last long and oil prices would reach the astronomical figure of US$72.3 per barrel in 1985 (this unrealistic figure was probably based on simple projections of past oil increases). Both assumptions were wrong, resulting in a large jump in the external public debt of the government and in the nation's overall debt servicing ratio.[2]

These processes undoubtedly occur in varying degrees and combinations in many societies. But in Malaysia, the political and cultural dynamics of ethnicity made them combine strongly to compromise policies that would build a strong national economy.

In the present economic debacle, it is unlikely that Malaysia can return to the liberal economic policies of the 1960s. The Malay business class has become a powerful lobby group. While the economic recession might have alerted them to a better understanding of economic vulnerabilities and constraints, they will probably insist on some form of state protection. Yet, the government desperately needs economic growth. The UMNO party gets the support of disparate economic groups, such as Malay businessmen and poor rice farmers, from an extensive system of patronage that depends on high growth and strong state resources.

The government has now turned to foreigners to re-crank the economy, while waiting for commodity prices to improve. It is a less controversial route than relying on the Chinese sector, and can be easily justified by the need for superior foreign technology. If foreign investment inflow is large, it will help generate employment, provide mobility for a broader strata of the population, and free state resources for subsidy schemes for the depressed rural and small business sectors. These benefits will help the present Prime Minister maintain and consolidate his power, and might blunt the need for authoritarian methods to deal with his challengers. The economic difficulties have contributed to the intensification of power struggles within UMNO as well as racial disaffection among the minority groups. Economic recovery, by making political competition less of a threat to the leadership, might allow the broad features of the previous political system to remain intact. These include electoral politics at the party and national levels, and the tolerance of opposition parties and their leaders. However, UMNO is unlikely to remain so dominant over the Malay population as in the past. State resources, even with commodity price improvements, may not be as plentiful in the future to permit the extensive patronage system to work with its previous effectiveness.

However, if foreign investment inflow is not adequate (such as less than $500 million annually) and commodity prices remain weak, there is the prospect of long-term economic stagnation. Sluggish investment could result from multinationals finding new sources of low-cost production, such as in Thailand, China, Mexico, and India, or even producing at home using new, cost-effective technologies. In a weak economy, several political consequences are possible. The most optimistic would be a realignment of political parties from predominant ethnic to multi-ethnic organizations because of greater political differentiation within the Malay élite. Such a scenario might emerge from a weakened or factious UMNO unable to maintain the long-standing unity of the Western-educated Malay élite. Some Malay leaders might then be prompted to join or forge coalitions with non-Malay groups. However, it would be too far-fetched to expect a smooth evolution toward multi-ethnic political organizations since poor economic conditions could first lead to authoritarianism à la Guyana or ethnic conflict à la Sri Lanka. Already the Mahathir regime has placed new controls on the judiciary and arrested opposition leaders and critics. A weak economy and continued political challenges to the current regime could lead to the severe curtailment of political activity and greater reliance on the security apparatus for rule. The commitment of the élite to democratic norms is not deep in Malaysia, neither is their desire to give up power easily. The twenty-five years of political pluralism of sorts were based on fortuitous circumstances, such as the racially accommodative approach of the first Prime Minister and high economic growth rates.

The other danger of a depressed economy is that the economic route to Malay group power and worth will have been punctured. This psychological defeat might create the base for radical Malay chauvinism. In politics, PAS could emerge as a major force. To pre-empt it, the power-holders might be tempted to take an extreme racial and religious position. For a while, this strategy may prove effective in mobilizing broad strata of the Malay population. One can only hope that some form of rationality will prevail over the all too familiar type of power struggle that feeds on the evocation of deep primordial urges and prejudices.

In conclusion, two general points can be made from our study of Malaysia. First, it is imperative to examine domestic policies and priorities in shaping development rather than resort to models of external causation. External actors and structures, such as multinationals and international financial and commodity markets, do have important implications for development possibilities. However, what is more critical is whether a country is able to initiate actions that maximize the benefits and anticipate the potential problems of its engagement in the international economy. In Malaysia, the government strained its financial and administrative resources during favourable times for its political and ethnic goals to the neglect of building greater resilience in the economy. As for the frequently criticized role of multinationals, the great irony was that it was precisely when the leaders decided to selectively control and buy them out that problems began to emerge over time.[3] This resulted from poor entrepreneurial substitution and the high reliance on foreign borrowing to carry out the substitution. Neglecting domestic social structures, indigenous cultural aspirations, and policy-making processes cannot lead to an adequate explanation of national development outcomes.

Secondly, the recent trend of explaining successful economic development in terms of the state possessing relative autonomy from dominant economic élites needs qualification. The argument is based on the need for the state to intervene on behalf of national economic rationality against the short-term, profit interests of the private sector. However, it is important to realize that a state which is insulated from the pressures of the dominant economic groups is not autonomous from all social groups and free to concentrate on economic growth. It is critical to consider what state élites choose to do when they are not constrained by existing, dominant economic groups. States are ultimately political entities; perhaps in homogenous countries, states can carry out rational economic strategies better, but in ethnic societies, such state autonomy can be detrimental to successful economic development. In Malaysia, the state was relatively autonomous from the dominant foreign and Chinese business groups, but the logic of group competition and political support-building led the state to create a new Malay business and managerial class. This effort had short-run political pay-offs but it imposed significant costs on the economy. A state that had been more responsive to the views of the Chinese and foreign groups might have served the economy and the society better in the long run.

1. In 1967, Malaysia's per capita income was US$324, Taiwan's $272, and South Korea's $159 (United Nations, 1971: 177). In 1978, the figures were US$1,090, $1,400, and $1,160 respectively (*World Bank*, 1980: 110–11, Table 1).

2. The external public debt rose from 6.1 per cent of GNP in 1970 to 37.5 per cent in 1986. The national debt servicing ratio in 1986 was 20.7 per cent, a great jump from 3.8 per cent in 1978 (Ministry of Finance, 1986: Table 1.2: vi, vii; 27; Bank Negara, 1979: 20).

3. We are not arguing here against building up the skills of national actors to replace and compete successfully with multinationals.

Select Bibliography

Abdul Aziz Ishak (1977), *Special Guest: The Detention in Malaysia of an Ex-Cabinet Minister*, Singapore: Oxford University Press.

Abdul Razak Abdul (1984), 'Joint Venture between Malaysian Public Corporations and Foreign Enterprise: An Evaluation', pp. 263–99 in Lim Lin Lean and Chee Peng Lim, eds., *The Malaysian Economy at the Crossroads: Policy Adjustments or Structural Transformations*, Kuala Lumpur: Malaysian Economic Association.

Allen, G. C. and Donnithorne, Audrey G. (1954), *Western Enterprise in Indonesia and Malaya*, London: Jarrold and Sons.

Allen, James de V. (1967), *The Malayan Union*, Southeast Asian Studies Monograph Series No. 10, New Haven: Yale University Press.

Andaya, Barbara W. and Andaya, Leonard Y. (1982), *A History of Malaysia*, London: Macmillan.

Arasaratnam, S. (1970), *Indians in Malaysia and Singapore*, 1st ed., London: Oxford University Press.

Associated Chinese Chambers of Commerce and Industry Malaysia (ACCCIM) (1978), Working Papers, Malaysian Chinese Economic Conference, Kuala Lumpur.

Bank Negara Malaysia (1979), *Money and Banking in Malaysia*, Kuala Lumpur.

——— (1986), *Annual Report 1985*, Kuala Lumpur.

Bauer, P. T. (1948), *The Rubber Industry. A Study in Competition and Monopoly*, Cambridge: Harvard University Press.

Beaglehole, J. H. (1969), 'Malay Participation in Commerce and Industry: The Role of RIDA and MARA', *Journal of Commonwealth Political Studies*, 7(3): 216–45.

Bennett, Douglas C. and Sharpe, Kenneth E. (1985), *Transnational Corporations Versus the State: The Political Economy of the Mexican Auto Industry*, Princeton: Princeton University Press.

Block, Fred (1977), 'The Ruling Class Does Not Rule: Notes on the Marxist Theory of the State', *Socialist Revolution*, 7: 6–28.

Bornschier, Volker and Ballmer-Cao, Thanh-Huyen (1979), 'Income Inequality: A Cross-National Study of the Relationship Between MNC-Penetration, Dimensions of the Power Structure and Income Distribution', *American Sociological Review*, 44 (June): 485–506.

Bowring, Philip (1978), 'Buying Back the Plantations', *Far Eastern Economic Review*, 13 January: 48–55.

Cardoso, Fernando H. and Faletto, Enzo (Trans. M. M. Urguidi) (1979), *Dependency and Development in Latin America*, Berkeley: University of California Press.

Chang, Y. S. (1971), 'The Transfer of Technology: Economics of Offshore Assembly, the Case of the Semiconductor Industry', UNITAR Research Report No. 11, New York: United Nations.

Chin, P. Y. (1984), 'Significant Recent Developments in Ownership Linkages and Control of the Banking Sector', pp. 195–213 in Lim Lin Lean and Chee Peng Lim, eds., *The Malaysian Economy at the Crossroads: Policy Adjustments or Structural Transformations*, Kuala Lumpur: Malaysian Economic Association.

Chin, Poky (1978), 'Appraisal of the Economic Status and Problems of the Malaysian Chinese in the Context of National Economic Development', in *Malaysian Chinese Economic Problems*, Kuala Lumpur: Selangor Chinese Chamber of Commerce.

Clapham, Christopher (1985), *Third World Politics: An Introduction*, Madison: University of Wisconsin Press.

Comber, Leon (1983), *13 May 1969: A Historical Survey of Sino-Malay Relations*, Kuala Lumpur: Heinemann.

Courtenay, P. P. (1972), *A Geography of Trade and Development in Malaya*, London: G. Bell and Sons.

Davenport, Andrew (1976), 'Battle for Sime Darby', *Far Eastern Economic Review*, 3 December: 38–42.

Department of Statistics (1971), *Survey of Manufacturing Industries*, Vol. 1, Kuala Lumpur.

＿＿＿ (1975), *Report of the Financial Survey of Limited Companies Malaysia*, Kuala Lumpur.

＿＿＿ (1985), *Report of the Financial Survey of Limited Companies Malaysia*, Kuala Lumpur.

Doering, Otto Charles III (1973), 'Malaysian Rice Policy and the Muda River Irrigation Project', Ph.D. dissertation, Cornell University.

Domhoff, William G. (1970), *The Higher Circles: The Governing Class in America*, New York: Random House.

Dos Santos, Teotonio (1970), 'The Structure of Dependence', *American Economic Review*, 60(5): 231–46.

Drabble, J. H. and Drake, P. J. (1981), 'The British Agency Houses in Malaysia: Survival in a Changing World', *Journal of Southeast Asian Studies*, 12(2): 297–328.

Drake, P. J. (1969), *Financial Development in Malaya and Singapore*, Canberra: Australia National University Press.

Drummond, Stuart and Hawkins, David (1970), 'The Malaysian Elections of 1969: An Analysis of the Campaign and the Results', *Asian Survey*, 10 (April): 320–35.

Duvall, Raymond D. and Freeman, John R. (1981), 'The State and Dependent Capitalism', *International Studies Quarterly*, 25(1): 99–118.

Eckstein, Harry (1975), 'Case Study and Theory in Political Science', in Fred Greenstein and Nelson Polsby, eds., *Handbook of Political Science*, Vol. 7, Philippines: Addison-Wesley.

Edwards, C. T. (1970), *Public Finances in Malaya and Singapore*, Canberra: Australian National University Press.

Edwards, Christopher B. (1975), 'Protection, Profits and Policy—An Analysis of Industrialization in Malaysia', Ph.D. dissertation, University of East Anglia, England.

Emerson, Rupert (1937), *Malaysia, A Study in Direct and Indirect Rule*, New York: Macmillan.

Evans, Peter (1979), *Dependent Development: The Alliance of Multinational, State, and Local Capital in Brazil*, Princeton: Princeton University Press.

Federal Industrial Development Authority (FIDA) (renamed Malaysian Industrial Development Authority or MIDA), *Annual Report*, various issues.

Fifth Malaysia Plan 1986–1990 (Fifth MP) (1986), Kuala Lumpur: Government Press.

First Malaysia Plan 1966–1970 (First MP) (1965), Kuala Lumpur: Government Press.

Fourth Malaysia Plan 1981–1985 (FoMP) (1981), Kuala Lumpur: Government Press.

Frank, Andre Gunder (1967), *Capitalism and Underdevelopment in Latin America: Historical Studies of Chile and Brazil*, New York: Monthly Review Press.

Freedman, Maurice (1961), 'The Handling of Money: A Note on the Background of the Economic Sophistication of the Overseas Chinese', pp. 38–42 in T. H. Silcock, ed., *Readings in Malayan Economics*, Singapore: Eastern Universities Press.

Freeman, John R. (1982), 'State Entrepreneurship and Dependent Development', *American Journal of Political Science*, 26(1): 90–112.

Funston, John (1980), *Malay Politics in Malaysia: A Study of UMNO and PAS*, Kuala Lumpur: Heinemann Educational Books.

Gale, Bruce (1981a), 'Petronas: Malaysia's National Oil Corporation', *Asian Survey*, 21(11): 1129–44.

———— (1981b), *Politics and Public Enterprise in Malaysia*, Singapore: Eastern Universities Press.

———— (1985), *Politics and Business: A Study of Multi-Purpose Holdings Berhad*, Singapore: Eastern Universities Press.

Gereffi, Gary (1983), *The Pharmaceutical Industry and Dependency in the Third World*, Princeton: Princeton University Press.

Gill, Ian (1980), 'Lim Uses Gambling Profits to Expand Genting', *Insight*, June: 20–6.

Goh Joon Hai (1962), 'Some Aspects of the Chinese Business World in Malaya', *Ekonomi*, 3: 84–95.

Golay, Frank H. (1969), 'Malaya', in Frank H. Golay *et al.*, eds., *Underdevelopment and Economic Nationalism in Southeast Asia*, Ithaca: Cornell University Press.

Gold, Thomas B. (1981), 'Dependent Development in Taiwan', Ph.D dissertation, Harvard University.

Gosling, L. A. P. (1983), 'Chinese Crop Dealers in Malaysia and Thailand', pp. 131–70 in Linda Lim and Peter Gosling, eds., *The Chinese in Southeast Asia*, Vol. 1, Singapore: Maruzen Asia.

Gullick, J. M. (1958), *Indigenous Political Systems of Western Malaya*, London: The Athlone Press.

Hamilton, Nora (1982), *The Limits of State Autonomy: Post-Revolutionary Mexico*, Princeton: Princeton University Press.

Hansen, Roger D. (1971), *The Politics of Mexican Development*, Baltimore: Johns Hopkins University Press.

Hawkins, David (1969), 'Britain and Malaysia—Another View: Was the Decision to Withdraw Entirely Voluntary or Was Britain Pushed a Little', *Asian Survey*, 9(7): 546–62.

———— (1972), *The Defense of Malaysia and Singapore: From AMDA to ANZUK*, London: Royal United Services Institute for Defence Studies.

Helleiner, Gerald K. (1973), 'Manufacturing for Export, Multinational Firms and Economic Development', *World Development*, 1 (July): 13–21.

Heng Pek Koon (1983), 'The Social and Ideological Origins of the Malayan Chinese Association', *Journal of Southeast Asian Studies*, 14(2): 290–311.

Hintzen, Percy (1985), 'Ethnicity, Class and International Capitalist Penetration in Guyana and Trinidad', *Social and Economic Studies*, 34(3): 107–96.

Hirschman, Albert (1970), *Exit, Voice, and Loyalty: Responses to Decline in Firms, Organizations, and States*, Cambridge: Harvard University Press.

——— (1973), 'The Changing Tolerance for Income Inequality in the Course of Economic Development', with a mathematical appendix by Michael Rothschild, *Quarterly Journal of Economics*, 87(4): 544–66.

——— (1986), *Rival Views of Market Society: And Other Recent Essays*, New York: Viking Penguin.

Hoffman, Lutz and Tan Siew Ee (1980), *Industrial Growth, Employment, and Foreign Investment in Peninsular Malaysia*, Kuala Lumpur: Oxford University Press.

Horowitz, Donald L. (1985), *Ethnic Groups in Conflict*, Berkeley: University of California Press.

H'ng Hung Yong (1979), 'The Future of MCA', presented in and compiled under 'MCA Political Seminar: The Future of the Chinese Community in Malaysia', Kuala Lumpur.

IMP. See *Medium and Long Term Industrial Master Plan Malaysia 1986–1995*.

International Bank for Reconstruction and Development (IBRD) (1955), *The Economic Development of Malaya*, Baltimore: Johns Hopkins University Press.

Ismail Muhd. Salleh (1983), 'Sources, Performance, and Incidence of Taxation in Malaysia', pp. 93–112 in Sritua Arief and J. K. Sundaram, eds., *The Malaysian Economy and Finance*, New South Wales: Rosecons.

Jagjit Singh Sidhu (1980), *Administration in the Federated Malay States 1896–1920*, Kuala Lumpur: Oxford University Press.

James, Kenneth (1986), 'The Malaysian Economy: The Shadow of 1990', *Southeast Asian Affairs*, Singapore: Institute of Southeast Studies, 208–22.

Jones, Edwin (1981), 'The Role of the State in Public Enterprise', *Social and Economic Studies*, 30(1): 17–44.

Junid Saham (1980), *British Industrial Investment in Malaysia 1963–1971*, Kuala Lumpur: Oxford University Press.

Konggeres Ekonomi Bumiputra Malaysia (First Bumiputra Economic Congress) (1965), Kertas² Kerja (Working Papers), Kuala Lumpur: Government Printers.

Konggeres Ekonomi Bumiputra Kedua (Second Bumiputra Economic Congress) (1968), Memorandum Dari Persaorangan (Memorandum from Participants), Kuala Lumpur.

Kuala Lumpur Stock Exchange (KLSE), *Annual Companies Handbook*, 1974, 1978, 1980, and 1984, Kuala Lumpur.

Kumar, Krishna and McLeod, Maxwell G., eds. (1981), *Multinationals from Developing Countries*, Lexington, Mass: Lexington Books.

Kumar, N. (1975), 'Foreign Investment in Malaysia: Problems and Prospects', *The Economic Bulletin*, December: 13–14.

Lal, Deepak (1985), *The Poverty of 'Development Economics'*, Cambridge: Harvard University Press.

Laws of Malaysia (1983), Act 156, Industrial Coordination Act 1975, Kuala Lumpur: Government Press.

Lecraw, Donald J. (1981), 'Internationalization of Firms from LDCs: Evidence from the Asean Region', Chap. 3 in Krishna Kumar and Maxwell G. McLeod, eds., *Multinationals from Developing Countries*, Lexington, Mass: Lexington Books.

Lee Kam Hing (1980), 'The Peninsula Non-Malay Parties in the Barisan Nasional', in Harold Crouch, Lee Kam Hing and Michael Ong, eds., *Malaysian Politics and the 1978 Election*, Kuala Lumpur: Oxford University Press.

Li Dun Jen (1982), *British Malaya: An Economic Analysis*, 2nd ed., Kuala Lumpur: Insan. First published 1955.

Lijphart, Arend (1969), 'Consociational Democracy', *World Politics*, 2(2): 207–25.

_____ (1977), *Democracy in Plural Societies*, New Haven: Yale University Press.

Lim Chong-Yah (1967), *Economic Development of Modern Malaya*, Kuala Lumpur: Oxford University Press.

Lim, David (1973), *Economic Growth and Development in West Malaysia 1947–1970*, Kuala Lumpur: Oxford University Press.

Lim Hyun-Chin (1982), 'Dependent Development in the World-System: The Case of South Korea, 1963–1979', Ph.D. dissertation, Harvard University.

Lim Kit Siang (1986), *BMF: The Scandal of Scandals*, Petaling Jaya: Democratic Action Party.

Lim Mah Hui (1981), *Ownership and Control of the One Hundred Largest Corporations in Malaysia*, Kuala Lumpur: Oxford University Press.

_____ (1985), 'Contradictions in the Development of Malay Capital: State, Accumulation and Legitimation', *Journal of Contemporary Asia*, 15(1): 37–63.

Lim Mah Hui and Canak, William (1981), 'The Political Economy of State Policies in Malaysia', *Journal of Contemporary Asia*, 11(2): 208–24.

Lim Teck Ghee (1976), *Origins of a Colonial Economy: Land and Agriculture in Perak, 1874–1897*, Penang: Universiti Sains Malaysia.

_____ (1977), *Peasants and their Agricultural Economy in Colonial Malaya, 1874–1941*, Kuala Lumpur: Oxford University Press.

Lindblom, Charles E. (1977), *Politics and Markets: The World's Political-Economic Systems*, New York: Basic Books.

Lindenberg, Marc M. (1973), 'Foreign and Domestic Investment in the Pioneer Industry Program, Malaysia 1965–1970', Ph.D. dissertation, University of Southern California.

Loh, Philip Fook Seng (1975), *Seeds of Separatism: Educational Policy in Malaya, 1874–1940*, Kuala Lumpur: Oxford University Press.

Mahathir bin Mohamad (1970), *The Malay Dilemma*, Singapore: The Asia Pacific Press.

Malaysian Industrial Development Authority (MIDA), *Annual Report*, various issues.

_____, *Malaysia Industrial Digest*, various issues.

_____ (1984), *Modern Malaysia*, brochure.

Malaysian International Chamber of Commerce and Industry (MICCI), *Yearbook*, various annual issues.

_____ 'Basic Facts About MICCI', c.1984, brochure.

Mauzy, Diane K. (1983), *Barisan Nasional: Coalition Government in Malaysia*, Kuala Lumpur: Marican and Sons.

Mamajiwala, Rukhyabai K. (1968), 'Ownership and Control of Public Limited Rubber Planting Companies Incorporated in the Federation of Malaya, 1948–1958', MA thesis, University of Malaya, Kuala Lumpur.

McGee, T. G. (1986), 'Domains of Analysis: Perspectives on the Study of Inequality and Economic Growth in Malaysia', *Pacific Affairs*, 59(4): 655–64.

Means, Gordon P. (1976), *Malaysian Politics*, 2nd ed., London: Hodder and Stoughton. First published 1970.

Medium and Long Term Industrial Master Plan Malaysia 1986–1995 (IMP), prepared by UNIDO/MIDA for the Malaysian Government (1985): *Electronics and Electrical Industry*, Vol. 2, Part 8; *Executive Highlights*; *Textiles/Apparel Industry*, Vol. 2, Part 12; *Transport Equipment Industry*, Vol. 2, Part 8.

Mehmet, Ozay (1986), *Development in Malaysia: Poverty, Wealth, Trusteeship*, London: Croom Helm.

Mid-Term Review of the Second Malaysia Plan 1971–1975 (MRT SMP) (1973), Kuala Lumpur: Government Press.

Mid-Term Review of the Fourth Malaysia Plan 1981–1985 (MTR FoMP) (1984), Kuala·Lumpur: Government Press.

Miliband, Ralph (1969), *The State in Capitalist Society*, New York: Basic Books.

Milne, R. S. (1976), 'The Politics of Malaysia's New Economic Policy', *Pacific Affairs*, 49(2): 235–62.

Milne, R. S. and Mauzy, Diane K. (1978), *Politics and Government in Malaysia*, Singapore: Federal Publishers.

Milne, R. S. and Ratnam, K. J. (1965), 'Politics and Finance in Malaya', *Journal of Commonwealth Political Studies*, 3(3): 182–98.

Ministry of Finance (1975), *Economic Report 1975/1976*, Kuala Lumpur: Government Printer.

———— (1976), *Economic Report 1976/1977*, Kuala Lumpur: Government Printer.

———— (1985), *Economic Report 1985/1986*, Kuala Lumpur: Government Printer.

———— (1986), *Economic Report 1986/1987*, Kuala Lumpur: Government Printer.

———— (1987), *Economic Report 1987/1988*, Kuala Lumpur: Government Printer.

Ministry of Labour (1984), *Labour and Manpower Report 1981/82*, Kuala Lumpur.

Mohamed Amin and Caldwell, Malcolm, eds. (1977), *The Making of a Neo-Colony*, Nottingham: Spokesman.

Mohamed Suffian (1972), *An Introduction to the Constitution of Malaysia*, Kuala Lumpur: Government Press.

Mohd. Jali Tajuddin (1974), 'Bumiputra Participation in Commerce and Industry', paper presented at MARA–USIS seminar on 'Aids for Small Businesses in Malaysia'.

Mohd. Noordin Sopiee (1974), *From Malayan Union to Singapore Separation: Political Unification in the Malaysian Region 1945–1965*, Kuala Lumpur: University of Malaya Press.

Mohd. Raza Ali (1969), 'Legislative and Public Policy Developments in Malaysia's Industrial Relations', *The Journal of Developing Areas*, 3 (April): 355–72.

Morais, J. V., ed. (1972), *Blueprint for Unity: Tun Tan Siew Sin* (selected speeches), Kuala Lumpur: MCA Headquarters.

Moran, Theodore (1974), *Multinational Corporations and the Politics of Dependence: Copper in Chile*, Princeton: Princeton University Press.

———— (1978), 'Multinational Corporations and Dependency: A Dialogue for "Dependentistas" and "Non-Dependentistas" ', *International Organization*, 32: 79–100.

Nkrumah, Kwame (1966), *Neo-Colonialism: The Last Stage of Imperialism*, New York: International Publishers.

Nonini, Donald M. (1983) 'The Chinese Truck Transport "Industry" of a Peninsula Malaysia Market Town', pp. 171–206 in Linda Lim and Peter Gosling, eds., *The Chinese in Southeast Asia*, Vol. 1, Singapore: Maruzen Asia.

Olson, Mancur (1982), *The Rise and Decline of Nations: Economic Growth, Stagflation, and Social Rigidities*, New Haven: Yale University Press.

The Oriental Economist (1981), *Japanese Overseas Investment: A Complete Listing by Firms and Countries*, Tokyo.

Osman-Rani, Anuwar Ali and Toh Kin Woon (1986), *Effective Mechanisms for the Enhancement of Technology and Skills in Malaysia*, Singapore: Institute of Southeast Asian Studies.

Ozawa, Terutomo (1979), *Multinationalism, Japanese Style: The Political Economy of Outward Dependency*, Princeton: Princeton University Press.

Parkinson, C. Northcote (1960), *British Intervention in Malaya, 1867–1877*, Singapore: University of Malaya Press.

Parmer, Norman J. (1964), *Colonial Labor Policy and Administration: A History of*

Labor in the Rubber Plantation Industry in Malaya 1910–1940, New York: J. J. Augustine for the Association for Asian Studies.

Pernas (1984), *Annual Report*, Kuala Lumpur.

Petras, James (1976), 'State Capitalism and the Third World', *Journal of Contemporary Asia*, 11(2): 432–43.

Popenoe, Oliver (1970), 'Malay Entrepreneurs: An Analysis of the Social Backgrounds, Careers and Attitudes of the Leading Malay Businessmen in Western Malaysia', Ph.D. dissertation, London School of Economics.

Pura, Raphael (1986a), 'Malaysia Plan to Control Tin Led to Disaster', *Asian Wall Street Journal*, 22 September.

────── (1986b), 'Daim May Make Big Gain on Bank Sale', *Asian Wall Street Journal*, 26–27 September.

Purcell, Victor (1965), *The Chinese in Southeast Asia*, 2nd ed., Kuala Lumpur: Oxford University Press. First published 1951.

Puthucheary, James J. (1960), *Ownership and Control in the Malayan Economy*, Singapore: Eastern Universities Press.

────── (1977), 'Changes in Ownership and Control in Malaysia', 4th Malaysian Economic Convention, mimeo.

Puthucheary, Mavis (1979), 'The Control of Pubic Enterprises with Special Reference to State Economic Development Corporations', in K. C. Cheong, S. M. Khoo and R. Thillainathan, eds., *Malaysia: Some Contemporary Issues in Socio-Economic Development*, Kuala Lumpur: University of Malaya Press.

Rabushka, Alvin (1973), *Race and Politics in Urban Malaya*, Stanford: Hoover Institution Press.

Raja Mohammed Affandi, (1978), 'Public Enterprises in Malaysia: Roles, Structure and Problems', Occasional Paper No. 6, Kuala Lumpur: Jabatan Perdana Menteri.

Rao, V. V. Bhanoji (1980), *Malaysia: Development Pattern and Policy 1947–1971*, Singapore: Singapore University Press.

Ratnam, K. J. and Milne, R. S. (1967), *The Malayan Parliamentary Election of 1964*, Singapore: University of Malaya Press.

Report of the Committee for Rational Development (1986), in S. Tambiah, *Sri Lanka: Ethnic Fratricide and the Dismantling of Democracy*, Appendix 3, Chicago: University of Chicago Press.

Reid, Anthony (1969), 'The Kuala Lumpur Riots and the Malaysian Political System', *Australian Outlook*, 23 (December): 258–78.

Roff, William R. (1967), *The Origins of Malay Nationalism*, Kuala Lumpur: University of Malaya Press, and New Haven: Yale University Press.

Rogers, Marvin L. (1975), 'The Politicization of Malay Villagers: National Integration or Disintegration?', *Comparative Politics*, 7(2): 205–25.

Rowley, Anthony (1984), 'The Politics of Business', *Far Eastern Economic Review*, 10 May: 83–90.

Rudner, Martin (1975), *Nationalism, Planning, and Economic Modernization in Malaysia: The Politics of Beginning Development*, Beverly Hills: Sage.

────── (1980), 'Trends in Malaysian Development Planning: Goals, Policies and Role Expansion', *Review of Indonesian and Malaysian Affairs*, 14(12): 48–91.

Schmitter, Phillippe C. (1974), 'Still the Century of Corporatism?', in Federick Pike and Thomas Stritch, eds., *The New Corporatism: Social–Political Structures in the Iberian World*, Notre Dame and London: University of Notre Dame Press.

Scott, James C. (1985), *Weapons of the Weak: Everyday Forms of Peasant Resistance*, New Haven: Yale University Press.

Selangor Chinese Chamber of Commerce (SCCC) (1978), 'Malaysian Economic

Problems', Memorandum submitted to the Associated Chinese Chambers of Commerce and Industry of Malaysia, Kuala Lumpur.

Second Malaysia Plan 1971–1975 (SMP) (1971), Kuala Lumpur: Government Press.

Short, Anthony (1975), *The Communist Insurrection in Malaya 1948–1960*, London: Frederick Muller.

Simandjuntak, B. (1969), *Malayan Federalism 1945–1963: A Study of Federal Problems in a Plural Society*, Kuala Lumpur: Oxford University Press.

Slimming, John (1969), *Malaysia: Death of a Democracy*, London: John Murray.

Smelser, Neil J. (1976), *Comparative Methods in the Social Science*, Englewood Cliffs: Prentice-Hall.

Smith, M. G. (1965), *The Plural Society in the British West Indies*, University of California Press.

Smith, Patrick (1981), 'A Colonial Chapter Closes', *Far Eastern Economic Review*, 18 September: 144–7.

Smith, Tony (1981), *The Pattern of Imperialism: The United States, Great Britain, and the Late-Industrializing World since 1815*, Cambridge: Cambridge University Press.

Snodgrass, Donald R. (1970), 'A Survey of Labour Utilisation in West Malaysia 75', EPU Manpower Section.

—————— (1980), *Inequality and Economic Development in Malaysia*, Kuala Lumpur: Oxford University Press.

Stenson, M. R. (1970), *Industrial Conflict in Malaya: Prelude to the Communist Revolt of 1948*, London: Oxford University Press.

Stepan, Alfred (1978), *The State and Society: Peru in Comparative Perspective*, Princeton: Princeton University Press.

Stone, John (1985), *Racial Conflict in Contemporary Society*, Cambridge: Harvard University Press.

Sundaram, Jomo Kwame (1977), 'Class Formation in Malaya: Capital, the State and Uneven Development', Ph.D. dissertation, Harvard University.

—————— (1986), *A Question of Class: Capital, the State and Uneven Development in Malaya*, Singapore: Oxford University Press.

Swettenham, Frank (1920), *British Malaya: An Account of the Origin and Progress of British Influence in Malaya*, London: Bodley Head. First published 1907.

Tan Boon Kean (1980), 'Formation of Small Malay Capital', mimeo.

—————— (1982), 'The State and the Transition to Dependent Development: Malaysia 1957–1970', mimeo.

Tan Ee Leong (1961), 'The Chinese Banks Incorporated in Singapore and the Federation of Malaya', pp. 454–79 in T. H. Silcock, ed., *Readings in Malayan Economics*, 2nd ed., Singapore: Eastern Universities Press. First published 1953.

Tan Tat Wai (1982), *Income Distribution and Determination in West Malaysia*, Kuala Lumpur: Oxford University Press.

Tham Seong Chee (1977), *Malays and Modernization: A Sociological Interpretation*, Singapore: Singapore University Press.

Thillainathan, R. (1976), 'Malaysia', in Nguyen-Truong, ed., *Public Enterprise in National Development in Southeast Asia: Problems and Prospects*, Pt. 1, Singapore: RIHED.

Third Malaysia Plan 1976–1980 (TMP) (1976), Kuala Lumpur: Government Press.

Thoburn, John T. (1977), *Primary Commodity Exports and Economic Development: Theory, Evidence and a Study of Malaysia*, New York: John Wiley and Sons.

Toh Kin Woon (1982), 'The State in Economic Development: A Case Study of Malaysia's New Economic Policy', Ph.D. dissertation, University of Malaya.

Toh Kin Woon and Sundaram, J. K. (1983), 'The Nature of the Malaysian State and Its Implications for Development Planning', pp. 22–44 in K. S. Jomo and R. J. Wells, eds., *The Fourth Malaysian Plan: Economic Perspectives*, Kuala Lumpur: Malaysian Economic Association.

Tugwell, Franklin (1975), *The Politics of Oil in Venezuela*, Stanford: Stanford University Press.

Turnbull, Mary (1964), 'The Nineteenth Century', pp. 128–37 in Wang Gungwu, ed., *Malaysia: A Survey*, New York: Frederick A. Praeger.

United Nations (1971), *World Economic Survey, 1969–1970*, New York: United Nations.

Vasil, R. K. (1972), *The Malaysian General Election of 1969*, Singapore: Oxford University Press.

_____ (1980), *Ethnic Politics in Malaysia*, New Delhi: Radiant Publishers.

Verchere, Ian (1978), 'The Changing World of Robert Kuok', *Insight*, August: 8–17, 54–5.

Vogel, Ezra F. (1979), *Japan as Number One: Lessons for America*, Cambridge: Harvard University Press.

Vokes, Richard W. A. (1978), 'State Marketing in a Private Enterprise Economy: The Padi and Rice Market of West Malaysia, 1966–1975', Ph.D. dissertation, University of Hull.

Von Vorys, Karl (1975), *Democracy Without Consensus: Communalism and Political Stability in Malaysia*, Princeton: Princeton University Press.

Wallerstein, Immanuel (1974), *The Modern World-System: Capitalist Agriculture and the Origins of the European World Economy in the Sixteenth Century*, New York: Academic Press.

_____ (1976), 'A World-System Perspective on the Social Sciences', *British Journal of Sociology*, 27(3): 345–54.

Wells Jr., Louis T. (1981), 'Foreign Investment from the Third World', Chap. 2 in Krishna Kumar and Maxwell G. McLeod, eds., *Multinationals from Developing Countries*, Lexington, Mass: Lexington Books.

Wheelwright, E. L. (1965), *Industrialization in Malaysia*, Melbourne: Melbourne University Press.

Who's Who in Malaysia and Singapore (1983), Vol. 1, Malaysia, Kuala Lumpur: Who's Who Publications.

World Bank, *World Development Report*, 1987, 1986, 1980, New York: Oxford University Press.

Wu Yuan-Li and Wu Chun-Hsi (1980), *Economic Development in Southeast Asia: The Chinese Dimension*, Stanford: Hoover Institution Press.

Yip Yat Hoong (1969), *The Development of the Tin Mining Industry of Malaya*, Kuala Lumpur: University of Malaya Press.

Yong Poh Kon (1980), 'The Economic Challenges of the 80s', presented in and compiled under 'MCA Political Seminar: The Challenges of the 1980s', Kuala Lumpur.

Zaidi, S. J. H. (1974), *Malaysian Trade Union Congress, 1949–1974*, Kuala Lumpur: MTUC Publication.

Newspaper and Magazine Sources

Newspapers

Asian Wall Street Journal, Hong Kong
Business Times, Malaysia
Business Times, Singapore

Economic Times, Bombay
New Nation, Singapore
New Straits Times, Malaysia
Singapore Monitor
Straits Times, Malaysia (before 31 August *1974*; precursor to *New Straits Times*)
Straits Times, Singapore
The Star, Malaysia

Magazines

Asian Business, Hong Kong
Asian Finance, Hong Kong
Business Week
Far Eastern Economic Review, Hong Kong
Insight, Hong Kong
Malaysian Business, Kuala Lumpur
Suara Pernas, magazine of the Pernas Group

Index

ABDUL AZIZ ISHAK, 54–5
Abdul Rahman, Tunku: and Anglo-
  Malayan Defence Agreement, 52;
  economic policy, 53–5, 73, 193; and
  National Operations Council, 70–1; and
  UMNO, 44
Abdul Razak, Tun: and Barisan Nasional,
  77; foreign investment policy, 53; and
  Malay economic development, 75;
  Minister of Finance, 78; Minister of
  National Development, 65; and NEP,
  130; leader of National Operations
  Council, 70–1; and Robert Kuok, 61;
  and Tengku Razaleigh Hamzah, 86
Abdul Razak Abdul, 138, 185
Abdullah Ibrahim, 108
Abu Bakar Lajim, 103
ACCC, see Associated Chinese Chambers
  of Commerce
ACCCIM, see Associated Chinese
  Chambers of Commerce and Industry
  Malaysia
Agriculture: government assistance for,
  50–1, 84, 115; plantation, 30–2, 58–9
Ajinomoto, 58
Alliance, 44–5, 67, 69
Amanah Saham Nasional, 115–16
American Sociological Review, 166
Andaya, Barbara W., 31
Andaya, Leonard Y., 31
Anglo-Malayan Defence Agreement, 52
Anglo-Oriental, 33
Ansul, 58
Arab–Malaysian Development Bank,
  106–7
Asian Wall Street Journal, 120
ASN, see Amanah Saham Nasional
Associated Chinese Chambers of
  Commerce, 63, 130–1
Associated Chinese Chambers of
  Commerce and Industry Malaysia,
  132–3, 136–40, 142, 147, 162, 165
Australia: investment by Malaysian

Chinese in, 154; investment in Malaysia,
  145, 182
Azman Hashim, Datuk, 106–7

BABA CHINESE, 30
Balance of payments, 135
Ballast Nedam Groep, 92
Ballmer-Cao, Thanh-Huyen, 166
Bandar Raya Developments, 156
Bank Bumiputra, 51, 64, 66, 86, 105, 120,
  126
Bank Islam, 101
Bank Kemajuan Perusahaan, 101
Bank Negara, 60, 78–9, 87, 93, 101, 127
Bank of Tokyo, 60
Bank Pembangunan Malaysia Berhad, 101,
  105
Bank Rakyat, 105, 120
Banks: Chinese, 35, 46, 60, 63–4; foreign,
  33–4, 60; government control of, 93
Barisan Nasional, 77–8
Barlow Holdings, 91
Birla, 183
BMF Inquiry Committee Report, 120
Board of Commissioners of Currency, 28,
  50
Boon Siew Sdn Bhd, 153
Bornschier, Volker, 166
Boustead, 48
Boustead–Buttery, 32
Brazier, John, 4
Brazil, 2, 6, 8, 20
Bright, Keith, 90
British agency houses, 30, 32–3, 48, 57, 60
British–American Tobacco, 57
British East India Company, 26
British in Malaya, 26–45, 52–3
British investment in Malaysia, 57–8,
  180–1
British Oxygen, 57
British Petroleum, 57
Bumiputra Economic Congresses, 65–6, 115
Business Week, 168–9

Cantonese, 34
Capital Issues Committee, 79, 90, 96, 105
Carrian, 120
Castrol, 57
Central Bank, see Bank Negara
Central Indian Association of Malaya, 40
Central Securities, 61
Central Sugars Refinery, 151
Chang, Brian, 108
Chang Ming Thien, 156
Charter Consolidated, 33, 59, 89
Chartered Bank, 33, 60
Chase Manhattan Bank, 60
Chettiar, 33–4
Chia, Eric, 62
Chinese banks, 35, 46, 60, 63–4
Chinese businesses: large, 60–4, 150–5;
    small, 147–50
Chinese businessmen, 31, 34–5, 147–55;
    in agriculture, 30; attitude to foreign
    investment, 56; in banking, 35, 60,
    63–4; and British, 30–45; and
    competition from Malays, 132; and
    competition from state enterprises, 132;
    in construction, 63; and Industrial
    Coordination Act, 134–47, 149, 152; and
    Malay partners, 64, 129–30, 147–9; and
    Malaysian government, 17, 128–30; in
    manufacturing, 60–2, 134, 142–6,
    152–3; and MCA, 156; and MPH, 155–6;
    and NEP, 130, 133–4, 147–55, 195; in
    1960s, 60–4; and overseas expansion,
    154; in property development, 60–2,
    152–3; in rubber industry, 32, 35–6,
    61–2; in tin-mining, 33, 35–6
Chinese Chambers of Commerce, 43
Chinese Commercial Bank, 35, 46
Chinese in Malaysia: as business leaders,
    1, 31; ownership of rubber estates, 32;
    percentage of population, 1, 29; role in
    government, 129; and special rights of
    Malays, 68; and tin-mining, 27
Chinese migration to Malaya, 27, 29
Chinese organizations: and business, 31;
    and MCA, 43; and state policies, 17–18
Chinese Protectorates, 40
Chinese secret societies, 27
CIC, see Capital Issues Committee
Citibank, 60
Civil Service, 28, 37
Clan associations, 43
Coffee planters, 32
Colgate Palmolive Far East, 58
Commodities, 98, 117–18, 191, 194
Communist Party of Malaya, 40–1
Compulsory arbitration, 57
Consolidated Plantations, 59

Constitution: amendments to, 77
Constitution for independent Malaya
    (1957), 44
Consultative Committee on Trade and
    Industry, 140
Consumer Price Index: and wages, 171
CPM, see Communist Party of Malaya
Credit Guarantee Corporation, 101

Daim Zainuddin, Datuk Paduka, 107
Dainippon Ink and Chemicals, 185
Daishowa Paper Manufacturing, 58
DAP, see Democratic Action Party
Davenport, Andrew, 89
Deficit financing, 49
Democratic Action Party, 123, 124, 158–9,
    163, 169, 190
Dependent development theories, 6–8,
    14–16, 84, 166–7, 172
Desa Pachik, Haji, 87
Development and Commercial Bank, 106
Dirigisme, 104–5
Drabble, J. H., 30
Dragon and Phoenix, 178
Drake, P. J., 30
Dunlop Holdings, 57, 89, 157
Dutch East India Company, 25

Eckstein, Harry, 20
Economic Planning Unit, 78–9, 81, 86,
    117, 127
Education, 40, 170, 187
Elections, 44, 69–70, 109–11, 157–9
Electronics industry, 173–6, 186–7
Emergency (1948–60), 41
Employees Provident Fund, 49, 81
Employment, 58, 167–8, 173–4, 177–80,
    191, 195–6
EPF, see Employees Provident Fund
EPU, see Economic Planning Unit
Esso, 57–8, 169
Ethnic groups: and development, 1–4,
    9–19; and politics, 44
Ethnic polarization, 68–9, 74, 198
Eu Tong Sen, 35
European banks, 33–4
European Economic Community, 181
Evans, Peter, 6–8, 14–18, 20
Export sector, 30, 32, 36, 59–60, 120–1,
    173–4
Exxon, 82

Fawanis, 108
Federal Flour Mills, 61
Federal Industrial Development Authority,
    141
Federal Land Consolidation and

Rehabilitation Authority, 102
Federal Land Development Authority, 51, 61, 102
Federated Malay States, 28
Federation of Malaya Agreement, 43
Federation of Malaysian Manufacturers, 139–40, 161–2
Felcra, see Federal Land Consolidation and Rehabilitation Authority
Felda, see Federal Land Development Authority
FIC, see Foreign Investment Committee
FIDA, see Federal Industrial Development Authority
Fiji, 4
Five Year Plans, 50
Fleet Group, 87, 107
FMM, see Federation of Malaysian Manufacturers
Foong Seong, 35
Foreign debt, 81–4, 121–2, 194, 198–200
Foreign investment: fall in, 186–7; and government stability, 189–91; incentives for, 45, 56–7, 72–3, 187–9, 196; in manufacturing, 56–60, 131, 134–5, 144–6, 173–89; policy, 53, 162–3, 187–9, 198
Foreign Investment Committee, 79, 88, 96
Free enterprise system, 52–6
Free Trade Zones, 173, 177, 179, 188
FTZs, see Free Trade Zones
Fumakilla, 153

Gajras, 183
Gale, Bruce, 169
Gambier, 30
GDP, see Gross Domestic Product
General Labour Union, see Pan-Malayan Federation of Trade Unions
General System of Preferences, 176
Gerakan Party, 69, 133
Germany: investment in Malaysia, 145, 174
Ghafar Baba, 135
Ghazali Shafie, 71, 169
Glaxo–Allenburys, 57
GNP, see Gross National Product
Godrej, 183
Goodyear Malaysia, 93
Government economic policy: of British, 32, 36, 38, 48; interventionist (1970–90), 1–2, 76–124, 194–6; laissez-faire (1957–69), 1, 47–74, 193–4
Grenfell Holdings, 151
Gross Domestic Product, 20; growth, 118, 171; manufacturing share of, 20, 58, 134, 147; rubber percentage of, 47; tin

percentage of, 47
Gross National Product: exports share of, 50; growth of, 135; manufacturing share of, 3; public investment share of, 50; public sector financing share of, 80
Guinness, 57
Guthrie, 32–3, 48, 59, 91
Guyana, 4

Hainanese, 34
Hakka, 34
Hall Thermotank Ltd, 160
Hamilton, Nora, 16, 77
Hamzah Abu Samah, Datuk, 135
Hansen, Roger D., 116
Harper Gilfillan, 48
Harrisons and Crosfield, 32–3, 59, 91
Harun Idris, Datuk, 107, 120
Haw Par Brothers International, 88–9
Heavy industrialization, 118–19
Heavy Industry Corporation of Malaysia, 118, 145, 160–1, 184–5
Helleiner, Gerald K., 18
Hewlett–Packard, 174
HICOM, see Heavy Industry Corporation of Malaysia
Hirschman, Albert, 4–5, 11, 154
Hitachi, 174
Ho Hong Bank, 35, 46
Hokkien, 34
Honda, 62
Hong Kong: investment by Malaysian Chinese in, 154; investment in Malaysia, 176–8
Hong Kong and Shanghai Bank, 33, 60
Horowitz, Donald, 10–12, 38, 111
Huaren Holdings, 156
Huay kuan, see Clan associations
Hussein Onn, Tun, 100, 144

Ibrahim Mohammed, Datuk, 108, 150
ICA, see Industrial Coordination Act (1975)
ICI, 57, 181
ICU, see Implementation and Coordination Unit
Imperial, 178
Implementation and Coordination Unit, 86, 98
Import-substitution programme, 57, 187
Independence of Malaya Party, 44
India: investment in Malaysia, 183–4
Indians in Malaysia, 1, 29, 32, 41–2
Industrial Advisory Council, 142
Industrial Coordination Act (1975), 79, 91–2, 130, 135–47; amendments to, 141–2, 162, 188; Chinese protest

against, 134–5, 137–47; and foreign
investors, 167–8
Intel, 174
Internal Security Act: arrests under, 123,
190
International economy: effect on Malaysian
economy, 117–18
Investment Incentives Act (1968), 173
Irrigation projects, 38, 50
Islam: introduction of, 24–5; and politics,
127; as state religion, 44
Ismail Ali, Tun, 86–7
Ismail Mydensah, 103
ITT, 174

JA'AFA ALBAR, TAN SRI, 56
Japan: investment in Malaysia, 57–8, 145,
152–3, 173–4, 177, 182, 184–5, 189
Japanese Chamber of Trade and Industry
in Malaysia, 189
Japanese Occupation, 41
Johor Flour Mills, 61
Joint ventures, 58, 138, 182, 184–5
Jones, Edwin, 14
Judiciary: reduction in power, 190, 199

KAH MOTORS, 62
Kamunting, 178
Kanebo, 178
Kanematsu–Gosho, 177–8
Kanetso Malaysia, 177–8
Kee Huat Radio, 153
Kelantan, 69–70
Kesatuan Melayu Muda, 42
Kesatuan Rakyat Indonesia Semenanjung,
42
KH Consolidated Pty Ltd, 92
Khalid, Haji, 54–5
Khoo Kay Peng, 151–2
Kirloskar, 183
KKP Holdings, 152
Koh Pen Ting, 130
Kongsi, 31, 37
Kontena Nasional, 93
Koperasi Bersatu Bhd, 150
Krian Irrigation Scheme (1905), 38
Kumar, Krishna, 18
Kuok Brothers Sdn Bhd, 61
Kuok, Robert, 61, 63, 154
Kuomintang Malaya, 40, 43
Kwong Lee Bank, 151
Kwong Yik (Selangor) Bank, 35

LABOUR PARTY, 44
Lal, Deepak, 4–5
Land development schemes, 50–1
Land tenure, 28

Lau Pak Kuan 35
Lebanon, 4
Lee, Sir H. S., 35, 43–4, 49, 106
Lee Kong Chian, 35
Lee Kuan Yew, 68
Lee Loy Seng, 36, 59, 155
Lee San Choon, 158
Lee Wah Bank, 35
Lee Yan Lian, 63
Lever Brothers, 181
Licensed Manufacturing Warehouses, 188
Lien Hoe Industries, 152
Lim Goh Tong, 34, 63
Lim Kit Siang, 120
Lion Corporation, 58, 185
Local capitalists, 6–7, 20
Loh Boon Siew, 34–5, 62
Loke family, 35
Loke Yew, 35
London City Takeover Panel, 90
London Metal Exchange, 88, 119
London Tin Group, 33, 59, 88–9
Loy Hean Heong, 61–2

MAGNUM CORPORATION, 156
Mahathir bin Mohamad, Datuk Seri Dr:
and ACCCIM, 142; and BMF, 120;
and changes in government, 190; and
Chinese, 144; and commodity prices,
119; and Daim Zainuddin, 107; and
divisions in UMNO, 109, 123, 124, 135,
190; and early Malay commerce, 25;
economic policies, 117–19, 169; and
foreign investment, 144, 188–9; and
HICOM, 118, 161; and Ibrahim
Mohammed, 108; and ICA, 141; and ISA
arrests, 190; and position of Malays, 12,
80, 105; and Tunku Abdul Rahman, 71
Majlis Amanah Rakyat, 51–2, 66, 85, 90,
101, 103, 126
Malay: as national language, 44
Malay Administrative Service, 37
Malay associations, 40, 42–3, 80
Malay bourgeoisie, 2, 105–8
Malay business development, 64–7, 100–9,
195
Malay Chamber of Commerce and
Industry, 21, 136
Malay College, 37
Malay élite: under British, 30, 37–9; and
bureaucracy, 37; and business, 51–2,
65–7; managers, 97, 101; and NEP,
72–3, 105, 197; traditional role, 25–6;
and UMNO, 43, 199
Malay Nationalist Party, 42
Malay Reservations Enactment (1913), 38
Malay smallholders, 47

Malay sultans: under British, 28; and constitution for independent Malaya, 44; and Federation of Malaya Agreement, 43; traditional role, 25-6
Malay Trading and Craft Company, 38
Malay traditional social system, 24-5; and British, 27
Malayan Banking, 105-6, 126
Malayan Civil Service, 28
Malayan Manufacturers' Association, 56
Malayan People's Anti-Japanese Army, 41
Malayan Sugar, 61
Malayan Tin, 33
Malayan Union, 42-3
Malayan United Industries, 151-2
Malayan Veneer, 61
Malayawata, 93
Malays: attitude towards Chinese, 39-41, 64, 68-9; and colonialism, 29-30, 36-9; in construction, 63, 102; contractors, 66, 102-4; education, 113-14; and government contracts, 132; group worth, 116-17; income, 114; and Japanese Occupation, 41; jobs in private sector, 67-8, 111-12; land ownership, 38; in manufacturing, 58, 134; in mining industry, 66; and multinational corporations, 167; ownership of companies, 79; and PAS, 194; and politics, 42; percentage of population, 1, 29; professionals, 112; shareholdings, 66, 105, 109; special position of, 43-4, 68, 77; in timber industry, 66; and trade unions, 42; traders, 25, 30-1; traditional occupations, 36, 38, 64; in transport industry, 66, 102; and UMNO, 194
Malaysia: history, 24-30
Malaysia National Insurance, 86, 92
Malaysia National Reinsurance, 93
Malaysia Plan: First, 50-1, 54, 84; Second, 71, 82, 84, 91, 101, 130, 134; Third, 82, 84; Fourth, 82, 84, 146; Fifth, 162
Malaysian Chinese Association: and Barisan Nasional, 78; business activities, 147, 155-9; economic policy, 73; and elections, 44, 67, 69, 157-9; formation of, 42-3; and Independence of Malaya Party, 44; loss of power, 71, 131, 133; and NEP, 154-9; in 1960s, 129; and UMNO, 44, 53-5, 162-3, 169, 193
Malaysian Indian Congress, 44
Malaysian Industrial Development Authority, 168
Malaysian Institute of Micro-Electronic Systems, 176
Malaysian International Chamber of Commerce and Industry, 88, 136-8, 140, 142
Malaysian Mining Corporation, 89, 93, 97
Malaysian Rubber Corporation, 148
Malaysian Trade Union Congress, 42, 44, 75
Malaysianization of private companies, 88-98
Manufacturing: Alliance government policy, 48; British policy, 32, 36; Chinese investment in, 142-6; foreign investment in, 56-60, 131, 134-5, 144-6, 167-91; share of GDP, 58, 134, 147; share of GNP, 3; and ICA, 135-47; Malay investment in, 145-6; plan for 1970-90, 87, 134; state investment in, 145-6
MARA, see Majlis Amanah Rakyat
Market economy: role in Third World development, 4
Matsushita Electric, 58, 173, 183
MCA, see Malaysian Chinese Association
McGee, T. G., 180
McLeod, Maxwell G., 18
Melaka, 25-6
Mercantile Bank, 33
Mexico, 20
MIC, see Malaysian Indian Congress
MICCI, see Malaysian International Chamber of Commerce and Industry
MIDA, see Malaysian Industrial Development Authority
Ministry of Commerce and Industry, 64
Ministry of Finance, 78-9, 131, 141
Ministry of National and Rural Development, 65-6
Ministry of Public Enterprises, 98-100
Ministry of Trade and Industry, 78-9, 104, 130-1, 135-7
Ministry of Works and Public Utilities, 101-3
Mitsubishi Motor Corporation, 62, 119, 161, 184-5
Mitsui, 58, 178
Mohd. Noah, 63
Moran, Theodore, 16
Mostek, 174
Motorola, 174
MPH, see Multi-Purpose Holdings Bhd
MTUC, see Malaysian Trade Union Congress
MUI Bank, 151
Multi-ethnic societies: economic process, 2-3
Multi-Fibre Agreement, 177
Multinational corporations, 6-8, 18-19, 166-7
Multinational corporations in Malaysia, 18-19, 167-91; British, 57, 180-1; from

developing countries, 182–3, 186, 196;
and employment, 18–19, 167–8, 177,
179–80, 191, 196; in FTZs, 177, 179;
government policy, 196, 199; Hong
Kong, 176–7; Indian, 183–4; Japanese,
58, 172–4, 177–8, 184–6; and Malays,
167; and NEP, 167; role in development,
19–21, 167–72; Singapore, 177, 183;
and state, 84, 161–4, 167; United States,
57–8, 172–4, 181–2; West European,
185
Multi-Purpose Holdings Bhd, 107, 155–9
Musa Hitam, Datuk, 71, 100, 124, 190
Mustapha, Tun, 106
Myrdal, Gunnar, 4–6

NATIONAL CAR PROJECT, 119, 161, 195
National Chamber of Commerce and
Industry, 139–40, 166
National Corporation, see Perbadanan
Nasional
National Electricity Board, 92
National Equity Corporation, see
Permodalan Nasional Berhad
National Front, see Barisan Nasional
National Investment Company, 64
National Operations Council, 70–1
National Semiconductor, 174
'National Timber Industry', 64
National Unit Trust Scheme, see Amanah
Saham Nasional
NEC, see Nippon Electric Company
Negeri Sembilan, 28
Neil and Bell, 33
Neo Yee Pan, 158
NEP, see New Economic Policy
New Economic Policy: aims of, 1–2, 71–3;
changes in government for, 76–8; and
Chinese businesses, 195; and CIC, 79;
and company restructuring, 79, 88–90;
control of criticism against, 77; and EPU,
78–9; and FIC, 79; and ICA, 79, 137;
and Malay leaders, 79–80, 194; and
multinational corporations, 168; revenue
for, 82; and state enterprises, 85–100
NGK Spark Plug, 185
Nikkei Business, 168
Nippon Electric Company, 92, 174, 185
Nippon Steel Corporation, 184
Nissin Sugar Manufacturing, 58, 61
NOC, see National Operations Council
Nonini, Donald M., 149
NS Gula, 184

OIL PALM, 59
Olson, Mancur, 12–13
Omron, 174

Onn Jaafar, Dato, 43–4
Osborne and Chappel, 33
OTIS Elevators, 93
'Outline Perspective Plan 1970–1990', 87,
91, 134
Overseas Chinese Banking Corporation, 90

PADI AND RICE BOARD, 148
Pahang, 28
Pan-Electric Company, 158
Pan-Malayan Cement Works, 151
Pan-Malayan Federation of Trade Unions,
41
Pan-Malayan Islamic Party, 44, 47, 49
Pangkor Treaty of 1874, 27
Parliament: loss of power, 117
Parti Islam SeMalaysia: and Barisan
Nasional, 77, 124; change of platform,
109; and elections, 69, 109–10; future
of, 199; leaders arrested, 123, 190; and
poor Malays, 194, 196; and UMNO, 169
PAS, see Parti Islam SeMalaysia
Pegi Malaysia, 157
Pen-Group, 177
Penang, 26, 69
Penang Yellow Bus Company, 34
People's Action Party, 68
People's Progressive Party, 44
Pepper, 30
Perak, 27–8, 70
Perbadanan Nasional, 85–97, 107, 132,
145, 148–9, 151, 156–7, 160
Perlis Plantations, 61
Permodalan Nasional Berhad, 85–91, 93,
96–7
Pernas, see Perbadanan Nasional
Petroleum Development Act (1974), 130–1,
168–9
Petroleum industry, 82, 117–18, 187–8,
194, 196, 198
Petronas, 82, 168–9
Phaltan Sugar Works Ltd, 99
Pilgrims Fund, 90
Pioneer Industrial Scheme, 56, 58, 62
Pioneer Ordinance (1958), 56–7
Plantation companies, 88–91
Plantation Holdings, 156
PMIP, see Pan-Malayan Islamic Party
PNB, see Permodalan Nasional Berhad
Popenoe, Oliver, 66
Population, 1, 29; growth, 47
Portugal, 20
Portuguese in Melaka, 25
Poverty: decrease in, 114–15; NEP and, 71
Prime Minister's Department, 78, 86, 176
Promet, 108
Promptshipping, 158

Public development expenditure, 50–1, 80–3, 122, 147
Public Works Department, 102
Puthucheary, James J., 32, 36, 59

RABUSHKA, ALVIN, 39
Race riots, 1, 70, 194
Rafidah Aziz, Datin Paduka, 100, 162
Rational economic models, 4–8, 193
Razaleigh Hamzah, Tengku: and BMF, 120; chairman of Bank Bumiputra, 86; chairman of Pernas, 86–7; chairman of Petronas, 82, 169; and divisions in UMNO, 109, 124, 135, 190; and Ibrahim Mohammed, 108; and Malaysianization, 131; Minister of Finance, 169; and multinational corporations, 182; and private sector, 144; and Tun Abdul Razak, 86
RCA, 174
Real national income, 117
Registrar of Companies, 79
Rice cultivation, 38
Rickwood and Company, 61
Rothmans, 57
Rothschilds and Sons, 89, 91
Rowe and Pitman, 91
Rubber industry, 32, 49
Rural and Industrial Development Authority, 65–6

SAMBU CORPORATION, 92
Satria Utara Sdn Bhd, 148–9
SCCC, see Selangor Chinese Chamber of Commerce
Schmitter, Phillippe C., 77
SEDCs, see State Economic Development Corporations
Seikisui Chemical Company, 185
Selangor, 27–8, 70
Selangor Chinese Chamber of Commerce, 131–3, 139, 156
Selangor Dredging, 59
Selangor Properties, 150
Selangor State Development Corporation, 103
Sensitive Issues Act, 133
Shahriman Sulaiman, Tunku, 86
Shell Company, 57, 82, 181
Siemens, 174
Sime Darby, 32–3, 35, 57, 97; and Pernas, 89–91, 93
Singapore, 26, 73, 75; investment by Malaysian Chinese in, 154; investment in Malaysia, 57–8, 177, 182–3
South Korea, 2, 20, 73, 189
Southern Banking, 156

Sperry Univac System, 93
Sri Lanka, 2–4
State and economic development, 4–8, 14–16, 20
State Economic Development Corporations, 85–6, 98–100, 126, 145
State enterprises, 6, 14–16, 19, 84
State enterprises in Malaysia, 16, 67, 72, 84–100, 194–5
Stepan, Alfred, 16, 76
Straits Chinese British Association, 43
Straits Settlements, 26
Straits Trading Company, 33, 59
Sugar, 30
Suhaimi Kamaruddin, 157
Sultan of Kedah, 63
Sultan of Pahang, 63
Supreme Corporation, 155
Swettenham, Frank, 31, 38–9
Syed Kechik, Datuk, 105–6

TAIPING TEXTILES, 106–7
Taiwan, 2, 73, 189
Tan Cheng Lock, 35, 43
Tan Koon Swan, 155–6, 158–9
Tan Siew Sin, Tun: and Chinese business, 56, 129; and foreign investment, 53; MCA leader, 43; Minister of Finance, 49, 54, 78; politician, 35; and Treasury, 78
Tan, T. H., 130
Tan Tat Wai, 60–1, 63
Tapioca, 30
Tariff protection, 48
Tata, 183
Taxation system: Alliance government, 49; Barisan Nasional government, 81–2; under British, 27; traditional, 25–6
Tee family, 152
Telecommunications Department, 92, 102
Teo family, 34, 63
Teochew, 34
Texcham Trading, 153
Textile Alliance Limited, 176–7
Textile industry, 176–9
Tin-mining, 27–8, 30, 33, 36, 46, 49, 59, 88
Tong Bee Finance Bhd, 151
Tong Bee Finance Bhd, 151
Toray Industries Inc, 177
Toshiba Corporation, 153, 173–4
Trade in early Malaya, 24–5
Trade unions, 41–2, 46, 57, 169–71, 173
Treasury, 78–9
Trinidad, 2–4
Tugwell, Franklin, 85
Tunas Satria, 103

UMNO, see United Malays National Organization

Unemployment, 47, 67, 168, 171, 174, 187–9
Unico Holdings Bhd, 165
UNIDO, 160
Union Carbide, 58
United Malay Contractors, 64
United Malayan Banking Corporation, 93, 107, 156–7, 165
United Malays National Organization: and Barisan Nasional, 77–8; and bureaucracy, 80; and DAP, 163; divisions within, 109, 123, 124, 135, 190–1, 198; economic policy, 116; and elections, 44, 67, 69–70, 109–11; formation of, 42–4; and the future, 198–9; and Malay élite, 43, 199; Malay support for, 124, 194, 196, 198; and MCA, 44, 53–5, 162–3, 169, 193; in 1980s, 109, 116; and National Operations Council, 71; and PAS, 109–10, 127; and PMIP, 47, 49; and poor Malays, 194, 196; and SEDCs, 98–100; and workers, 170–1; Youth Division, 80, 156–7

United States: investment in Malaysia, 57–8, 145, 173–4, 181–2
Universities, 113–14, 187
Urban Development Authority, 85, 101, 107

WAGES, 171
Wallerstein, Immanuel, 21
Wen, Dato T. K., 150
Western Europe: investment in Malaysia, 185–6
Wilkenson Process, 57
Wong Brothers Electrical and Refrigeration Sdn Bhd, 160
World Bank, 3, 20, 48

YANGTZE-KIANG, 176
Yong Shook Lin, 43
Yuasa Battery, 153

ZAIDNER, DAVID, 119
Zimbabwe, 2–4

DATE DUE

		JAN ~~18 1997~~	
~~DEC 0~~ 1994		~~OCT 26 1998~~	
~~FEB 12 1996~~			
	~~1996~~		
~~MAR 19 1996~~			
~~MAY 1 4 2000~~			
		Printed in USA